BUSINESS

The Key Concepts

Here is a practical and accessible guide to the essentials of business. This book provides everything you need to know about the key concepts and terms, from accountability to zero-sum game. Subject areas include management, economics and finance, marketing, organizational behaviour and operations. Each entry is written in a clear style to make business intelligible.

- Combines detail and accessibility.
- Considers new developments in business, notably e-business and contemporary business ethics.
- Covers established subjects, taking an international and strategic perspective that balances theory and practice.
- Suggests specific further reading for many concepts and also includes an extensive bibliography.

Whether you're already in business and you could do with a handy reference guide, or you're a student needing an introduction to the fundamentals, *Business: The Key Concepts* is the perfect companion.

Mark Vernon writes on business for the *Financial Times*. He also contributes articles on the subject for a wide range of other publications on both sides of the Atlantic. He holds degrees from the universities of Oxford and Durham and is currently undertaking research at Warwick University.

ROUTLEDGE KEY GUIDES

Routledge Key Guides are accessible, informative and lucid handbooks, which define and discuss the central concepts, thinkers and debates in a broad range of academic disciplines. All are written by noted experts in their respective subjects. Clear, concise exposition of complex and stimulating issues and ideas make *Routledge Key Guides* the ultimate reference resources for students, teachers, researchers and the interested lay person.

BUSINESS

The Key Concepts

Mark Vernon

London and New York

First published 2002
by Routledge
11 New Fetter Lane, London EC4P 4EE

Simultaneously published in the USA and Canada
by Routledge
29 West 35th Street, New York, NY 10001

Routledge is an imprint of the Taylor & Francis Group

© 2002 Mark Vernon

Typeset in Times by Taylor & Francis Books Ltd
Printed and bound in Great Britain by Biddles Ltd, Guildford and King's Lynn

British Library Cataloguing in Publication Data
A catalogue record for this book is available from the British Library

Library of Congress Cataloging in Publication Data
Vernon, Mark.
Business: the key concepts/Mark Vernon.
Includes bibliographical references and index.
1. Business–Encyclopedias. I. Title.
HF1001 .V47   2001
650′.03–dc21   2001019934

ISBN 0–415–25323–3 (hbk)
ISBN 0–415–25324–1 (pbk)

CONTENTS

PREFACE

This book is a resource. It provides an explanation and exploration of the key concepts in the study of business. The list includes subjects from the areas of management, marketing, finance, economics, organizational behaviour and operations. Care has been taken to present an international viewpoint, to consider contemporary perspectives on business such as strategic approaches, and to balance theory and practice. The exciting though often hyped developments associated with e-business and ethical business are also assessed. Throughout, I have endeavoured to apply the ethic of transparency to the business of writing, that is to provide clarity.

The book is written to be used. Three groups of people in particular have been held in mind. The first are students of business, whether beginners looking for an introduction or those who are more advanced and need a resource to extend their studies. The second are practitioners of business who could do either with a desktop reference book to help them understand their work more thoroughly, or simply with a resource to provide them with material, say for that presentation next week. The third group of people are interested general readers who hear words like 'innovation' or phrases like 'neoclassical economics' bandied around and wonder quite what is meant by them.

The entries in this book cover the subjects that would be included in most business studies or MBA courses. When a subject is fundamental the entry aims to explain it. When a subject is more controversial the entry provides a critique and balanced viewpoint. Each entry begins with a definition, followed by a description and discussion of the concept that is designed both to ground the subject firmly and outline avenues in which it is being developed.

Entries are of different lengths, reflecting the relative importance of the subject. For example, utility has a short entry since whilst it is a word employed in business studies it is also more generally used. Alternatively, zero-based budgeting has a short entry since, in terms of this book, it is a secondary, if important, subject in relation to accounting.

Long entries vary in aim to ensure that as many subjects, and angles on subjects, as possible are covered. For example, the marketing entry provides a high-level introduction to the many subjects that fall under that heading. These can be followed up in other parts of the book. Alternatively, the management entry offers a discussion of the study of management rather than management *per se*, since that seemed a more useful thing to do. Again, areas of management are discussed thoroughly under separate headings. Or again, the long entry under technology discusses the close relationship between technological advances and economic advances; it is therefore different from the long entry under information and communications technology which takes more of a technical slant; this is in turn different from the long entry under e-business, which addresses the question of what difference electronic networks make to business and how they might be used.

Every entry ends with at least one of two notes. The first, 'See also', points to other related entries in the book which either develop the subject further or point to entries that have a lateral but interesting link with it. The second, 'Further reading', suggests relevant material from the bibliography. With these two pointers, the book aims to help the reader in their ongoing exploration of business concepts.

The detailed index provides another starting point. In particular it will help readers find hundreds of additional subjects that are not listed among the entries. For example, the finance entry contains discussions of payback period and of net present value that are listed in the index.

The bibliography is extensive. It includes a long list of important business books published in the last three years, key reference books in the areas of management, business and economics, and classic texts, from historic thinkers as well as modern exponents of business. Many of them are referenced at the end of the entries, but the bibliography also provides suggestions for further reading. The idea is that in it, and indeed in the book as a whole, readers will find rich resources to continue their study of business.

ACKNOWLEDGEMENTS

I am indebted to the British Library for providing me with a place in which to write and many of the materials with which to research the book. I would also like to thank Stuart Draper, who first introduced business to me, and Craig Mackenzie, with whom I have enjoyed long hours of discussion about the subject since.

Mark Vernon
London
January 2001

ACCOUNTABILITY

The obligation placed on employees and organizations to be answerable for their actions.

In practice, the term denotes a framework of responsibilities covering various decisions and actions within which individuals or groups work. The goal is to ensure that standards, methods and timeframes are adhered to.

Accountability finds its roots in classical management theory, with its militaristic belief in lines of command and specialization that governs the division of labour. However, the concept has been modernized so that accountable management today is a practice that seeks to manage by holding employees to performance measures or objectives, agreed wherever possible with the individuals concerned. Cost and profit centres are closely associated with this style of management – the establishment of units within the organization based on function or location for which costs or profits can be reliably calculated and, therefore, controlled. Shareholders and other third parties are also developing means of holding firms to account, often over ethical concerns.

See also: **Audit, Ethics, Performance**

Further reading: Klatt *et al.*, 1999

ACCOUNTING

The discipline that provides information about a business based on financial data.

Accounting information can be used by anyone making decisions about the organization or their relationship to the business. Accounting is a massive subject area embracing a variety of methods that have a profound impact upon the way a business is viewed. Here, the fundamental principles are reviewed along with some pointers as to how the subject is currently evolving.

The results of accounting procedures can range from a simple balance sheet to a voluminous record of a corporation's entire commercial activity, but the discipline as a whole can be broken down into two broad areas. The first is financial accounting, the preparation of reports for shareholders, tax authorities and business reports. Accounts must therefore be intelligible to these third parties according to rules that might be enforced by law. The second is managerial accounting, the use of financial data within an organization to assist in decision making and driving profit and growth. Financial accounting varies according to legal, economic and social context. This can present a number of problems to businesses. For example, accounting principles as Americans put it, or accounting practices for the UK, differ dramatically. In the UK, four principles are basic: the going concern principle, that is a company is at least initially assumed to be viable; the self-explanatory principle of prudence; the matching principle which says that records are entered in the period in which they arise not when actually transacted; and the principle of consistency which advises adherence to precedent.

Accounting standards are agreed by national professional associations to assist in the auditing process. However, these give rise to another source of variation: standards are legally enforceable in Canada and often in the US, but are voluntary in the UK.

Accounting for goodwill and foreign currency exchanges also contributes to diverse practices. Hence there are many initiatives to promote accounting harmonization. For example, it is an important driver in European Economic and Monetary Union.

Managerial accounting originates in the need to control costs. It is not necessarily subject to external rules, and variations in practice are common, typically due to inherited anomalies, although best practices are often deployed. Models such as cost volume profit analysis (CVP), that calculates financial economies of scale, are fundamental. More sophisticated tools, such as activity based costing (ABC), seek to enhance this basic information. Others deal with less tangible factors that demand a degree of personal judgement as well as objective standards. For example, cost-benefit analysis assesses the enhancement of a product or service accrued from a particular cost. Firms also implement accounting software tools, such as Enterprise Resource Planning (ERP), to overcome gaps in corporate knowledge.

The central accounting discipline has sprouted a number of branches to meet particular needs. For example, cash flow accounting provides an alternative to transaction analysis by calculating the difference between a company's cash outlays and income over the accounting period. Inflation accounting incorporates measures that are able to deal more meaningfully with businesses working in areas in which monetary values fluctuate significantly. Infamously, creative accounting uses techniques to improve the financial profile of the firm (though whenever even two conservative accountants are looking at the same data, at least three different reports will result).

Today, the academic study of accounting embraces a number of tensions, such as the arguments between those who advocate the importance of value in accounting and those who prefer to stick to hard costs. Accounting practices are also likely to continue to develop as factors such as the demands of international capital markets grow. Further, as the firm's relationship with its banks evolves, accounting for financial products such as swaps and derivatives will increasingly be taken in-house, making the accountant's tasks more complex.

See also: **Activity-based costing, Audit, Cash, Finance, Foreign exchange risk, Goodwill, Income statement, Inflation accounting, Opportunity cost, Transfer pricing, Zero-based budgeting**

Further reading: Bishop *et al.*, 1999; Kaplan and Atkinson, 1998; Jagolinzer, 2000; Rashad Abdel-Khalik, 1998; A. Thomas, 1999

ACCULTURATION

The process whereby a foreign culture is assimilated without losing the benefits of the original or the other.

In international business, acculturation is a tricky issue. Informal management styles in Silicon Valley, for example, do not work well with Japan's preference for extensive deliberation. Alternatively, global labour markets demand a greater understanding of the stresses and strains on employees negotiating different cultures. The effectiveness of a workforce can be severely impaired if cultural preferences are ignored.

A further issue concerns that of cross-cultural marketing. There are relatively few genuinely global brands, with most varying according to locale. Occasionally, things go very wrong. For example, dogs associated with toilet paper works well in the West, but not in the Middle East, where the animals are regarded as dirty.

See also: **Culture, Geocentricism, Joint venture**

Further reading: Beechler and Stucker, 1998; Morosini, 1998

ACTIVISM

The initiatives of employees, shareholders, stakeholders or pressure groups to influence the decisions or actions of a company. The demonstrations of activists protesting at the meetings of the World Bank and IMF have recently stolen the headlines. Powered by communications technology, these various groups are highly organized and arguably effective at raising their concerns. However, this kind of very visible activism is only one, contested, way in which people try to influence the operation of businesses.

For example, shareholder activism has long been a feature of American corporate life. Mackenzie describes it as shareholder action, a loose term that covers attempts to influence corporate decision making through the shareholder process. It can cover action by individuals, small campaigning groups, large national pressure groups, and institutional investors like pension funds. This kind of shareholder action is different from the traditional concerns of shareholders with dividend payments. It refers to attempts to encourage a company to think about a range of social and ethical policy questions.

Shareholder action in the pursuit of social interests has become increasingly common in the last two decades, particularly in the US. Today, several hundred companies face ethically motivated shareholder action campaigns at any one time. While the overwhelming majority of these campaigns take place in America, a growing number of companies in other countries have faced pressure from shareholder activists too. Institutional investors that are increasingly interested in ethical fund management, companies that want to be seen to be more accountable for their actions, and other kinds of activism, will ensure that shareholder action is a trend set to grow.

See also: **Environmental audit, Ethics, Social audit, Stakeholder**

Further reading: Mackenzie, 1993; Pringle and Thompson, 1999; Weinreich, 1999

ACTIVITY-BASED COSTING

An accounting method that aims to assess and include the real costs of processes, called activities, in the production of products, called cost objects.

Activity-based costing is the most important of the new accounting techniques that have emerged since the early 1980s. It developed to rectify faults with traditional cost management solutions. In particular, ABC allows the costs of products to be assessed more clearly in relation to identifying profits and economic break-even points, as well as with other managerial purposes such as improving strategic decision making and implementing business plans. ABC lends itself well to situations in which overheads are high, where accounting errors are sensitive or competition is high, and where cost objects themselves are complex.

The total cost of a product is the sum of its direct cost, such as labour and materials, and associated overheads. It is this second element that ABC addresses in particular. Traditional cost accounting arbitrarily allocates overhead costs by assuming that they can be calculated according to volume-based measures, such as machine time and labour hours. ABC focuses on tracing expenses accrued by objects and treating them as direct costs.

Understanding the relationship between cost objects, activities associated with them and the resources they consume is central. ABC requires five steps: identification of activities, determination of cost of activities, determination of cost drivers, collation of activity data and calculation of product cost.

The adoption of ABC by organizations varies, although why firms that would otherwise apparently benefit from the virtues of ABC do not adopt its practices is an open question.

See also: **Accounting**

Further reading: Brimson, 1999; Forrest, 1996; Innes and Mitchell, 1998; Turney, 1996

ADAPTABILITY

The flexibility of a company's aims.

Adaptability is important to business in certain specific senses. An adaptive strategy is one in which negotiation and compromise characterize the achievement of goals that are themselves adaptable. This mode of operation is typically suited to public sector or charitable organizations. However, adaptability is increasingly recognized as a valuable quality even for organizations used to fixed targets and strict aims.

A second less significant application of adaptability refers to employees' ability to cope with change, and is deployed in the screening of employees for work abroad. Tests include assessing the ability to handle stress and the ability to make decisions on limited knowledge.

See also: **Aptitude test, Mission statement**

Further reading: Birkinshaw and Hagström, 2000

ADHOCRACY

The type of organization associated with an open-ended style of decision making.

An adhocratic structure seeks to allow all staff in the organization to work together across traditional divides for the achievement of the goals of the company. The reason behind such a complex environment is to produce the dynamism necessary to make decisions that face high degrees of uncertainty or chance. For example, administrative staff might have insights on an issue that production managers alone would overlook. Alternatively, an innovative organization might adopt adhocratic methods so that good ideas can surface from a variety of sources.

Garbage can models of decision making are a famous variation. Here, the value of chaos within the organization is recognized, with management's task being to steer the creativity that results.

See also: **Creativity, Innovation**

Further reading: Carter, 1999; Stredwick and Ellis, 1998; Syrett and Lamminman, 1998

ADVERTISING

The paid-for use of mass media to promote goods and services to influence customers.

Although it should immediately be added that an accurate definition of advertising, with its assumptions about the use of media, and the rationale and effectiveness of the advertisement, is notoriously hard to come by. There are a number of reasons for this, reflecting the complexity of the subject.

For example, advertising is not solely concerned with selling products. This has been the argument of the tobacco industry as it fights in various parts of the world to maintain its right to advertise: here advertisements are designed to maintain loyalty to brands and win smokers from other brands, not to sell cigarettes *per se*. Advertisements are also designed to establish legitimacy or significance, and to animate a company, service or product.

Another important point is that whilst advertisers use mass media, they do not in general seek to reach mass audiences. Advertisements are generally targeted at small groups of individuals who are susceptible to the message they carry.

The origins of modern advertising lie in the Industrial Revolution and the mass production of goods. The problem manufacturers had was to find or create new mass markets, and then manage them using techniques such as segmentation. Mass media provided the means and the development of brands was perceived as achieving the ends; indeed, some would argue that it was advertising that created consumer culture.

Advertising contributes to the overall marketing mix, although how much depends on who you ask. One hundred years ago, the British advertising agent S. H. Benson wrote, 'the results of advertising are not discernible', and the study of the interaction of audiences and advertisements has been extensive and contested ever since. Academics contribute a theoretical perspective using disciplines such as semiotics. Practitioners, especially media buyers, constantly struggle to quantify the effectiveness of advertisements. Pre-testing with focus groups and post-evaluation by polling are common methods. Reach, frequency and impact are the variables that are taken into account. Effectiveness is a particularly current critical issue for new media, the aim being to justify the spending on online banner ads, for example, upon which so many of the so-called dotcoms depend.

The links between advertising and the media run deep. Andy Warhol believed that the perfect magazine would consist of nothing but advertisements, making the point that the dependency of publications on advertisements and vice-versa is often uneasy. The newspaper brand must be maintained, but advertisers represent an important source of revenue, and they will advertise more if editorial works in their favour, but then that will tend to erode the brand.

The regulation of advertising is another area of contestation. Many national laws have an impact, in addition to which in most parts of the Western world self-regulatory codes are enforced, in part to stave off periodic demands for tougher legislation. Global media create regulatory problems for advertising on satellite television or the internet. For example, in continental Europe, children are not used as extensively in advertisements as in the UK and US.

The limits of advertising, whether set by taste or code, have been incorporated into the increasingly sophisticated tricks that advertisers play, notably to win so-called below the line advertising. Here the point is to stimulate interest in the advertisement itself, thereby massively increasing its reach. Versace is a leading exponent of this art.

Recently, the advertising industry has been in something of a crisis. The hegemony of advertising agencies has been broken as the industry fragments and as the relationships between advertising specialisms change. The definition of what constitutes advertising is also being stretched, as advertisers exploit new techniques such as the 'infomercial' and product placement to stimulate an increasingly ad-wise public.

See also: **Brand, Consumer, Marketing, Segmentation, Semiotics, Socioeconomics, Subliminal advertising**

Further reading: Brierly, 1995; Cronin, 2000; Fletcher, 1999; Jones, 1998; Wilmshurst and Mackay, 1999

ANTITRUST LAW

The action of a government to sustain lively competition in a marketplace. Also called action against anticompetitive practice.

In America, the first antitrust law, the Sherman Act, was passed in 1890, making it illegal to set up monopolies that reduce competition or build cartels that limit trade. A number of laws have been enacted since, the most important being the Clayton Act and the Federal Trade Commission Act, both of 1914. In Europe, the most significant body of legislation is found in the European Union's 1957 Treaty of Rome, especially Articles 85 and 86. One of the key differences between the US and Europe is that in Europe small- and medium-sized enterprises are allowed to operate as cartels to compete with large firms. This is forbidden in the US.

These laws have also become a powerful tool in combating exclusionary marketing tactics. As long ago as 1912 NCR (National Cash Register) was successfully prosecuted. The most recent and ongoing case concerns the operations of Microsoft. However, antitrust laws are typically of a general nature, or, when covering a large trading area, incorporate the principle of subsidiarity, which means that the enforcement of legislation often proves very difficult.

Legal debate on antitrust focuses on issues such as whether these laws are concerned solely with the operation of markets or whether they aim to stem the eroding effect that large corporations wielding significant economic power might have on the functioning of democracy. The economic theory upon which these laws are based is also questioned, for example, in relating efficiency to organizational size. This confusion in turn gives rise to concern about the effectiveness of recourse to the law when markets are threatened.

See also: **Barrier to market, Competition, Monopoly**

Further reading: Howard, 1983; Kovaleff, 1990

APTITUDE TEST

Aptitude is the ability to learn. Aptitude tests measure that capacity in individuals, often in relation to specific tasks.

Aptitude tests are often used during recruitment or in the management of an individual's career by HR (human resources) departments. Basic tests assess numerical and verbal ability with more sophisticated measures covering elements such as mechanical or administrative capacities. Psychological profiling is also employed by many firms, to assess intelligence or temperament, factors which are not only important in themselves but also in relation to team building.

One example of a test that is generally agreed to deliver good results is the General Aptitude Test Battery (GATB) which the US Employment Service adopted in 1947. It was extensively revised in the 1980s. It consists of a 2½-hour series of tests covering a wide range of aptitudes of use to employees.

See also: **Occupational psychology, Training**

Further reading: Anastasi, 1988; Parkinson, 1999

ARBITRATION

The resolving of disputes by bringing in an independent third party on whose judgement the disputing parties agree to abide.

Arbitration has become one of the most common methods of

dispute resolution, since it potentially offers a way to short-circuit lengthy and damaging recourses to law. Many countries have set up publicly acceptable arbitration services. International bodies also exist which are particularly attractive as an alternative to legal systems that favour national interests or local business knowledge. Other advantages of using arbitration include the maintenance of secrecy, the employment of specialist third parties who know the nature of the business concerned, and a certain degree of flexibility it brings in relation to time and place which eases the human sources of conflict in disputes.

Further reading: Elkouri and Elkouri, 1985; Litka, 1991

ARTIFICIAL INTELLIGENCE

The capacity of computers to act like human beings, particularly in relation to logical reasoning.

AI can take many different forms. Improving the way computers interact with humans is one that deploys technology such as 'fuzzy logic' on website search engines. This allows individuals to misspell an entry or use an entry with similar meaning without jeopardizing the result. AI also covers the ability of computers to handle intractable calculations, vital to many forms of forecasting. For example, decision support systems and other analytical tools increasingly use AI to predict likely future scenarios or to identify otherwise hidden patterns in data. Using so-called heuristic knowledge, larger amounts of data from more extensive sources can be incorporated into calculations without rendering them impossibly large to complete. The uses to which this information can be put range from targeting customers in direct marketing campaigns to anticipating computers crashing before they actually do so.

Expert systems are AI applications that capture the knowledge of workers with some expertise and make it available to non-experts in the same or different field.

Neural networking is a related area in which AI is developing fast, the characteristic feature being that it provides the computer with the ability to learn. Neural networks are typically built of many computation units, called nodes, working in parallel, that is simultaneously and independently. An array of these nodes can be 'trained' by adjusting the nodes to alter the way the network responds to various inputs until the correct output results. The system can then be thought of as a tailor-made algorithm with the significant advantage that it can be used to perform calculations very speedily.

See also: **Data, Forecasting, Information and communications technology**

Further reading: Smith, 1998

ASSET

An asset is anything that can be expected to return a financial benefit. It is the opposite of a liability.

The fundamental accounting equation is often said to be the balance between assets and liabilities plus equity used to pay for things owned. A balance sheet places assets on one side and liabilities plus equity on the other so that the accounting records balance. From this, the double entry system follows, since any transaction recorded in the general ledger can be said to have an impact upon assets, called a debit, and liabilities, called a credit. Hence all entries require at least two lines of data.

Many things owned or controlled by a company may count as an asset. Accountants will agree on those that can be measured in monetary terms, bank deposits or property being two obvious examples. However, an established brand or loyal staff, whilst also clearly an asset to a company, are not so easily accounted for. These latter cases can be more readily evaluated in a so-called 'buy and sell' scenario, since then a price is agreed to reflect value. But since they are usually regarded as 'going concerns', when control of the asset is held over time, future benefit may be hard to ascertain and associate with a quantifiable value. The asset may then be regarded as having an intangible benefit. For example, in many high technology companies, an ability to assess the value of R&D spending might be very important when reporting profits. The alternative is simply to publish R&D expenditures and let readers make up their own minds.

Asset quality is a way of assessing the realistic value of an asset which may differ from the reported value on a balance sheet. For example, assets may be segregated according to their risk, with more liquid assets representing less risk. If most of the company's assets are high risk, then the overall value of the company to investors is likely to be reduced.

Asset stripping is buying a company, not with a view to developing its viability, but in order to sell off its assets and pocket the profit. Ethically, this is a questionable activity when it is undertaken with little regard for the needs of customers or employees.

Asset management is aimed at maximizing the way a company exploits its assets. This division of management theory seeks to develop methods by which assets can be effectively allocated. Market forecasting models, for example, assist asset managers in deciding how to invest in various financial instruments to maximize yield over time. Alternatively, decisions will be made over how an organization can best use its buildings or equipment.

See also: **Accounting, Capital, Cash, Labour, Value**

Further reading: Bishop *et al.*, 1999; Chorafas, 2000; Thomas, A., 1999

AUCTION

An auction is a competitive trading environment in which goods of an unspecified price are simultaneously offered to many buyers with the sale being made to the buyer who bids most. It offers an alternative to fixed or negotiated price trading.

Auctions exist in various forms. The so-called English auction is one in which the bidding is transparent. A Dutch auction is one in which the auctioneer begins at a high price that is lowered until a first participant accepts it. First-price sealed auctions consist of bids made in secret with the most attractive bid winning. A variation on this type is the second-price sealed auction, in which the winner under the first-price sealed rules pays the amount bid by the runner-up.

Auctions are used in a variety of situations. The first-price sealed auction is used to secure many public sector contracts. The traditional open-outcry method of selling on financial market trading floors is of the English auction type. However, whilst this practice is tending to die out as stock markets adopt electronic systems that arguably make the market more efficient, the emergence of online marketplaces is seeing a reinvigoration of the form. In business-to-business procurement, these marketplaces are electronic 'hubs' that bring together buyers and suppliers into a trading community. The online auction is a variation on this model, designed to facilitate one-off transactions for one-off needs, with the goods going to the highest bidder. Auctions are good for spot sourcing goods. So they are useful if a company has a one-off purchase or when it is buying a new product.

Further reading: Small, 2000

AUDIT

The independent assessment of the current state of the business. This usually includes a process of verification that stated facts are true. Conclusions are presented in the auditor's report.

Traditionally, auditing has applied itself to the domain of finance, but organizations are increasingly finding value from internal audits that monitor other aspects of their activity. Environmental and social audits, for example, have been championed by firms such as Shell in response to the ethical concerns of both shareholders and the public in relation to the company's impact upon the locality. Financial auditing is growing in importance too, partly in response to recent major scandals such as the collapse of the banks BCCI and Barings, and also in order to monitor the increasingly complex demands being made upon accountants.

However, auditing remains something of a mystery to those outside of the profession, and has become more specialized as accounting has become more sophisticated. For example, whilst best practice has evolved certain tools for analytical review or establishing audit trails, an element of subjective judgement remains as auditors decide what evidence to include. Further, rules of thumb can never be ruled out.

Audit risk has developed as an issue too, as the models for reducing the probability of mistakes being made on sampling, for example, become more subtle. In countries such as Canada these have changed dramatically. Here, a Bayesian approach was introduced in 1980.

Auditors recognize the limitations of their science. They are not held responsible for detecting fraud, for example. Auditing provides a degree of assurance, but not insurance, as to the financial position of the firm.

See also: **Environmental audit, Finance, Social audit**

Further reading: Ashton and Ashton, 1994; Bell and Wright, 1995; Lower, 1998; Power, 1997

AUTOMATION

The process of change whereby tasks formerly carried out by humans are carried out by machines. Any definition also requires a conception of degrees of automation because, especially with information technology, functions can said to be increasingly automated as they are carried out by increasingly independent systems.

Whilst automation has been one of the key drivers for businesses since the Industrial Revolution, the term is widely acknowledged as having been coined by D. S. Harder when he was vice president of the Ford Motor Company. This origin in itself says a lot about the philosophy of traditional manufacturing automation and its relationship to mass production. Here it is mechanical devices that carry out specific repeated tasks, either to assist or replace human beings.

The term has broadened out with the advent of computer control, since machines can now be programmed to carry out a far wider range of operations. In goods manufacturing, for example, this has led to increased economies of scale and faster times to market for new products. Indeed, so-called batch production, where different types of products are manufactured in separate lots to meet market demand, is the norm in Western operations.

More recently, automation has extended its reach again. It is now common to talk of office automation, for example, that covers everything from word processing to advanced workflow systems that push and pull electronic documents and information around the organization. Here automation does not so much imply the replacement of human beings as support for, or enhancement of, the tasks they carry out. The most recent phase of office automation is the birth of the intranet, self-help online systems that allow employees to bypass the human intervention that would traditionally have been necessary to complete tasks from filing sick notes to internal procurement.

See also: **Fordism, Technology**

Further reading: Noble, 1984

BALANCED SCORECARD

A management control system for measuring performance that does not rely solely on financial data, developed by R. S. Kaplan and D. P. Norton.

Kaplan and Norton recognized that managers often have a problem assessing staff on factors that, whilst critical to financial returns, are not directly reflected in financial transactions. The four key factors that have a bearing and which are incorporated into the balanced scorecard are: first, the customer perspective or how customers see the company; second, the internal perspective that is the company's own core competencies and excellences; third, the innovation and learning perspective which is the company's capacity to develop and progress in the future; and fourth, the financial perspective or how other stakeholders, notably shareholders, view the company.

Scorecards seek to redress the use of excessive quantities of transactional information for measuring performance that often build up when no alternatives are available. They are also held to be valuable because they enable the company to develop a long-term strategic view of itself: financial information alone tends to lead to reactive responses dictated by the vicissitudes of the markets rather than to proactive planning that focuses on strategy and vision.

The trick is to bring financial and non-financial information together and present it in ways that allow, say, profit figures and customer satisfaction ratings, or product quality and share price fluctuations, to be meaningfully compared. Computers greatly facilitate this capacity, and ERP (enterprise resource planning) applications are proving particularly suited to putting real-time scorecard interfaces on the desktops of managers.

Scorecards are also a useful tool for determining the value of a company since value is increasingly associated with non-financial indicators too.

See also: **Control, Performance, Strategy, Value**

Further reading: Creelman, 1998; Graeser *et al.*, 1998; Kaplan and Norton, 1996

BANKING

In its narrowest sense, banking is the provision of deposit or loan facilities. But the institutions that provide these services, banks, may be engaged in a wide range of associated activities, from receiving, collecting and exchanging to investing, dealing and servicing money – veritable financial department stores.

Banks play major roles in the key functions of any financial system, notably managing resources and risk, dealing with wealth exchange and market incentives, price transparency, and clearing and settlement mechanisms. Commercial banks are often referred to as investment banks in the US and merchant banks elsewhere. Investment banks are different as a result of the contested Glass-Steagall Act of 1932. They provide all the services mentioned above except clearing and settlement.

Banks can also be thought of as providers of liquidity. Businesses fund themselves by borrowing money to invest in the development of their commercial activities that will in due course provide an agreed rate of return to those from whom money has been borrowed. Banks can be involved in this process at a number of levels. At one level they may assist in day-to-day cash flow with overdraft facilities where the cost of borrowing is reflected in the interest rate. However, banks are major investors too, creating profits out of the money deposited with them. They are therefore also important institutions in maintaining macroeconomic stability. Legislation such as Europe's Capital Adequacy Directive is designed to ensure that the risk banks take does not pose a threat to business, in short so that in all reasonable financial scenarios banks will be able to maintain liquidity in markets.

Related to this is the role of central banks. Apart from performing banking functions for commercial banks, central banks hold the national reservoir of reserves and assist governments in running monetary and fiscal policy. Indeed, in relation to the former, Western economies typically allow monetary factors, notably the raising and lowering of interest rates, to be controlled by central banks.

Internationally, the style and principles that underpin banking vary enormously. For example, Islamic banking is currently attracting a lot of attention in the West, with its policy of offering interest-free financing according to Shariah law. Instead, Islamic banks invest directly in the business or become business partners. Islamic banks do well not only in countries dominated by the Islamic system but also in other Arab states and various parts of the Far East.

Japan is home to one of the world's three major financial markets in Tokyo, and the country dominates the list of largest institutions in the world. Although commercial banks now look very similar to Western firms, a mutual principle of *keiretsu* – cross-holdings between banks and businesses – still operates, although it has been severely scrutinized following recent bank failures.

The banking industry in the West is currently in a tremendous state of flux. M&As are common, seeking to exploit recent waves of deregulation, with the general tendency being to create larger institutions and so capitalize on economies of scale and larger markets. So-called new entrants, particularly in the retail banking space, are another source of instability, leveraging brands to offer better customer service. The emergence of online banking is another driver of change, in both the retail and merchant/investment spaces. In worst-case scenarios, online banking threatens to turn banks into mere commodity brokers, as traditional banking services are offered by non-banks or simply taken in-house by businesses.

See also: **Cash, Finance, Liquidity**

Further reading: Munn *et al.*, 1991

BANKRUPTCY

This occurs when a business can no longer service its debts, that is when a negative net worth is registered on a balance sheet, although bankruptcy may be indicated by a number of additional factors including uncontrollable operating losses, insufficient working capital, and an inability to borrow.

Insolvency laws that govern the winding up of a bankrupt company vary from country to country but work, with arguable success, at defending the interests of creditors and minimizing additional costs. In the US, businesses threatened with bankruptcy can file for Chapter 11, also known as being under administration, when debt repayments are delayed. Culturally, being a past bankrupt can carry a major stigma. Although famously, in Silicon Valley, working through one or two failed businesses is regarded as an asset.

Research shows that rates of business failure have increased in recent years, which, apart from macroeconomic factors such as recession, is often blamed on a high debt culture.

Auditors work with various indicators to calculate the likelihood of impending business failure. A good example is E. Altman's Z-Score, which weights a number of financial measures to provide a score that determines the probability. However, it should also be noted that firms can be technically bankrupt according to these indicators but still be regarded as going concerns. Many of the so-called dotcoms, for example, ran simply on their presence in a new industry, although there was a high probability of future failure.

See also: **Exposure, Finance, Risk**

Further reading: Altman, 1993; Davies, 1999

BARRIER TO MARKET

An impediment preventing a company from participating in a market.

Also called barriers to entry, they may take many forms. Natural obstacles include the costs that a firm incurs as a potential entrant or the limitations inherent in a particular market, such as shop space on the high street.

Strategic barriers to market are erected by current market participants to try to protect their interests. They might include the instigation of price wars based upon economies of scale against which small or newer players cannot hope to compete, or the reinforcement of dominant brands.

Artificial barriers to entry can be contrived by current market participants to prevent new entrants. They may be subject to antitrust laws. Artificial barriers also exist because of market regulation that wittingly or not protects cartels and monopolies.

See also: **Antitrust law, Capacity, Competition, Growth, Liberalization, Marketing, Monopoly, Porter's five forces, Protectionism, Saturation**

Further reading: Bain, 1956

BEHAVIOURAL THEORY

Theory derived from observations of the way individuals or groups act.

Behavioural theory has been applied to a wide range of business functions. For example, behavioural decision models seek to describe the influence of an individual or group's character or makeup upon decision making. They contrast with rational models of decision making, that emphasize the way an entity should act, with actual descriptions of how decisions are made.

One result of this different approach is captured in the neologism 'satisficing'. It stems from the observation that individuals often make decisions not on the basis of what optimizes outcomes, as a rational model would suggest, but merely on the basis of what is sufficient or will bring enough satisfaction. The point is that decisions are often made in complex environments in which there are high degrees of uncertainty. This is particularly likely in organizations. The oft-given analogy is that people will not look for the sharpest needle in the haystack but opt for the first one they find that is sharp enough.

Behavioural theory has in turn led to a greater sophistication in areas such as agency theory. Here, ideas about agency are extended beyond the usual economic assumption that individuals act in their own best interest. The indications are that individuals act on their own, or on someone else's behalf, according to a variety of principles similar to those that govern more general social relations. Ethical concerns, for example, might count.

Behavioural theory is sometimes turned to the problem of the so-called black box, the hidden mental processes that control human behaviour that some regard as having a powerful hold on decision making.

See also: **Cognition, Decision making, Guru, Human resources management, Maslow's hierarchy, Occupational psychology**

Further reading: Bowie and Freeman, 1992; Cyert and March, 1963; Simon, 1976

BENCHMARKING

The practice of comparing performance against a recognized standard.

Benchmarking can be applied to products, services or processes with the aim of identifying areas where the opportunity exists to improve overall. The practice is widely credited to the Xerox Corporation, which in the 1970s sought to understand why Japanese competitors were successfully underselling it. The process which the company developed provides the foundation for benchmarking to this day. It is built of five phases: planning clarifies the need for benchmarking; analysis identifies relevant performance gaps; communication carries the message to relevant parties in the firm; action initiates plans to implementation; and maturity measures outcomes and begins the cycle again.

The main change since then is that today benchmarking is usually carried out by independent organizations who compare against industry best practices. This enables companies to use benchmarking as an ongoing process, and also prevents jeopardizing trade secrets that provide competitive advantage in the field. Researchers test all the participants in a particular sector and then rate them according to key factors. Individual businesses are then able to interpret the results for themselves.

Some commentators have pointed out that a culture of benchmarking can have a detrimental effect. The problem they point out is that benchmarking tends to lay blame at the door of managers, ignoring economic or cultural factors that inhibit productivity.

Benchmarking has also taken on a specialized meaning in the world of computers, as industry-wide standards against which the performance of hardware or software can be gauged.

See also: **Effectiveness, Performance, Productivity, Quality**

Further reading: Bendell *et al.*, 1998; Bogan and English, 1994; Codling, 1998; Jorion, 1997; Xerox Corporation, 1987; Zairi, 1998

BENEFITS

Non-monetary remunerations awarded to an employee on top of their salary.

The sum of benefits excluding salary is often referred to as the compensation package. Benefits come in various kinds. Employee benefits, also known as fringe benefits, might include health insurance, pension provision and compensatory agreements to meet various eventualities. Some employee benefits are required by law, such as (in the US) remuneration as a result of becoming unemployed through no fault of the individual.

Discretionary benefits are of a different sort. They are used by the employer to act as incentives, either to attract labour or to motivate individuals. Examples of the former that are currently widely discussed include child care benefits or maternal and paternal leave.

Some benefits, such as certain pension plans, are contributory. Employers promise to pay a certain amount proportional to that contributed by the employee.

See also: **Labour, Motivation**

Further reading: Armstrong and Murlis, 1998

BEST PRACTICE

Ways of conducting business processes that are generally agreed to be the most efficient or effective.

Best practice originated in the General Electric company. GE management was looking for ways to overturn an entrenched culture that was preserved by middle management in particular. CEO Jack Welch instigated the workout programme that developed activities such as 'bureaucracy bursting' with the CRAP detector (Critical Review Appraisal). The style and energy of his initiative is characteristic.

More recently, best practice has come to be associated with an ongoing management style that focuses on processes. The idea is that an organization should not be stymied by being oriented towards people or product. The argument is that best practice in processes is what delivers improvements in the most important business indicator, customer satisfaction.

Best practice has gained additional status with the implementation of electronic supply chains. Its encouragement to treat suppliers as partners, fits with the increased transparency electronic supply chains provide between organizations.

See also: **Innovation**

Further reading: Tichy and Sherman, 1993

BIG BANG

Originally the deregulation of the various London financial exchanges and institutions in October 1986. But now taken to mean an approach that instigates change synchronically, the opposite of a phased or gradual approach.

The Big Bang of 1986 revolutionized the London Stock Exchange through a range of measures that took effect at a particular time by abolishing minimum commissions, ending the relationship that existed between stockbroker and stockjobber, and widely extending membership.

Since then, a big bang approach has been generalized to various scenarios, notably in relation to the introduction of the Euro, but it is often associated with the implementation of computer systems, when the old system is turned off one night and the new one starts up the next morning. Here the advantage of not having to run multiple systems simultaneously is thought to offset the risk of faults with the new system.

See also: **Project management**

Further reading: Lintz and Rea, 1999; Lock, 2000; Tinnirello, 2000

BOSTON CONSULTING GROUP MODEL

A methodology for enabling strategic thinking.

The Boston Consulting Group is a leading company of management consultants. The BCG Model, also called the growth share matrix, is probably its unique contribution. The matrix is a grid upon which products can be placed to assess their worth, present and future, for the company. A new product starts as a question mark because it is associated with high costs and low revenues. If the right decisions are made over which question marks to back some products will become stars, generating large revenue streams in growth markets though requiring a high spend to maintain. Cash cows represent products in their mature stage, generating large profits but requiring little in terms of expenditure because the market is not growing. Dogs complete the picture, products with low market share in low growth markets. According to the model, dogs are either exhausted cash cows or redundant question marks and should be divested.

See also: **Product, Strategy**

Further reading: Costin, 1998; Morse, 1998; Trott, 1998

BRAINSTORMING

A group decision technique that seeks first to generate ideas and only later to assess them.

Individuals that are perceived as being able to reflect, perhaps obliquely, on the problem at hand gather in an environment in which the constraints on free associating are minimized. The creative energies of the group are thereby thought to be maximized so that, when the brainstorming is over, it can turn to ordering what has been thrown up with a view to generating a solution.

Brainstorming is particularly useful as a way of subverting hierarchies. However, the belief that more original thinking can be done in a group has been questioned by research which indicates that individuals alone generate more innovative solutions, if less frequently.

See also: **Decision making**

Further reading: Kuhn, 1988

BRAND

The distinguishing characteristics of a product or service that inspires loyalty in customers and differentiates it from rivals.

The evolution of the Nike brand is illustrative. At first the brand was identified with the particular design in the sole of Nike shoes. The brand then became attached to the name of the company and its distinguishing logo. Finally, the essence of the company has come to be represented in the logo alone, or even the 'noise' of the logo.

Brands work on a number of different levels. To consumers, they can carry a number of factors that affect choice, from quality to lifestyle, and build customer loyalty. To the company, brands can offer ways of targeting different market segments with the same or similar products, for example Cadbury's range of sweets. Alternatively companies can market a range of products under one brand, such as Gillette. Brands typically have the legal status of trademarks.

Since the 1980s, when brands first appeared on asset sheets, they have increasingly come to be recognized as the most valuable part of some products or services. The Coca-Cola brand, for example, is valued in the region of $50 billion. During takeovers, high brand equity can be the most important factor on the price paid, in some cases pushing the value of the company to multiples of its stock market value and many multiples of its earnings. Strong brands can also appear to defy usual business rules. In one famous case on 2 April 1993, Philip Morris cut the price of Marlboro cigarettes to 20 per cent in response to a contracting market and rival products selling at less than half the price of a packet of Marlboro. However, the market responded negatively, the company's stock value falling by $13.4 billion on 'Marlboro Friday', since an otherwise logical move was perceived as damaging to the brand (although the company has since recovered and grown).

Each brand the company owns will have a brand manager. That individual or group will be interested in everything that affects the product, from development to customer feedback. In global markets, this is particularly complicated, especially since there are relatively few global brands. The manager's job focuses on influencing strategies to maintain brand coherence. Advertising is the main way a brand is established and maintained, achieving its so-called positioning. Advertisers talk of brands reinforcing a set of beliefs that are held by the target audience, that is they add value. This increase in the worth of the commodity is what distinguishes the brand from the product or service. Advertisements seek to build brand recognition or awareness, that is an acknowledgement on the part of the target audience that the product is 'for them', both in terms of how it feels and what it says. Advertisements can utilize a variety of subtle ploys to get the message across and achieve similarly complex or even contradictory results. At their peak, for example, Levi jeans appealed because they gave the wearer both individuality and commonality. Arguably the most successful brands are those that carry their customers with them, keeping just one step ahead of their tastes and values, so-called brand extension.

Having said that, brands also stand or fall on the products they represent. Brand is eroded if the price of the product is not right or its performance slips.

Marlboro Friday is regarded by some as a something of a watershed, exposing the chimera of this intangible asset. And yet brands appear to go from strength to strength. They have renewed their vitality in the online world, being the main contributor to the market valuations of firms such as Yahoo! and Amazon, and even in traditional businesses, such as Virgin, brand is clearly the most significant contributor to ongoing success.

See also: **Advertising, Category management, Differentiation, Intellectual property, Loyalty, Marketing, Positioning, Value**

Further reading: Chernatony, 1998; Dearlove and Crainer, 1999; Keller, 1998; Pringle and Thompson, 1999; Rook, 1999; Sherrington, 1999

BRAND EXTENSION

The application of a brand to a new product.

Companies use brand extension when they are introducing a new product to the market. It should be distinguished from line extension which is when a new product is targeted at a new market segment, and category extension which is when an existing brand is used to market different kinds of products labelled with it.

There are a variety of possible strategies for brand extension, such as adding the new product to a family of products already established, but it is managing the change that is complex. For example, a majority of customers will generally resist something that is new. Brand extension seeks to overcome this by giving the marketing department something familiar – the brand, from which to launch something new – the product. The familiar brand can also encourage retailers to stock the new product. Further, certain brand characteristics increase the chance of a new product being successful. If the brand portrays trust and comfort this can encourage customers to take the unfamiliar steps of buying the new product. Longevity and service reduce the sense of risk that customers have with the new product.

Brand extension carries risks too. For example, an ill-chosen extension cannot only lead to the failure of the new product but to damage being inflicted upon the parent brand too. Customers may similarly not only not buy the new product but become confused or irritated with the parent brand.

See also: **Brand, Leverage, Segmentation**

Further reading: Keller, 1998

BROKER

An entity that acts on behalf of a party in a buying or selling scenario.

Brokers can be employed for a variety of reasons. Sometimes they simply stand in for an individual who cannot be present. Sometimes they are able to offer expertise that enables the transaction. Some brokers called market makers, especially in financial markets, buy products themselves hoping to sell at a later time and make a profit. Brokers usually charge a commission as a percentage of the sale or purchase.

BUREAUCRACY

A measure of the administrative burden borne by an organization.

However, the pejorative meaning, that a bureaucracy is somehow inefficient, is contemporary. To the sociologist Max Weber, bureaucracies were the embodiment of the rationalist principle within an organization, making for consistency and good decisions. The modern drive to reduce costs is often taken to mean cutting bureaucracy, hence the negative connotation.

But this is a simplistic approach, and something can be learnt by re-examining Weber's definition. Bureaucracy is governed by two key principles: the division of labour and authority. A division of labour ensures that individuals perform tasks to which they are best suited. Authoritarian structures reintegrate these differentiated roles for the purposes of the organization by standardizing, rationalizing and routinizing processes. The company develops an administrative core responsible for this functioning. Loyalty to the bureaucracy which ensures coordinated, efficient action is encouraged by incentives and various intangible qualities such as respect for seniors.

Contemporary organization theory has focused on the problems of these so-called centralized organizations. Sociologists since Weber have demonstrated how the depersonalizing character of bureaucracy tends to cause the introduction of more and more rules and regulations, forming a vicious circle manifested in escalating amounts of paperwork. Economists have pointed out that organizational transactions that are the result of the workings of the bureaucracy alone increase in volume in the absence of market forces and so bureaucracies tend to become increasingly inefficient. Others have pointed out that in bureaucracies means can easily become ends in themselves.

As a result, decentralization has become a key driver in organizational reform. Here the idea is to move away from activity-based structures to relatively autonomous business units focused upon profits or customers. Decentralization follows since decisions are not hierarchically driven, though some top-down elements will remain, because the power to act is devolved to where it is closest to the processes concerned.

Government programmes to privatize public sector organizations are also driven by the critique of bureaucracy given above, although there is a growing body of work which indicates that not all service organizations are best governed by market principles, since these have their own internal dynamics that can tend to undermine public sector goals.

See also: **Centralization, Efficiency, Liberalization, Organization, Public sector**

Further reading: Pfeffer, 1981; Rathgeb Smith and Lipsky, 1995; Weber, 1979; Wilson, 1989

BPR

Business process re-engineering, defined by the authors Michael Hammer and James Champy as 'the radical redesign of business processes to achieve dramatic improvements in performance' in their 1993 book *Re-engineering the Corporation: A Manifesto for Business Revolution.*

Their programme centres on the drive to get organizations to organize around processes not functions. So rather than having separate departments doing R&D and marketing, there should be one continuous process of product development. Their belief is that the real benefits of BPR come not by improving already existing processes, but by redesigning them from the ground up. An organization after BPR will be a very different entity from what it was before. Revolution, not evolution, is what is required.

The theory is that vertical structures in organizations are inefficient. They create silos and impede responsiveness. Horizontally integrated processes, on the other hand, are always focused on the ends that improve productivity. There is also an emphasis in the programme on multi-skilling employees so that decision making need not be unnecessarily delayed. BPR seeks to exploit the opportunities offered by new information technology. Indeed, it has been closely associated with the deployment of workflow technology that aids horizontal process integration.

Since Hammer and Champy, various attempts have been made at not so much redefining BPR as reworking the methodologies they devised. Perhaps the most significant contributions are Harrington's business process improvement and Davenport's process innovation. Discussion of the risks associated with BPR has been rich too. For example, because BPR tends to be led by top-down teams there can be many problems associated with employee ownership of the change. Further, because BPR tends to require a long period of time, there has been much argument about its effectiveness in rapidly changing marketplaces. Even Hammer and Champy acknowledge that between 50 and 70 per cent of projects do not achieve the desired results.

Whilst BPR has undoubtedly achieved much in some organizations, it has been subject to waves of fashion. In particular, several well publicized BPR failures have fed the suspicion that BPR is only the latest wrap for the services of consultants who had become pervasive in the period before and since Hammer and Champy wrote their book.

BPR has also been questioned from an ethical stance. It is closely aligned to downsizing and restructuring since, particularly in the early days, BPR was sold as a way of making quick cost savings by reducing head count. These moves have been seen to backfire on firms who more recently have come under pressure to improve their customer service levels or who, seeking to employ new staff, have come up against skills shortages.

See also: **Decision making, Downsizing, Effectiveness, Efficiency, Guru, Processes, Restructuring**

Further reading: Davenport, 1993; Dutta and Manzoni, 1999; Hammer, 1996; Hammer and Champy, 1993; Harrington, 1991

BUYER

A buyer is usually taken to mean the person in the organization responsible for procurement or purchasing. However, it also has the generic meaning of anyone who purchases goods.

A buyer in the stricter sense will manage every aspect of the relationship between the company and its suppliers, including strategic decision making affecting future directions.

A buyer's market is one in which supply exceeds demand. Power in the purchasing cycle passes to the buyer because demand has dropped or because supply has increased as a result of new entrants.

Buyer behaviour models seek to understand purchaser decision making. This information can be used to improve marketing. Various models have been proposed: the Nicosia model looks at how the individual moves from the point of first contact with the product to the moment of purchase; the Howard and Seth model is particularly illuminating in monitoring behaviour over time, since it seeks to understand how buyers learn.

Stochastic models are also useful for dealing with mass buying patterns. They deal with issues such as the probability of consumers switching brands because of various market factors. Economic models also exist that assume buyers are rational and work to maximize satisfaction within the limits of the income they have. However, behaviourist theories have tended to show that non-rational factors are often at work too.

See also: **Behavioural theory, Consumer, Supply and demand**

Further reading: Lamming and Cox, 1999

CAPACITY

The quantity of product that can be produced, usually measured in the throughput of units over time. A less common meaning is the ability to meet debts.

How much capacity a company has is a fundamental operational question. A common method managers use to gauge an answer consists in posing the so-called 'M' questions: what methods are in operation; what materials are available; what machinery is deployed; what manpower is ready and able; what money can support production?

Measuring throughput can be a complex task, especially when outputs are varied, as on modern assembly lines, or intangible, as in service industries. In these cases throughput is sometimes calculated by measuring inputs or assessing what role the 'M' factors play. Capacity must also be thought of in terms of timescales – meeting demand in the short term is very different from having a strategy to deliver ongoing capacity over months and years.

A number of specific terms have also been developed to assist capacity management. The design capacity is the maximum throughput that can be achieved if circumstances are ideal. This will clearly differ from the actual capacity, which is what can be expected in practice. Normal capacity differs again: this is throughput subject to external pressures, such as demand for product or supply of raw materials. Excess capacity occurs when demand drops due to unexpected market conditions, although it can also be used as a competitive device that acts as a barrier to entry for competitors. Excess capacity is sometimes used to describe unexploited intangible assets such as brand.

See also: **Logistics, Productivity, Operations management and strategy, Total capacity management**

Further reading: McNair and Vangermeersch, 1998; Menascé and Almeida, 2000; Vollmann *et al.*, 1992

CAPITAL

The assets that give rise to production. One of the three basic ingredients, along with labour and land, that are necessary for production.

Capital comes in a number of guises. Human capital, for example, is the assets in the form of the individuals that a company employs. Intellectual capital is the sum of the knowledge held by the company. Financial capital is its total monetary resources.

Capital powers production, though if managed well is not consumed by it, and so firms try to find ways to invest in their capital. This increases its yield and enables the company to stay ahead of rivals. Capital investment might include training employees or enhancing a brand. Capital budgeting is the process by which managers decide how limited investment resources should be allocated. The payback period is the time it takes to recover the value of the initial investment, after which a return on the investment (ROI) can be expected. ROI is then a measure of whether the investment is worthwhile.

A more sophisticated investment assessment is the net present value tool. This incorporates calculations of the risk that an investment represents over time, resulting from factors such as changes in the value of currency. However, it can still only act as a guide in capital budgeting.

Capital investment in securities is the most important non-productive way that a company can make money out of its financial assets. However, it too brings returns over time, which means that returns are always to some degree uncertain. The capital asset pricing model (CAPM) is one way of managing this risk. CAPM breaks the investment into its risky and risk-free constituents and so tries to calculate the return the capital investment should yield. This figure can then be used to assess actual returns and make adjustments to the capital investment.

The assumptions that underlie CAPM have recently come under attack. In a famous article, 'Bye-bye Beta' published in *Forbes* in March 1992, the economist David Dreman pointed out that CAPM depends upon historical data; it is not necessarily a good measure of future returns. However, as no one has come up with a better model, CAPM is still widely used.

Firms employ a number of other terms when discussing capital. The cost of capital is the amount it must spend to maintain control of capital assets. It includes costs such as interest payments. Capital restructuring takes place when a firm alters the balance between capital of different types, perhaps by using cash to buy back shares or pay off debt. A capital gain is the profit made when a capital asset is sold.

Although fashionably discredited, an interesting point of departure in a theoretical discussion of capital is the work of Karl Marx. He held to the classical economic view of capital, which defined it as the sum of raw materials, the means of production, and that which sustains production – that is, accumulated labour. But he added a new ingredient to denaturalize capital. He pointed out that labour only becomes capital within a certain set of social relationships, those that form bourgeois society. This enabled him to develop a theory which showed how capital is commoditized. Raw materials, for example, have a use-value, that is, what they do in themselves. But they also have an exchange-value: their worth in a market. Capital is then the sum of exchange-values; or to put it another way, labour must be hired by capital to cause production. From this point, Marx was able to derive his critique of capitalist society, since, as he sees it, within this set of social relations, capital always has the upper hand.

See also: **Asset, Cash, Economics, Equity, Intellectual capital, Overcapitalize, Portfolio management, Restructuring, Risk, Venture capital, Yield**

Further reading: Brickley *et al.*, 2001; Carroll, 1998; Marx, 1999; Marx, 2000; Munn *et al.*, 1991; Singer, 1980; Vandermerwe, 1999

CAREER

The course of an individual's working life.

Career planning plays an important part in recruiting and retaining employees, acting as an incentive in the former case and as a motivator in the latter. Large firms often offer extensive programmes to educate staff and provide them with new experiences. One of the most recent developments in this respect stems from the deployment of HR technology. With an intranet, individuals are empowered to take responsibility for their own career path and are also able to deal with issues that research shows they may be hesitant to raise with their bosses directly, such as family commitments.

The taking of career breaks is much debated. The extension of the workforce, for example to include women, has made it a more common practice, in this case to raise children. But the blurring of the boundaries that surround working lives also tends to sensitize the issue for individuals.

See also: **Human resources management, Training**

Further reading: Maister, 1997

CARTEL

A group of businesses that collude to preserve their mutual interests in a market against external competition.

Cartels come in various forms; some are overt and legal, and even bring benefit to the market, as, for example, when R&D costs can be shared between participants. Other cartels are less enlightened. They generally work in one of two ways, either to maximize profits within the market as a whole or to maintain the market shares of the respective participants. Cartels function best when markets are stable and external threats are kept at bay. The maintenance of trust between colluders is important too, although a certain degree of competition between members of the cartel is possible, since they tend to exist in markets that are not overly sensitive to, say, small price changes.

The regulation of cartels varies from place to place. In the US, all cartels are in theory illegal, since antitrust laws outlaw any attempt to fix prices. The EU, on the other hand, only disallows cartels that actively reduce competition.

It can be hard to identify when a cartel exists, since – at least at a theoretical level – they might not be easily distinguished from a well functioning market. In this kind of cartel, market participants 'collude' not by arrangement but because competition is mediated by perfect signalling between market participants that forces them to act together.

See also: **Antitrust law, Barrier to market, Competition, Monopoly**

Further reading: Howard, 1983

CASE STUDY METHOD

The presentation of the activities of a particular company or market designed to highlight key factors that affect the way it operates.

Case studies provide useful, some would say essential, reading in business studies. Model case studies include Chandler's *Strategy and Structure*, which is still a core document in the study of the American firm. Empirical work of this type can be regarded as ground breaking.

The use of case studies in teaching varies from the merely illustrative of more theoretical points, to academics who use them as the only valid raw material from which conclusions can be drawn. Their importance to business studies has been emphasized by some schools in particular, notably the Harvard Business School, though not without being contested. Case studies, the critique runs, are only representative of business problems, and so tend to idealize scenarios, and then only those situations that lend themselves to the light of analysis.

There is also a trade-off between quantity and quality. Case studies that are not based upon individual cases but upon aggregated cases have the advantage of being more representative. However, individual case studies are able to present a richer picture that can explore specifics. Advocates of the case study method argue that it is this very understanding of specifics that is key to business success.

See also: **MBA**

Further reading: Chandler, 1962; Heath, J., 1998

CASH

The most liquid form of contract for value exchange. In general, money in hand.

Cash based accounting records transactions only when cash changes hands. It is therefore of limited value in describing the running of a business. However, cash flow – the provision of liquidity at the business's disposal – is essential to day-to-day trading and is critical to a functioning balance sheet. The cash flow statement takes on the same form as the balance sheet: something that requires cash on the right of the statement necessitates a reduction in the cash entry on the left, and vice-versa. In this way a balance is maintained. The cash flow statement can be used to answer various questions about the business, such as the relationship between earnings and cash flow, and it can guide managers in various operational and financing activities.

Cash flow analysis differs slightly and is a fundamental accounting measure. It seeks to answer the question of how much an asset costs and how much cash benefit it will bring to the organization over its lifetime. In order to complete the analysis, various questions must be asked of the asset, including its value and return, when this return can be expected and with what risk, and finally whether that will benefit the business.

Cash flow analysis differs therefore from other forms of cash based analysis, such as accounting profits. In this latter case, a healthy profit may be reported that disguises the fact that the business does not have the cash to invest in the assets it requires for the future. Failure to manage cash flow is a common cause of business failure. On the other hand, cash flow analysis is not the whole story either, since it does not account for non-monetary benefits, such as maintenance of brand, which may also be vital for future viability.

Cash flow analysis also does not account for depreciation, the rate at which some assets lose their value to a business, since the asset is accounted for by the initial transaction. And cash flow analysis can lead to a distortion in the way investment decisions are represented if account is not taken of the difference between financing investments, that need not be cash based, and the sum of investments made by the company over the given period.

Cash management is taking care of the cash needs of the organization and ensuring that cash is available in the right places and at the right times. Good cash management prevents a company from tripping up. For example, in a global economy the movement of cash across national boundaries can become a major issue because it costs, both in terms of fees and losses due to foreign exchange fluctuations. Removing these uncertainties is one of the benefits to business that would come with the introduction of the euro.

See also: **Accounting, Finance, Income statement, Inflation accounting, Liquidity, Returns**

Further reading: Munn *et al.*, 1991; Shim and Siegel, 2000; Shim *et al.*, 1997; Silbiger, 1994

CATEGORY MANAGEMENT

The administration of families of products, produced by a single large company, that are nonetheless associated with different brands. The idea behind category management is to ensure that whilst brands within the category compete successfully for different market segments, enabling the parent company to maintain its place within the category, the dangers of cannibalizing the market or eroding fellow brands are avoided. In large companies that own several brands within the same product category, the category manager complements the brand manager. The category manager sees that appropriate distances are maintained between brands, distances that brand managers may be tempted to traverse. And the category manager looks for opportunities when brands can work together for mutual advantage, something brand managers may never spot.

See also: **Brand, Marketing, Product**

Further reading: Doyle, 1998; Hill and O'Sullivan, 1999; Hooley, 1998; Lancaster and Massingham, 1999

CENTRALIZATION

The process of placing control of an organization in the hands of a few decision makers. Whilst decentralization is a more common route for companies to take in today's global markets, the amount of centralized control that should be exercised poses critical questions. For example, what economies of scale can be achieved with centralized management or production; can cost centres be established that introduce savings; what role does a centralized culture play in taking the corporation forward; are there issues peculiar to the business that can gain from centralization, such as R&D? Conversely, the issues that tend to cause companies to decentralize include the requirements of local regulations, the desire to get closer to local markets, the need to undo unwieldy bureaucracy, and a variety of reasons that lead to spinning off subsidiaries.

See also: **Bureaucracy, Organization**

Further reading: Ackoff, 1999b; Mendenhall *et al.*, 1995; Mudambi and Ricketts, 1998; Ostroff, 1999; Pasternack and Visco, 1998

CHANGE MANAGEMENT

The matter of steering a business from established to new modes of operation.

Change management has always been a critical issue for businesses, since there is no market that does not evolve and challenge companies to respond. However, the pervasive spread of information technology has led many to believe that change must become a way of life in organizations, not merely an activity that should occur at occasional intervals. The argument is that computer systems provide companies with the means to far greater knowledge of themselves and their markets. Those organizations that can use that information for themselves become proactive and dynamic, and will steal a march on competitors. The imperative, then, is for everyone to be good at change. In firms that have embraced change most radically, long-term planning is rejected in favour of portfolios of possible action which are constantly tested and rejected or evolved. Flux is the norm. Permanence the enemy.

It is widely agreed that people are the greatest challenge in change management, although to what extent people are actually resistant to change is a matter of debate. There is evidence, for example, that management, not people, has tended to be a conservative force in the sense of always looking for stasis, an attitude in large part motivated by fear of mistakes. It is perhaps for this reason that management consultants are nearly always sought when organizations are negotiating change: it not only brings in wider experience but provides scapegoats should things go wrong.

There are a number of management theories that deal with issues of change. A common type seeks to describe change in response to the development of the organization. This typically sees change as periods of evolution broken by a crisis of revolution, before regular growth continues again. For example, when a small company starts out it is driven by its own internal dynamic of creativity. However, with success comes growth, presenting the leadership with its first crisis. These individuals typically do not have the right management skills to negotiate this point, and so direction has to be brought in to take the firm to the next stage. The danger here is that the original creativity is compromised, so some kind of devolution has to occur to pass responsibility back. As the organization continues to grow, there are likely to be times when the matter of its control comes to the fore. Again, various management techniques will be tried, each dealing with the immediate problem but potentially threatening some other factor critical to continued growth.

It is the contraction of the periods of regular growth and the extension of the times of revolution that is promoted by those who believe change should be a way of life for modern businesses. Another category of change theories discusses how change can be most effectively brought about. These theories typically begin with an analysis of the situation along the lines that nothing can be achieved unless quality information is available about the organization and its functioning. They also stress the importance of staff owning the process of change from an early stage, perhaps with incentives, building motivation, or asking for contributions. How the change takes place is the next major concern. For example, McMahan and Woodman derive four categories: human processual, in which interpersonal relationships are used to drive change; technostructural, when the implementation of IT is the cause; strategic planning, when top management initiates change; and systemwide, when, for example, total quality management programmes are run.

Asking how organizations change is one thing. But whether they change for good or ill is another question entirely. The modern engine of change, information, can elude even the best computer systems. And with all the data in the world, predicting future patterns of growth is at best an imprecise science. It is therefore easy for organizations to change for the sake of change. The evaluation of changes that take place is therefore an important part of the process too. Again, business theory provides a number of options for carrying this out, but most theories stress that change evaluation depends upon the quality of the information about how the organization has changed and in what ways. Ways of checking the collection and interpretation of this data are essential.

See also: **Evolutionary change, Growth, Technology**

Further reading: Carnall, 1999; Clegg and Birch, 1998; Collins, 1998; Donaldson, 1999; Greiner, 1972; Kotter and Schlesinger, 1979; Macdonald, 1998; McMahan and Woodman, 1992

CHANNEL

The route that goods and services take from their originators to final purchasers.

Channel management is part of marketing, and deals with the various kinds of relationship that can exist along this distribution chain. The simplest channel is direct selling on the part of the manufacturer or service provider. Complexity is built up as various intermediaries appear between the two, such as retailers, agents and consultancies.

The reasons for not selling directly vary. It might be due to the traditional shape of the market, as with vehicle manufacturers. It might allow the producer of the product to concentrate on that core concern, leaving selling and end-user relations to others. This is common in the software industry. The channel also allows firms to access mass markets, as with those that sell on the high street.

The implementation of a channel strategy, that is the means by which a company can best exploit a channel to sell its products, can be fraught. For example, channel conflicts, when the interests of one participant in the channel are opposed by the actions of another, must be resolved. Channel strategy is also vulnerable when industries as a whole go through periods of change or new channels appear. For example, vehicle manufacturers are just one sector currently coming to terms with the emergence of the internet as a viable channel: some manufacturers are experimenting by dealing with customers directly, which has been interpreted by car dealerships as deliberately provocative. Disintermediation can be the result, when the role of some parties in the channel becomes redundant.

See also: **Direct operations, Retailing, Sales management**

Further reading: Friedman and Furey, 2000

CHARTISM

The belief that future share prices can be predicted on the basis of what has happened in the past.

Chartism gets its name because analysts use the patterns on historical price charts to describe likely price movements in the future. Mathematical modelling and neural networks have dramatically increased the complexity that can be brought to bear upon the problem of historically based market speculation.

Chartism stands in contradistinction to the predictive theories of the efficient market hypothesis (EMH), which states that all historical activity is already represented by the current price and so to look back provides no new information. Other market practitioners use a combination of tools in conjunction with their own intuitions, such as the famous and apparently random devices of Warren Buffett. For example, he has recommended investing in the five cheapest of the ten highest yielding shares from the Dow Jones Industrial Index.

See also: **Forecasting, Modelling**

Further reading: Paxson and Wood, 1997

CHURN

This is usually used to describe the rate of turnover of employees or customers. It also refers to artificially increased transaction rates in financial markets.

With regards to the first meaning, churn commonly carries a negative connotation. When there is a high employee churn rate, the implication is that that a company is unable to retain skills because staff leave. High customer churn is interpreted as indicative of the weakness of a brand or a crisis in customer loyalty.

Churning in financial markets, when brokers inflate buying and selling rates, increases uncertainty in prices and so tends to benefit the intermediaries who initiate the turbulence. Ascertaining whether churning has occurred can be difficult, since it closely imitates other, routine market conditions.

CLASSICAL ECONOMICS

The economic theories of the late eighteenth and nineteenth centuries.

In 1776, Adam Smith published *An Inquiry into the Nature and Causes of the Wealth of Nations*. He was the first to develop theories that supported the deregulation of trade, arguing that an 'invisible hand' governs groups of people operating in their own self interest, which brings about the unexpected result of good for all. His case is fundamental to the social acceptability of modern markets.

Smith sought to explain economic behaviour in terms of labour, land and capital. He believed that the goal of economic behaviour is consumption. He showed how the division of labour, that is specialization, increases productivity, which is in turn the only factor affecting the exchange value of products bought and sold. He illustrated this by his famous diamonds and water paradox: the former have little use but high exchange value, unlike the latter, because and only because they are hard to produce.

Smith's ideas were developed by David Ricardo, who argued a relativist case for exchange value by relating the value of exchange to the labour costs associated with production. He also introduced the principle of comparative advantage, a kind of division of labour on a national scale. This formed the theoretical basis for the promotion of international trade.

Thomas Malthus contributed a more pessimistic strain of thought. He is famous for having predicted the exponential growth of populations falling far behind increases in food production, since the latter are driven only by the comparatively weak incentive of profit.

The classical period is approximately concurrent with the Industrial Revolution. Its theories were important for freeing nations from the strictures of older mercantilism that demanded excessive government control, for example. However, whilst the classical writers are responsible for the principle of laissez-faire, which is that economic decisions are best made by individuals not governments, they also realized that companies operating in free markets need different kinds of regulation to be protected from threats such as monopolistic practices and any compromise to the labour force.

Other classical principles that persist include the stress on output in economics, notably the law of diminishing returns, which states that increasing inputs does not increase outputs indefinitely.

The classical period came to an end with the social crisis at the end of the nineteenth century. John Stuart Mill is usually thought of as signalling the end of it with his *Principles of Political Economy* in 1848. He believed that governments should intervene at certain times, in particular to manage the distribution of commodities. Mill also believed that demand played an important role in determining exchange value. Neoclassical economic theories were the result, and Marx added a pejorative connotation to the classical label when he accused Smith and others of theoretical myopia.

See also: **Keynesian economics, Monetarism, Neoclassical economics**

Further reading: Magill, 1997; Malthus, 1999; McAuliffe, 1997; Mill, 1998; Peach, 2001; Smith, 2000

COGNITION

An individual's perception of their environment. In business, cognitive sciences have contributed to understanding how individuals interact with the world around them so as to affect decision making.

The cognitive sciences seek to investigate the various forms of human reasoning. The underlying assumption is that human beings do not act wholly rationally but are influenced by attitudes, assumptions and biases. A cognitive error is a mistake made because of faulty reasoning that stems from these covert influences. Alternatively, a cognitive bias is the prejudice that results in decisions being systematically, if elusively, skewed. Cognitive dissonance is the discomfort an individual feels as a result of having to act in a way that conflicts with the beliefs or prejudices they hold.

Cognitive models of appraisal assess the performance of an individual in the light of these insights. They aim to account for all aspects that affect human performance and the way people interact with each other, including factors that are not immediately visible. Distributed cognition extends these insights to the level of the group.

The example of Myers-Briggs personality testing is illuminating. According to four criteria, individuals can be assessed for the way they relate to and function in the world. Particularly important for decision making are the two that show how people receive information from the world around them and how they process that information. With regards to the former, individuals receive information either through their senses or by using their intuition. With regards to the latter, they process information using either more emotional criteria or more rational argument. These combinations of type suggest, for example, that only certain individuals will be good at certain sorts of decision making.

See also: **Consumer, Decision making**

Further reading: Newell, 1990; Posner, 1989; Toplis *et al.*, 1991

COLLABORATION

Working together to achieve common or mutual ends. Collaboration is becoming an increasingly common feature in business as organizations operate in global, networked economies. Studying how firms collaborate is therefore an important gauge of the success with which they do it.

Various theories try to provide answers as to when companies should collaborate to best advantage. At a basic level, transaction-based cost economics shows how companies collaborate when they need a resource they do not have. A level of sophistication that is more appropriate to the global situation today is added by interorganizational relationships theory, which looks at how firms develop joint forms of government that assist in the collaboration.

The so-called virtual organization is the logical endpoint of collaboration. Here companies bring their core competencies along to the common enterprise.

See also: **Core competency, Network, Outsourcing, Virtual organization**

Further reading: Ackoff, 1999; Dussauge and Garrette, 1999; Francesco and Gold, 1998; Kock, 1999; Lee *et al.*, 1999; Mudambi and Ricketts, 1998

COMMUNICATION

The exchange of information within a company and with its partners, suppliers and customers.

Effective communication is vital to the well being of an organization. Without it, employees lack morale and direction, partners lose touch with common aims, and customers become discontent or indifferent.

Communication theory is founded upon the work of Claude Shannon. He identified seven factors at work during communication: a source encodes a message that is transmitted via a channel to a receiver that decodes the message and may provide some feedback. At any stage in this process, the effectiveness of the communication will be impacted by factors ranging from the cultural to the merely personal. Any of these could mean the communication goes wrong. The decoding stage is particularly important in business, since at that point the source has lost its ability to control how the message is received. In advertising, for example, great effort is made to understand how a target audience will interpret any message that the advertisement carries. Empirical research or even trial and error is often the only way to be sure.

Whilst many would agree with Shannon's basic model, there have been many different attempts to adapt his approach to different commercial applications. Sticking only with marketing, communication already takes many forms, including advertising, direct marketing, public relations and sales promotion. Together these are known as the communications mix. Different types of communication may be deemed more appropriate at different times. For example, more expensive or luxurious products may require direct marketing. Alternatively it might be regarded as wholly inappropriate for a company to communicate its regret for a mistake with an advert.

See also: **Advertising, Human resources management, Leadership, Marketing, Semiotics**

Further reading: Carysforth, 1998; Gronstedt, 2000; Jablin, 2001; Miller, 1999; Steinbock, 2000

COMPANY

The legal entity that exists to generate profits from commercial activities. Companies are usually required by law to be registered, for which they enjoy limited liabilities, notably that shareholders cannot be sued for debt repayment.

Company law is a massive subject in its own right. However, a few comments can be made here. Whilst legal requirements vary substantially from country to country, most jurisdictions have entities comparable to the UK's public limited company. The plc is required by law to publish details of its activities, called financial accounts. This responsibility is to provide the accountability that comes with the reduced liabilities a plc enjoys. The British Companies Act of 1985 sets out the minimum details that need to be published. Large companies must issue a balance sheet, a profit and loss account, and a cash flow statement. Small companies have to provide less, but the required information is mainly aimed at giving an indication of the company's worth, for the purposes of shareholders. Additional details are usually withheld to avoid supplying advantageous information to competitors.

Apart from their legal status, companies can be defined by a number of other characteristics. An important one is culture or ethos. Whilst this may or may not be consciously generated, it affects a wide range of attitudes to matters such as discipline and goals. It sets the tone that employees follow.

A related issue is that of company vision or mission. For example, in the 1980s Bill Gates saw Microsoft's goal as putting a 'computer on every desk in every home' – remarkable then, but the success of which can be judged by the fact that it is commonplace now. Company vision brings a long-term perspective on short-term management decisions.

See also: **Corporation, Mission statement, Organization**

Further reading: Goffee and Jones, 1998; Litka, 1991; Loose *et al.*, 2000; Pendlebury and Groves, 1999

COMPETITION

The rivalry that exists between firms operating in the same markets. However, a more technical meaning, from economic theory, sees competition as a necessary condition for the functioning of free markets.

The irony is that under theoretical conditions of perfect competition no rivalry can take place. Perfect competition is marked by completely transparent information flow between large numbers of market participants who can act without hindrance. Under these conditions, rivalry over price, for example, cannot take place because buyers will not tolerate even small increases by one company. The reason the conditions for perfect competition are worth studying nonetheless, is that they act as indicators for maximizing efficiency in the marketplace. On the other hand, some economists believe that models of perfect competition are limited because they cannot account for the most common features of real markets – the rivalrous behaviour of advertising, price-cutting, innovating and so on.

Regardless of theoretical contentions, the language of competition in business indicates that rivalry is alive and well. Competitive advantage is something all businesses seek: a relative lead on ideas or products that enables them to be more productive than their competitors. The theory of competitive advantage seeks to show how those with competitive advantage are more efficient than their rivals, which supports the common business practice of comparing productivity with rivals rather than with previous results from the same company.

Other related definitions are: competitive price – the amount arrived at after prices have been deliberately lowered to beat competitors; competitive tendering – the process of bidding for contracts, usually in the public sector, by private companies using sealed bids.

A number of ethical issues arise as a result of the rivalry inherent in competitive practice. These fall into at least two broad categories, one directly affecting the individual and the other dealing with the more general behaviour of companies. Classical economics states that competitive markets are good for societies and individuals. Whilst this principle is generally believed to hold, at least in the capitalist West, all markets are governed by rules. The governance of competitive environments must therefore be assessed ethically. John Rawls, in *A Theory of Justice*, argues that the rules of market association can be analysed by asking whether they act fairly and equally on all participants in the market, whether they be supplier, buyer, winner or loser. In general, it turns out that what counts as unethical behaviour, such as price fixing or erecting barriers to market, is also detrimental to competition.

The theory of perfect competition has been revived to a degree in recent years because of the pervasive spread of computer systems in business – with the implication that information flows more freely in markets as a result. The question is to what degree this is merely coincident with increased levels of competition in many sectors. Some claim that the pace of change is now such that the nature of competitive markets is altering fundamentally. For example, they point to evidence which suggests that even monopolies are not immune from competition. Whatever the theoretical implications, it is certainly true that the need to remain competitive has never been more keenly felt by business.

See also: **Classical economics, Monopoly, Neoclassical economics, Price, Supply and demand**

Further reading: Ball and McCulloch, 1999; High, 1990; Porter, 1998a, 1998b; Rawls, 1971; Salmon and Linares, 1999; Wagner and Hollenbeck, 1998

CONSOLIDATION

Combining business activities within and without the organization in order to cut costs.

Consolidation was originally applied to the practice in the shipping industry of companies linking together to fill containers and so reduce freight costs. However, it is now commonly applied more generally.

A more recent specialized application of the word concerns consolidated accounts. This refers to the integrated financial reports of a parent company consisting of a group of smaller companies that have previously been taken over. Each company in the group can keep its legal integrity even though the parent is obliged to produce consolidated accounts for the purposes of shareholders.

See also: **Downsizing, Holding company**

CONSUMER

A buyer or user of goods or services.

To this basic definition a number of others should be added. Consumer choice, for example, is a concept from marketing that seeks to increase sales by segmenting potential buyers of goods and diversifying their appeal through advertising, brand or price. Consumer acceptance is the point at which a product meets the approval of its buyers. Consumer goods are those products that retail domestically, as opposed to, say, industrial goods. A consumer panel is a group of consumers asked about their behaviour and taken to be representative of consumers as a whole. The consumer price index is a measure of the cost of consumer goods in an economy.

An important contribution to the many theories that try to understand consumers is consumer buyer behaviour. It points out that consumers have different relationships to the central act of purchasing. In a typical household there will be initiators, who suggest the act; influencers, who inform any decision; deciders, with the power to act; purchasers, who carry it out; and users, the actual consumers.

Understanding the role these individuals play in buyer behaviour can inform marketing and pricing in particular. The theoretical models of economists tend to veer between those who see consumers acting more or less rationally. But generally speaking it is empirical data that businesses value most. The use of information technology is particularly illuminating. Many projects, including such schemes as loyalty cards, are aimed at building massive databases that precisely record individual consumer's behaviour in order to be able to predict, respond and promote likely choices in the future. In marketing, the logical end point of these developments is one-to-one marketing, in which the company relates to the consumer as a single entity rather than one of a large group.

Consumerism is a diverse concept. It can be applied as the chief characteristic of a late capitalist society, generally reckoned to have emerged at the time when domestic goods became available to mass markets of middle-class consumers. Conspicuous consumption is a related concept, when a consumer displays their ownership of goods to excess, possibly implying comment on the consumer society in the process.

However, consumerism also refers to the movement that has seen consumers organizing themselves to demand more sovereignty. This idea has taken another turn in, for example, the emergence of environmentally concerned groups of consumers who organize to raise awareness of the ethical impact of production and consumption. So-called 'green' or 'organic' products are a direct result.

A related development stems from the growth of international markets. Here consumerism is concerned with individuals who are vulnerable to exploitation because of gross inequality in the relationship between the consumer and the business.

Consumer rights more generally are therefore recognized in law. In the US, for example, the Consumer Bill of Rights of 1962 identifies four key rights: consumption must be safe, informed, freely chosen, and with the right of reply. The onus of responsibility for the maintenance of these rights generally rests with producers. Many consumer groups exist to safeguard the interests of consumers. Arguably the most famous was the Public Citizen Group, which in the 1960s instigated an investigation of the car industry in the US. It led to laws being passed, and set a precedent for the activity of pressure groups on other industries too. Consumer rights are today routinely taken up in media investigations, and companies that are seen to be putting profits ahead of rights can expect to be damaged as a result.

See also: **Activism, Brand, Data, Decision making, Environmental audit, Marketing, Relationship marketing, Sales management, Social audit**

Further reading: Craig-Lees *et al.*, 1995; Dubois, 2000; Engel *et al.*, 1990; Kotler, 1994; Lambkin *et al.*, 1998; Rook, 1999; Webb, 1999

CONTROL

The exercise of power within an organization, in business, for the purposes of promoting outputs.

The matter of control within the organization clearly affects many aspects of commercial life, from keeping count of the rivets that enter the assembly line for which control systems might be implemented, to managing a brand which will draw on a whole range of techniques all aimed at keeping control of its development. Control takes on a more specific meaning when it comes to the regulation of corporations. Corporate control is concerned with the enormous power that large companies exercise as a result of their market capitalizations. Financial markets provide the most important mechanisms of control. But the ability of shareholders to exercise their power varies enormously, with the US being arguably the most effective and Far Eastern economies the least.

See also: **Finance, Operations management and strategy, Processes, Quality**

Further reading: Chorafas, 2000; Kinney, 2000, Lee *et al.*, 1998; Schönsleben, 2000; Vollmann *et al.*, 1992

CORE COMPETENCY

The business output that more than any other provides a company with its lead in a market.

Identifying core competencies and then organizing the company to exploit them to increase productivity has become a key strategy for competing in contemporary markets. The problem is that global markets tend to erode many traditional sources of competitive advantage. It is argued therefore that the modern company that can view itself as a source of resources can find new ways to compete.

The practice is closely associated with outsourcing. A company will form partnerships with others that can execute processes they require but do not wish to develop themselves, in order to be free to concentrate in-house resources on their core competency.

Core competencies can be difficult to identify because of the implication that other things the firm does it does not do well. However, they can include tangible and intangible assets, from manufacturing products to managing brands.

See also: **Economies of scale, Outsourcing, Productivity, Specialization**

Further reading: Gay and Essinger, 2000

CORPORATION

A generally large association of persons who can in law carry out business or legal activities.

Because corporations are large business enterprises, the matter of their control is a specialized issue of management. Corporate planning is a top-down process that seeks to highlight the overall strategies the corporation should adopt and how those plans might be implemented. This information is communicated to managers, who are encouraged to gather more data to assist in honing the plans and work on those that emerge as the favourites. In large organizations there is the particular danger of losing sight of the 'bigger picture' because managers can become preoccupied with fire-fighting the issues that confront them on a daily basis.

Corporatism is the movement that through the course of the last century saw corporations gain power. This was partly because of the removal of controls that formerly limited company activity, and partly because changes to corporate law separated ownership from management. In fact, in the US a corporation may refer to any company in which managers are not owners. The opening up of investment opportunities that was associated with this change led to enormous increases in the power of corporations as capital flowed in their direction.

The birth of the modern corporation has led to other important economic developments. For example, the corporate pension fund is an investment fund set up exclusively for the benefit of employees upon retirement. As the cost of state pensions has risen, so governments have developed various incentives to encourage these funds. Corporate pension funds have therefore become important sources of capital in their own right. They are also subject to rigorous scrutiny in order to make sure that the interests of employees are paramount.

See also: **Company, Enterprise, Fordism, Holding company**

Further reading: Altman, 1993; Cohen and Boyd, 2000; Davies, 1999; Fraser, 1998; Hopt *et al.*, 1998; Howard, 1998

CREATIVITY

The capacity to generate new ideas. Creativity is increasingly recognized in business as a way of staying ahead of competitors. The question is, how can it be nurtured in organizations?

Part of the problem is that creativity is viewed as a personal trait rather than an organizational characteristic. Cognitive theorists in particular have analysed the process that leads to the development of a creative product, defined as one that captures the imagination in terms of its relationship to brand and customers. It is generally agreed that various factors should be in place, such as a high degree of self-belief and freedom to pursue intuitions. The problem is that these qualities do not sit very easily in most organizations. Indeed, bureaucracies work to limit precisely these things.

Various techniques have been devised to transcend organizational limitations. Brainstorming and innovation are discussed elsewhere. Synectics is one more to mention, a technique that seeks to disturb conventional ways of thinking about problems by pushing scenarios to limits that then give rise to new, radical solutions.

See also: **Brainstorming, Innovation, Leadership, Product, R&D, Strategy**

Further reading: Kuhn, 1988; Runci and Albert, 1990; Sternberg, 1988

CRISIS MANAGEMENT

A style of management that is able to deal with unknown or precipitous events striking at the heart of the business.

Crises can be chronic or critical. Chronic crises that may last some time, but which the company anticipates being able to pull out of, require strong management by individuals who recognize the depth of the challenge and are prepared to take measured risks. Morale is another important issue, and so communications skills and visibility in the organization are crucial. There are generally two sides to the decisions that must be made in chronic crisis mode. The first concerns costs – finding ways of cutting them effectively and quickly. The second concerns outputs – finding ways of breathing new life into products so that customers become receptive to them once again. These principles are of course different from 'business as usual' only by degree. But therein lies success or failure.

Critical crises may take companies by surprise when they happen but they can be prepared for no less. An example is the public relations activity that surrounds a disaster in which a company is directly implicated in people's deaths. Air France exhibited good crisis management of this sort after the crash of Concorde in 2000. Here the company had the mechanisms in place to deal with the media without delay, transparently, and in a manner that was seen to be caring. Air France was therefore able to contain even this dire situation.

Another less specific use of the phrase describes a generally reactive style of management.

See also: **Bankruptcy, Morale, Public relations, Troubleshooting**

Further reading: Bland, 1998; Heath, R., 1998; Ramu, 2000; Reid, 2000; Seymour and Moore, 2000; Zimmerman, 1991

CRITICAL SUCCESS FACTORS

The factors on which a business project can succeed or fail.

Critical success factors are important because they are not always obvious, or can be eclipsed by apparently more pressing items of business. For example, it may turn out that customers value a service for very different reasons than those originally intended. Alternatively, certain products in a portfolio, whilst important as loss leaders, may be insignificant in terms of generating profit. Identifying critical success factors can also be a useful way of reviewing the management of the business too.

The term originally stemmed from IT projects. The problem here is that computer system implementations are frequently very complex. Identifying precisely the benefits that are sought for can therefore provide a useful steer on a project as it proceeds and has to negotiate various hurdles and decisions. These are critical success factors.

See also: **Core competency, Project management**

CRM

The implementation of computer systems – customer relationship management – to support an organization's attempt to be customer oriented.

CRM may be regarded at a number of different levels. At its most basic it is about providing an organization with the ability to analyse the reserves of customer data it may hold for the purposes of marketing and sales. A next level refines this activity so that customers are segmented, typically according to profitability, in order that the organization can weight its efforts in favour of its better customers. At the highest level CRM enables the organization to respond directly to individual customers, providing a personalized service rather than one that is confined to predetermined processes. It is the growth of databases and the powerful tools that manipulate the vast quantities of data they contain that has led to CRM being seen as an important way of enhancing productivity.

A common goal of CRM is the retention of customers in saturated markets. Supermarkets and banks are therefore leaders in the field. Research shows that it is far more cost effective to cross and up-sell products to customers with brand loyalty than it is to attract new customers from competitors. In this respect, CRM is an important ingredient in the success of M&As. Indeed, the customer databases of the merging firms are often one of their most significant assets.

CRM enables companies to improve service in a variety of ways. It may improve direct mailshots by providing the means of sending out specific rather than general marketing collateral. CRM systems may make customers personalized offers, perhaps connected to some personal event such as a birthday. Alternatively, CRM tools integrate the different systems that support a customer's contact with the organization via various channels so that consistent and up-to-date information is presented to agents, whether in the branch or on the high street. Advocates often describe CRM as bringing the qualities of face-to-face 'village' retailing to mass market, multiple-channel business.

See also: **Data, E-business, Marketing, M&As, Relationship marketing, Segmentation**

Further reading: Gosney and Boehm, 2000; McKean, 1999

CULTURE

The beliefs, norms, attitudes and customs that inform a particular group of people.

Culture plays a critical part in various commercial activities. In marketing, for example, the shared values and common experiences of a culture directly shape consumer buyer behaviour, the way people respond to advertising, and the success that different products may have. In terms of the organization, cultures will determine how people behave and how they regard important characteristics of the organization, such as its hierarchy and way of doing business.

Cultures can be divided along many lines. For example, youth culture, associated with young people, is regarded as being characterized by spending on modestly priced items belonging to particular brands but with little loyalty to them.

International business brings another dimension to the problem. In particular, being able to compare cultures is increasingly valuable for organizations operating in global markets. Hampden-Turner rates a number of national cultures according to five factors that represent issues important in business. For example, a universalism-particularism axis rates the relationship of the culture to rules and standards. This can be important to business both in terms of providing a stable operating environment and establishing working practices. Canada, the US and the UK are easily the most universalist. Colombia and Venezuela the most particularist. A second axis is specific-diffuse, specificity implying an exact and analytical approach to relationships, diffuseness implying a strong sense of rapport and intuition. Uruguay steals the lead on Canada, the US and the UK here, with Portugal and Chile being the most diffuse. Attitude to status plays a major role in business too. According to Hampden-Turner, most Western countries have an attitude that respects what people do, whereas Latin American and other countries are more interested in who people are, although the way this plays out in terms of business growth is complicated and evolving fast.

Understanding subcultures, minority groups within a large culture, can also be valuable to businesses. These groups may well behave very differently from the culture as a whole, or embody characteristics ahead of time. For example, gay culture in the West has been successfully exploited not only by businesses directly serving lesbians and gay men, but also by mainstream businesses looking for consumers who are regarded as trend setters in the culture as a whole.

Apart from comparative work, organizations may simply encourage an awareness of culture. This does not require descriptive precision so much as sensitivity towards differences. On this basis, organizational problems associated with culture, such as racism, can begin to be undone.

As a theoretical subject, culture is one laden with ambiguity, as it resists close definition. Kroeber and Kluckholn's book is often regarded as foundational. They studied the work of anthropologists, though having been published in 1952 it shows the problem with the advancing of the subject too.

See also: **Discrimination, Marketing, Organization**

Further reading: Dowling *et al.*, 1999; Francesco and Gold, 1998; Gemünden *et al.*,1997; Hampden-Turner, 'Perspectives on management in the Americas', in Warner, 2000, 44–59; Kroeber and Kluckholm, 1952; Lane *et al.*, 2000; Maddock, 1999; Morosini, 1998; Oddou and Mendenhall, 1998; Wartick and Wood, 1998

DATA

Information in a form that can be processed by a computer.

Data is often regarded as the life blood of the modern organization and the raison d'être of the knowledge economy, since exploiting data is a key means of increasing productivity, profitability and competitive advantage.

The systems at a company's disposal for managing its data resources have proliferated in recent years. The database management system (DBMS) provides the fundamental building block. Originally DBMS was designed to tackle problems such as redundancy – the duplication of data as a result of the same information being stored in different files without reference to each other. Successive advances have increased the capacity of databases to model the data they contain and so manipulate it. The most common today is the relational database, in which information about data, so-called metadata, dramatically improves data handling both in terms of speed and sophistication.

Datawarehousing is a more recent development, responding to the massive increases in data that the modern, networked organization can assimilate. The problem was that many companies found it virtually impossible to access all this information at one time since it was distributed around the organization, often in incompatible forms. The solution is the datawarehouse, a central store of all the information that has been gathered together. The idea is that a holistic view of the organization can be gained by managers of all kinds, perhaps wanting to cut it to analyse sales of a certain product by place and time, perhaps wanting to gain a high-level view of the firm to report to the board. Datawarehousing is, however, no panacea. Data capture is still a major logistical issue, and the integrity of the data, how 'clean' it is, complicates matters further. The tools for analysing the data, in a process called datamining, still often impose limits on results and, in a world in which it is not just data that counts but real-time data, datawarehouses can become out of date.

Data protection is a related issue, and one over which arguments intensify day by day. Most countries have data protection legislation that gives individuals the right to access the information that is stored about them. However, it is sometimes argued that the internet, which has increased the ease with which data can be gathered, manipulated and shared by an order of magnitude, has rendered these laws redundant.

See also: **Information and communications technology, Technology**

Further reading: Cabena *et al.*, 1998; Davis, 1997; Martin *et al.*, 1999; Shim, 2000; Stair, 1999

DECISION MAKING

The analysis of options in order to choose the course of action that is believed to represent the greatest benefit or chance of success.

The literature on decision making is vast, since the subject is regarded as a critical management activity, though fraught with danger. All stress the importance of gathering information prior to decision making, being aware of factors that have a bearing upon the process itself, and identifying ways of dealing with the uncertainty that is at the nub of the problem.

The theoretical analysis of decision making aims to clarify what goes on during the process so as to improve the quality of decision making. Here, we will consider the work of Koopman and Pool (in Cooper and Robertson, see below) who have described four types of decision making in relation to the environments in which they are best suited. The first is the neo-rational model. It takes note of the cognitive insights which suggest that decision making involves rational and non-rational processes. However, because it tries to account for intangible factors such as feelings, it tends to be suited to situations in which only a few decision makers are involved, such as top management. The second is the open ended model which takes note of the uncertainty that surrounds decision making, preferring a number of small reactive decisions to be taken in order to best shape the overall outcome to real circumstances. The emphasis on flexibility suits innovative organizations. The third, the bureaucratic model, is characteristic of large corporations where decision making is inevitably complex and involves many participants. The emphasis on rigour brings a thoroughness to the process, although at the expense of time taken to reach a conclusion. Finally, the arena model of decision making applies to organizations in which responsibility is widely distributed. Typically, different interest groups will make representations to the organization as a whole in the hope that a consensus can be reached as to the course that should be followed. This model is necessary to hold certain kinds of organization together, although it suits those that are least sensitive to compromise.

Decision trees provide a graphical representation of the decision-making process. They are designed to set out the options a decision maker has, and provide some analysis of the outcomes that various choices could lead to. Decision trees are in the form of probability diagrams. Each branch of the tree represents an outcome that follows from the premise to which it is attached. For example, two common outcomes are success or failure, and a probability can be assigned to these to provide a quantitative measure of the likelihood of each. Alternatively, decision trees can be used to represent cost, with each branch carrying an amount that that choice represents. A larger decision can in this way be broken down into a number of smaller steps, clarifying the implications for the business if decided one way or another. If, for example, the overall success of a decision depends upon the success of several smaller steps, then an overall probability of success can be calculated.

Decision trees are very useful in certain situations. If, for example, the decision under scrutiny is similar to decisions that have been taken in the past, then the quantitative aspect of their analysis is likely to be accurate, since probabilities can be derived from that experience. However, for the same reason they tend to fall down if the decisions being taken are strategic rather than routine. Strategic decisions are by definition steps into the unknown. Decision trees are also subject to prejudices of the decision maker who might, for example, make a more desirable outcome appear more probable. They are also prone to conceal qualitative aspects of decision making, especially human factors, which can be as important to success.

See also: **Behavioural theory, Cognition**

Further reading: Ashton and Ashton, 1994; Cooper and Robertson, 1990, 101–48; Davis, 2000; Dearlove, 1998; Dowell, 1998; Evans and Olson, 2000; Hosking and Andersen, 1992; Kinney, 2000; Porter and Norton, 1995; Smith, 1998; Wisniewski, 1997

DELEGATION

The art of passing authority to others.

Delegation can be thought of as an art, since to be successful it requires a manager who is sensitive to their own issues as well as those for whom they are responsible. It is closely related to the issue of empowerment, since employees must be given the right amount of authority and skills to tackle the task: too little and they are ill equipped, too much and they are swamped. Timing the process of handing over authority is important, as is defining the criteria of success, although it is hard to provide prescriptive advice since determining these factors depends on the temperaments of the individuals concerned. Whilst, however, workers then become accountable for the delegated work, the senior manager remains responsible for it.

Delegation carries many benefits, beginning with the likelihood of a more effective and efficient organization, but also promoting motivation and morale. For managers, perhaps the most important commodity delegation generates is time. The irony is that whilst virtually all managers are short of time, many resist delegating. This could be for a variety of reasons. Some are institutional, such as a belief that a certain distance should be kept between seniors and their subordinates. Others are personal, such as when managers simply want to keep all the credit for themselves.

See also: **Leadership, Management, Motivation**

Further reading: Schwartz, 1992

DELPHI METHOD

A technique for determining the likelihood of future events based upon past experience. The Delphi method assembles a panel of experts from different disciplines to comment upon the research of others in their own and different fields. It is typically used to arrive at high-level predictions, especially in relation to economics and politics. The aim is to account for the complex factors that affect long-range forecasting, or situations in which unknowns might play a major part, by generating a wide range of possible future scenarios. The method also claims to safeguard against the tendency of group discussions on these kinds of matters to arrive at a consensus. With the Delphi method experts respond to questionnaires at a distance.

See also: **Forecasting, Qualitative methods**

Further reading: Gummesson, 2000a; Linstone and Turoff, 1975

DEMOGRAPHICS

Statistical information about a geographical area that defines the population's characteristics.

The national book of demographic information is the bible of the marketing department. The population can be defined according to any information that is available, usually derived from national censuses. Gender, age, race, marital status, birth rates, income and expenditure are typical variables.

Demographics can be used very imaginatively by marketing departments to identify opportunities. An obvious example concerns the rising age of populations in Western countries. Industries in which youth defined marketing appeal, such as health and holidays, have been revivified as businesses have recognized the importance of older people to their growth. A more sophisticated use of demographic information is demonstrated by supermarkets who depend on a variety of demographic factors to stock and even design their stores accordingly.

For the UK, upyourstreet.co.uk provides a good example of the kind of detail demographic sources now provide.

See also: **Marketing, Segmentation**

Further reading: Annual Abstracts of Statistics, Central Statistical Office, London: HMSO; *Statistical Abstract of the United States, United States Bureau of the Census*, Austin TX: Reference Press

DIFFERENTIATION

The process of establishing differences between a product or service and its competitors. Differentiation usually consists of first identifying or manufacturing a difference, then drawing consumers' attention to it by marketing.

Differentiation is a fundamental tool of marketing. It might be a way of drawing attention to one offering in a market that is swamped with many versions of virtually the same product. Price, brand or quality can be used as differentiators here. Differentiation can also serve to revivify markets in which there are otherwise few opportunities for new offerings. Dental care products provide a case in point: different toothpastes might be sold as enamel whiteners, breath fresheners or fighters of decay. Differentiation can also add value to a product by bundling a premium service with it. Lifetime guarantees for an extra charge is typical.

See also: **Brand, Marketing, Positioning, Saturation, Segmentation, Value**

Further reading: Gummesson, 2000b; Hartley, 1998; Hill and O'Sullivan, 1999; Hooley, 1998; Lancaster and Massingham, 1999; Stauble, 2000

DIRECT OPERATIONS

A variety of commercial activities that tend to cut out intermediate processes or agents.

Direct sales are familiar. For example, the insurance industry was revolutionized in the early 1990s by the introduction of call centres that enabled customers to buy insurance from firms without going through a broker. Insurance firms gained on a number of fronts, making cost savings by using a less expensive channel to market and establishing relationships with customers that could be exploited in other ways.

Direct marketing is an alternative to mass marketing. The best example is direct mail, which by posting information out to targeted addresses greatly raises the chances that marketing collateral will be seen by potential customers.

In economics, the direct ascription generally implies a close identification between financial means and ends. A direct cost, for example, is one that can be attributed specifically.

See also: **Data, E-business, Information and telecommunications technology, Marketing, Sales management**

Further reading: Berry, 1998; O'Malley *et al.*, 1999

DISCRIMINATION

An unfair bias against or intolerance of a group of individuals that is often illegal.

In the US, the pioneering work of modern anti-discriminatory practice was driven through by Lyndon Johnson's Equal Employment Opportunity (EEO) legislation, notably the Civil Rights Act of

1964. So-called protected classifications were defined, such as race, sex or religion, against which it became illegal to discriminate. Protection was not only provided for the minority group: the law applies to men as well as women in relation to sex, for example. The law was updated in 1991, when employers found guilty could also be called upon to pay punitive and compensatory damages. These amounts have since escalated as American society becomes more litigious. The situation elsewhere tends to be somewhat different, in terms of being less rigorous and more reactive. The touchstone in the European Union, for example, is equal opportunities, although current legislation passing through the European Parliament looks more like American discrimination law. However, the onus is still more on the offended party to prove discrimination than for companies to ensure they do not discriminate. The effect is that organizations are rather less aware of discriminatory practices that might be deeply buried in the institution. Having said this, tensions between the European Union and member states, the former being more of a champion of the cause, have highlighted the issues. So-called glass ceilings, preventing women from rising to top management posts, are widely recognized if as yet not dismantled.

Developments since the 1960s have had a positive effect on organizational behaviour, as well as providing recourse when things go wrong. For example, human resources management is now routinely scrutinized in great depth. At an individual level, managers have to provide extensive documentary evidence in support of their decisions. And at the organizational level, ways of assessing employees have been tested to ensure they are not prejudiced.

See also: **Culture, Glass ceiling, Human resources management, Tokenism**

Further reading: Good, 1998; Karake-Shalhoub, 1999; Maddock, 1999; Peters *et al.*, 1998; Wolkinson and Block, 1996

DISTRIBUTION

The physical movement of goods from the manufacturer to the point of purchase.

Producers often have a wide choice of distribution channels at their disposal. Adopting the right strategy to get products to market is critical, since distributors have a large impact upon the effectiveness with which a product reaches its market and the profit it generates as a result.

The globalization and increased efficiency of modern distribution channels has also been important in terms of opening up markets to producers, although this can be overplayed: even the Romans imported oysters from Colchester to reach their capital in a day. But generally, the extension of channels has tended both to diversify the products available and reduce the impact upon seasonal fluctuations in supply. For example, small farm holdings in Africa are able to supply high street supermarkets in the West, although this case also points to the ethical issue of profit-taking at multiple points along the distribution channel, which can dramatically reduce the earnings of the original producers. Distribution channels can also provide the means for companies that are dominant in a market to exercise anticompetitive practices.

The internet has prompted another wave of evolution in distribution, since it opens up potential productivity improvements in relation to the informational aspects of distribution, that is knowing what is where and when. The ramifications are as yet unclear, but in retailing, for example, online distribution has in certain sectors tended to reduce the power stores have as a channel to market. Alternatively, in manufacturing, electronic supply chains have dramatically altered the way suppliers relate to their customers.

See also: **Channel, E-business, Logistics**

Further reading: Christopher, 1998; Cox, 1997; Tyndall *et al.*, 1998

DIVERSIFICATION

The development of commercial activities across a range of interests, usually as a way of offsetting the risk of being too dependent on one.

That one should not hold all one's eggs in the same basket is a truism that applies to business as any other sphere of life. For businesses though, diversification can hold distinct strategic advantages.

For example, diversification is a key means to growth. This can be in a proactive and reactive mode. Proactively, it might be that a company itself opens up a new line of business by developing its activities to enter new markets. Diversification may also take the form of merging with or acquiring new businesses. Here the strategy is to benefit from economies of scale, or to gain control of the assets that the new partner has for the advantage of the whole.

Reactively, diversification can be a way of addressing jittery shareholders. The belief here is that increased profits will always follow a growth in sales. Internal or external diversification, as described above, can therefore have a positive impact upon share value. Having said this, diversification has tended to fall out of fashion in recent years, as companies look more to their core competencies and other strategies for increasing their worth.

See also: **Growth, Marketing, Portfolio management, Product, Saturation**

Further reading: Channon, 1997; Pasternack and Visco, 1998; Trott, 1998

DOWNSIZING

A management strategy that seeks to restructure the business by outsourcing and by reducing the workforce.

The mantra of downsizing is 'leaner and meaner'. It was closely associated with a number of movements in the 1990s, such as business process re-engineering. Downsizing has been credited with much business success. Commentators point to the extensive downsizing that took place in the US at the end of the twentieth century, for example, and the way in which that country also retained its place as the world's most competitive economy.

However, it did not come without cost. Following the experience, many companies found themselves stripped of valuable assets, notably skills sets and loyal employees. Today, downsizing has tended to be replaced by the idea of 'rightsizing', building an organization that is neither too bloated nor too lean.

See also: **BPR**

Further reading: Gowing *et al.*, 1998; Karake-Shalhoub, 1999

E-BUSINESS

Business activities that are driven wholly or to a significant degree by the exploitation of internet-type technologies.

E-business is the child of e-commerce, though one that is rapidly eclipsing its parent. It has developed specifically from the adoption of the internet since the mid-1990s, and more generally from the importance of information as a provider of competitive advantage that has emerged since computers started pervading businesses.

Overall, e-business is generating the massive interest it is because it represents a major evolution, if not revolution, in the options available to businesses of all kinds for improving operations and productivity. Internally, e-business has initiated a new wave of cost-cutting opportunities. It integrates business and administrative processes, allows for more effective sharing of information either between individuals or across the supply chain, and opens up new economies of scale for companies to capitalize on. Externally, e-business lowers the barriers that prevent entry into new markets, provides a cheaper but more customized channel to reach markets, represents the chance to develop new models for sales and marketing with significant competitive advantage, and has proven to be a major strategy for increasing shareholder value.

Less specifically, whilst it is an exaggeration to compare the online revolution with the Industrial Revolution, e-business has boosted a spirit of innovation in many business sectors, to say nothing of the lease of life it has brought to the IT sector.

E-business is usually divided into that which affects business to consumer relationships, so-called B2C, and that which affects business to business, B2B. Although B2C has caught the public imagination and made some e-businesses household names, the more substantial change to date and more immediate potential for growth that turns profits comes in the B2B space.

E-business typically impacts businesses in three ways. The most obvious, which stems directly from its e-commerce origins, is as a new medium for carrying out not just transactions, but many if not all the activities of business. Transacting online and the associated concerns with security is the big story in e-business. Technological development, the securing of internal processes, and the creation of an acceptable international legal framework are all major issues that will continue to hinder e-business in the foreseeable future.

The second area might be summed up as bringing different parties closer together. In the supply chain, for example, it allows companies to deepen the knowledge they have of the other's ability to supply and need for demand. This accelerates the development of 'just in time' delivery but, more radically, is opening up new trading models, such as B2B marketplaces.

The third area in which e-business is making an impact is in internal business processes, typically across intranets. A good example is procurement. Online systems are enabling businesses to control, standardize and streamline procurement across the whole organization for the first time. Another example is HR. Intranets not only make the administrative element within HR more efficient, by reducing paperwork, but provide opportunities for employees to have greater responsibility for themselves.

E-business does carry risks. Apart from those commonly associated with technical projects, notably the issue of security, e-business also introduces risks that are associated with the development of any new product, service or marketplace. As ever, employees must always be carried forward too, something that has been harder to do in technologically dependent change since it is often taken to represent a threat to jobs. Maintaining controls over core processes, ensuring fulfilment and after-sales care, and understanding how to work in a 7×24 business environment are other significant challenges.

The risks of relying on an innovative business sector – that is start-up IT companies – must also be considered. Not only might new business partners not survive the early rounds of fierce competition, but new business ventures might not survive to maturity themselves, something that has been clearly demonstrated by the so-called dotcoms.

See also: **E-commerce, Information and communications technology, Technology**

Further reading: Deise *et al.*, 2000; Fellenstein and Wood, 2000; Larsson and Lundberg, 1998; Leebaert, 1998; Menascé and Almeida, 2000; Norris *et al.*, 2000; Small, 2000; Tapscott *et al.*, 1998; Westland and Clark, 1999

E-COMMERCE

The exchange of goods via electronic media, though now almost exclusively taken to mean the internet.

E-commerce has existed in many forms for many years. Financial institutions have led the way in terms of volume, using a variety of private electronic networks to transact and transfer money and financial products. EDI (electronic data interchange) systems have oiled the wheels of retail operations in many instances. Automatic teller machines are an example of how the general public has used e-commerce too.

But the adoption of internet-type technologies by businesses since the mid-1990s has made a crucial difference that justifies the narrower application of e-commerce today. Before then e-commerce was expensive and exclusive. It cost a lot of money both to install proprietary IT equipment and to set up complex business processes. E-commerce tended therefore to be a luxury for large organizations.

The internet transcended the limitations of traditional e-commerce by making electronic networks accessible on standard PCs via established telecommunications infrastructures. The interfaces of the internet – notably the browser – were similarly cheap, intuitive and highly adaptable to multiple business tasks. Furthermore, the browser possessed the almost unique property in computing of being blind to different computer systems, allowing companies perhaps for the first time to access information across heterogeneous environments, that is the hotchpotch of systems that exist in the real world. Therein lies the power of e-commerce and the reason that estimates of its growth routinely run into the tens of billions of dollars within ten years.

It is becoming increasingly common to refer to the commercial implications and applications of these developments as e-business, a trend that is followed here. However, in relation to e-commerce it is worth outlining the technological base and some basic uses of the internet itself.

The internet was developed by the US military as a network that could withstand nuclear attack. The solution devised was a network that was decentralized, so no single or even multiple strike could disable it. Data that travel across the internet are therefore sent in numerous small packages, each package finding its way across the network to its destination, where the data are reassembled to form coherent information once again. The rules that the data adhere to in order to achieve this are called Internet Protocol or IP.

The web was developed by scientists at CERN in Switzerland. They needed a ready, global means of sharing the graphical results of their research. The web browser was born, an interface that is able to receive pictures using IP.

Since then, web technology has been greatly enhanced to incorporate all the features with which users are familiar. It also promoted an important aspect of computing called thin client computing. Thin client computing allows applications, from office tools to corporate databases, to be run at one point but accessed at multiple points. This idea is a powerful one. For example, the Amazon.com bookstore 'shop front', its web page, can be kept constantly up to date, with access to all its books, and customized for the person online. This would simply not have been possible without thin client computing. Other benefits are that it is also generally easier to install and cheaper to maintain.

See also: **E-business, Information and communications technology**

Further reading: Korper and Ellis, 2000; Turban *et al.*, 2000; Westland and Clark, 1999

ECONOMIC AND MONETARY UNION (EMU)

The European Union's programme to bring about economic and monetary union.

EMU is probably the most important economic development of the late twentieth century. The majority of countries within the EU have already adopted the currency, and will move from the transition phase to the implementation of euro notes and coins, and the abolition of their national currencies, in 2002. The remaining countries within the EU are in various states of being 'pre-in' or simply out. However, since EMU represents the culmination of the single market rather than the initiation of it, all businesses operating in the EU, whether based in in or out countries, have to be prepared for handling the new single currency. Indications are that they are in various states of readiness for the eventuality.

The framework for the introduction of the euro is laid down in the Treaty of Maastricht. The main parts of the legal framework for the introduction and use of the euro are laid down in two Council regulations: Council regulation on the introduction of the euro, and Council regulation (EC) no. 1103/97 of 17 June 1997 on certain provisions relating to the introduction of the euro. Regulation 1103/97, which is based on Article 235 of the Treaty, came into force on 20 June 1997. It is the first regulation dealing with the single currency, the euro.

The political arguments for and against the euro are complex. However, the economic arguments are clearer. The dominant argument in favour is the completion of the European single market. This will allow organizations to compete across Europe more effectively, since in theory the market will be more transparent, and efficiently, since for example businesses will not carry exchange rate risk. The main arguments against EMU are, in the short term, the cost of conversion, and in the long term, the uncertainty about the currency itself. Indeed, since its birth, indications are that the euro mountain is proving a tough peak to climb. As an international currency it is designed to rival the dollar, increasing liquidity and reducing risk in the currency markets. However, at the time of writing, the value of the euro has fallen dramatically, so it has yet to realize this aim.

For businesses with an array of disparate, unconnected software systems, conversion to the euro has proved to be a hugely complex operation. Analysts predict that the full cost of EMU compliance could reach around $150 billion world-wide, several times more expensive than accommodating the Year 2000 (Y2K) date change. Many are dependent upon their financial software suppliers. The cost of compliance has been steep for IT suppliers too. It is no trivial matter to provide triangulation, work to six decimal figures, or add a new base currency to the system.

Most consultants believe that an EMU project should be driven as an opportunity for business. Whether to be a euro leader or follower is an important managerial question. Euro leaders in a sector might be able to steal a march on competitors, whereas euro followers can learn from the mistakes of others.

See also: **Foreign exchange risk, Government**

Further reading: Chesworth and Pine-Coffin, 1998; Eltis, 2000; Reuters, 1998

ECONOMICS

The study of the supply of resources to meet demands.

Economics generally deals with issues at a social level, rather than individual, and systems of supply and demand and the relationships between different systems. As a science, the 'dismal science', it tests principles and laws that attempt to describe how resources, limited at source or in distribution, might satisfy various, often limitless or competing, appetites.

Economics is divided into microeconomics and macroeconomics. The former is the study of smaller units within an economy, notably businesses and market sectors. The latter is the study of larger systems of economic players, typically on a national and international level.

For businesses, a number of economic themes are important mostly from the microeconomic sphere. The relationship between supply and demand, represented by price and controlled by various forces, is the heart of the matter. On this basis a number of key concepts emerge. Because supply and demand rarely balance each other, or to use the technical term, reach equilibrium, businesses have to make choices about how they can manage the discrepancy. These choices result in opportunity costs, the loss of profit that the company incurs because it is unable to match perfectly supply to meet demand. However, equilibrium can be approximated to, and the fine tuning that businesses make to stay close to that balance results in marginal costs and marginal revenues, the small changes in total costs and total revenues associated with a product that fluctuations in supply and demand result in. In general, marginal revenues should always exceed marginal costs. A related measure is that of marginal utility, which seeks to express fluctuations in demand in terms of how useful extra supply would prove to the market. An exhausted market has zero marginal utility.

The ability to supply a product and the demand for it depends on price. If the price is decreased demand rises but supply is compromised because it cannot cover costs, and vice-versa. However, for some products this relationship is far tighter than for others: even a small price rise results in a substantial fall in demand. These products are termed elastic. Other products for which marginal changes in price make little difference are termed inelastic. The whole subject is called elasticity.

Markets produce economic conditions that affect supply and demand too in terms of competition. The ability of a company to meet the challenges of competition and make a profit or be attractive to investors is called its economic rent. At the highest level, markets can be characterized as falling within two extremes, pure competition and pure monopoly. Where market forces alone are at work in determining supply and demand, the situation is said to be one of perfect competition. Here the many market participants take the price they charge from the market itself, that is they are price-takers. Where demand is met by one supplier alone, the situation is a pure monopoly and the supplier is a price-maker.

A number of economic theories dominate the subject. Classical economics, Keynesian economics and Monetarism are discussed elsewhere. Whilst they differ dramatically in certain respects, they also hold certain principles in common. The law of demand states that if price rises, demand falls. The tricky question is, what is the relationship between the desirability of product and the ability of purchasers to buy it? The law of supply deals with the perspective of the supplier. The complexity here stems from the incentive suppliers require to satisfy their desire for profit. Economists also agree that there are three factors that determine production: capital, land and labour. Capital is discussed elsewhere. Land is essentially that which is necessary for production that humans cannot create themselves. Labour is that which is necessary for production that humans can create themselves.

See also: **Capital, Cartel, Classical economics, Keynesian economics, Mixed economy, Monetarism, Monopoly, Neoclassical economics, Opportunity cost, Price, Profit, Socioeconomics, Supply and demand, Value**

Further reading: Brickley *et al.*, 2001; Magill, 1997; McAuliffe, 1997; Png, 1998

ECONOMIES OF SCALE

Reductions in unit cost as a result of increases in volume of production.

Economics of scale stem from a basic law of production: operating costs and capital requirements do not increase in direct proportion to output but at some percentage less. This difference can be converted into profits by increasing volume of output. In order to achieve economies of scale of this sort, companies may therefore seek to become the dominant or at least a large player in one market.

However, economies of scale can also be gained simply by becoming more efficient. For example, if a company is over-staffed or does not utilize other assets fully, output can be increased at little extra cost, creating economies of scale. Supermarkets have been very good at this, letting redundant store space to non-competitive retailers. Alternatively, companies can spread fixed costs over a greater range of outputs. For example, it might be possible to spread R&D or marketing costs over a number of different products. Economies of scale of this sort can be realized by companies merging or acquiring competitors or new lines of business.

Economies of scale are usually harder to achieve in small businesses because they are closely associated with the division of labour and the specialization of employees, and small businesses tend to encourage generalization.

Economies of scale can also be made in the purchase of raw materials by agreeing volume discounts with suppliers. One of the most interesting developments in this field at the time of writing is in the emergence of B2B online marketplaces. Here, different firms with common suppliers can club together to make bulk purchases and share discounts. Alternatively, large non-competing buyers with many small, common suppliers are developing online models that enable them to buy together. This opens up economies of scale for goods that they would otherwise only buy in small quantities, simultaneously benefiting the suppliers who can capitalize on bulk orders.

Another way that economies of scale can be generated is by utilizing waste from inputs to generate secondary profitable outputs. This in effect reduces the unit cost of the main line of business.

EFFECTIVENESS

A measure of the performance of an individual or organization in terms of the ability to meet expectations.

Effectiveness is hard to assess. The quantitative measure of performance is tricky enough to calculate, but effectiveness is coupled to a wider range of expectations. These qualitative factors can conceal true effectiveness. It is, however, one of the most frequently cited indicators of progress, particularly in organizations that have already made big inroads into increasing their efficiency.

The problem is that in many companies there will be a clash of interests over effectiveness. Shareholders, for example, will be concerned that the company is effective at generating profits. Customers, on the other hand, may be more interested in the ability of the company to improve its products or services, in effect demanding higher R&D spends, eating into profits. Senior management usually works on the company's effectiveness in the areas that reflect the values and preferences of the more powerful constituency.

Progress has been made in recent years in terms of quantifying effectiveness, particularly in relation to IT projects for which proven increases in effectiveness are an important measure of ROI (return on investment). The first question that is asked is, what should the company be doing to achieve its aims and is it doing them? It is quite possible for an organization to evolve in such a way that it becomes very effective but in all the wrong areas, simultaneously kidding itself that it is effective. When these core activities have been clearly identified, the next step is to consider the processes that support them and then ask how effective they are at delivering the required results. Benchmarking is particularly useful in this respect, although again, it must be ensured that the performance indicator being assessed is one that the company really needs to work on to be truly effective.

See also: **Benchmarking, BPR, Performance**

Further reading: Cameron and Whetten, 1983; Denton, 1998; Hammer, 1996

EFFICIENCY

A measure of the relationship between inputs and outputs. An efficient organization is one in which inputs are minimized and outputs maximized.

The most common application of the term in business refers to what is more properly called productive efficiency, that is efficiency as defined above. So, many companies have sought to increase their efficiency by downsizing. The aim is to cut costs at the same time as increasing revenues and competitiveness. However, experience has shown that whilst organizations may in this way make processes cheaper, overall efficiency can be detrimentally impacted, since the processes themselves are not the most efficient way of completing tasks. It has become usual, therefore, for efficiency drives to be coupled to questions about effectiveness too. The mantra, though ugly, is, 'do the right things right'.

Related to productive efficiency is allocative efficiency, also called market efficiency. In short, if a market is efficient there are the customers to buy the goods that the market produces. Economists talk about 'Pareto optimality' which assesses whether the goods produced can be sold at a price that represents the optimal balance between the economic needs of the supplier and the economic means of the buyer.

There are two more technical applications of the term efficiency that should also be mentioned. The first is x-efficiency. It describes the relationship between costs and competitiveness. When the former rises, the latter falls. x-efficiency highlights various problems that can afflict the organization. Sources of x-inefficiency can be internal to the organization, for example, surplus staff or extravagant buildings. And they can be external to the organization, such as cartel practices between companies that should be competing. x-efficiency is often associated with Harvey Leibenstein.

The second is y-efficiency. It describes the relationship between revenue and competitiveness, in essence saying that a company is y-efficient if the market allows it to expand as much as it could.

See also: **Effectiveness, Pareto effect**

Further reading: Leibenstein, 1975; Pindyck and Rubinfeld, 1995

ENTERPRISE

A general term for any organizational engagement in business activities, though often merely referring to larger companies.

The concept of the enterprise has become particularly important in relation to information technology. Enterprise Resource Planning (ERP) systems were originally developed to keep track of materials in the supply chain, but today have become complex solutions capable of supporting and enhancing virtually all transactional and non-transactional processes within the enterprise.

The critical issue at the present stage is that large organizations consist of many computer systems that are not straightforwardly compatible with one another. However, if all the data generated by these networks, regardless of where it exists in the heterogeneous environment, can be accessed then there is tremendous potential to be gained from the knowledge that can be derived as a result. ERP systems are at the forefront of these developments, supporting activities as diverse as cash management and CRM, HR and financial market relationships.

See also: **Company, Corporation**

Further reading: Chandler, 1962; Norris *et al.*, 2000

ENTREPRENEURSHIP

The particular qualities of an individual who initiates the innovative processes that can lead to the creation of wealth in business.

The concept of entrepreneurship has become so central to contemporary business practice that many economists now regard it as a fourth ingredient of production, along with capital, land and labour. Great effort is made to identify and nurture the combination of leadership, creativity and risk-taking that make up the entrepreneurial characteristics of these individuals. Governments increasingly provide incentives for entrepreneurs, as well as ensuring that the commercial environment encourages rather than hinders them. And within the organization there has been much effort to dismantle the hurdles that can stifle the entrepreneur's efforts – often referred to as intrapreneurship.

In the studies of entrepreneurs, they are typically thought to carry characteristics such as independence and initiative, effectiveness in relation to resources, competitiveness and risk-taking, sensitivity to market feedback, and an ability to learn from and not to be crushed by mistakes. In addition to providing an environment in which these characteristics can flourish, entrepreneurs need to be able to directly benefit from the rewards of their efforts. Equity stakes are the most usual way of providing this, since linear salary increases alone are not a good way of rewarding exponential entrepreneurial success.

The confrontation that arises between the entrepreneur and the organization can be summed up as fundamental difference of spirit. The entrepreneur has an attitude of creative destruction. It is interesting that in Chinese, 'entrepreneur' is similar to the word for crisis. In short, nothing must stand in the way of the entrepreneurial goal. The organization, on the other hand, is designed to be conservative and cautious in order to instantiate the reliability and the security that matter so much to customers, shareholders, and employees respectively.

Studies of entrepreneurial businesses suggest a number of possibilities for developing an entrepreneurial organization. Typically, it needs to be thought of as resource-based to emphasize its creative potential. This does not just include gearing capital assets to entrepreneurial activity, but reordering organizational assets too. So, business processes need to incorporate mechanisms for constant improvement. Employees should be encouraged to share knowledge, learn from each other, and embrace new technology fast. Rewards should be associated with performance and innovation, rather than loyalty and reliability.

Entrepreneurial qualities are regarded so highly because they offer the best hope of success in the competitive environments within which most businesses operate. Flexibility, innovation and speed are the rules of the game, and entrepreneurs are the people best suited to play it. The point is that entrepreneurs are now not only required to get businesses started, but are needed in the ongoing struggle to keep businesses viable because change is continuous. The great management challenge is how to engage entrepreneurship as part of strategic management, since keeping an established organization alive to entrepreneurial opportunities is very different from embodying this spirit at start-up.

See also: **Creativity, Flexibility, Innovation, Learning organization, Risk, Synchronicity, Venture capital**

Further reading: Birkinshaw, 2000; Julien, 1998; Meyer and Heppard, 2000; Sundbo, 1998; Timmons, 1999

ENVIRONMENTAL AUDIT

A process that takes stock of a company's impact upon the environment. Audits of this kind are generally quite innovative in nature, and so they will not only include mechanisms to ensure that environmental legislation is complied with, but that the record of a firm's good ethical behaviour is communicated to stakeholders and the general public.

Environmental audits have existed since the 1970s. However, the green politics of the 1990s have substantially raised their profile. Companies such as Shell and BP now think of the environment as a strategic issue, partly because of their own sensitivity towards the public's perception of them, but increasingly because engaging with environmental concerns is seen as a way of gaining competitive edge and developing new markets.

Additional indications that environmental auditing could become a routine part of corporate life include the development of new auditing services within management consultancies specifically for this task, and the growth of ethical units within financial institutions, encouraging so-called 'active engagement policies' with the firms that they invest in.

See also: **Audit, Ethics, Social audit**

Further reading: Brinckerhoff, 2000; Fuller, 1999; Marinetto, 1998; Pringle and Thompson, 1999

EQUITY

In general, ownership of a company, though usually and specifically relating to the ownership of stock, also called shares or securities.

Equity typically comes in two forms. Common stock refers to equity that is valued after all the other financial obligations of the company have been met, notably bonds. Holders have voting rights. Preferred stockholders receive a higher priority in the payment of dividends and at liquidation. Stocks have no contractual requirements to pay dividends and they do not mature. Dividend payments are at the discretion of the company concerned, though most adopt policies that pay out when adequate profits are made. Stocks themselves are classified according to the company whose ownership they represent: growth stocks are in rapidly expanding companies; blue chip stocks in large organizations; cyclical stocks are sensitive to fluctuations in the economy as a whole; penny stocks are typically in start-up companies.

See also: **Finance**

Further reading: Hennell and Warner, 1998; Munn *et al.*, 1991; Paxson and Wood, 1997; Wallace, 1998;

ERGONOMICS

The study of the workplace and its impact upon employees.

The term covers a wide range of activities, from the design of computer interfaces to the layout of a control room. As a discipline, ergonomics grew out of the post-war realization that simple intuition was not adequate in determining how well suited equipment was for human use. For example, research showed that many human errors could be put down to bad design. Alternatively, productivity could be greatly enhanced by displays that were easier to understand. More recently, health concerns in the workplace have led to the introduction of such devices as ergonomic keyboards that are designed to reduce the stress that causes repetitive strain injuries.

A recent development is the concept of hotdesking. Modern networked computer systems mean that employees who work at a PC do not need to have a machine that is dedicated to their own use, but can logon from any computer terminal. The network recognizes the particular user and customizes the PC in front of them, there and then. This, it is argued, brings certain ergonomic advantages. For example, employees can choose where they work according to what they are doing.

Alternatively, hotdesking encourages a sense of dynamism in the organization, since people do not stay put but move around. Further, hotdesking can provide a way for companies to cut employee costs, since the organization only needs to have enough PCs for people working at any one time, not enough for all employees all the time. However, some firms that have experimented with hotdesking have found that employees tend to establish work patterns that are virtually identical to those used when desks were fixed.

See also: **Office management**

Further reading: Clements-Croome, 2000; Corbett and Wilson, 1995; Horgen *et al.*, 1999; James and Arroba, 1999

ETHICS

Ethics in business usually refers to the study of socially responsible and morally justifiable behaviour in managers and companies.

However, ethical considerations play a greater role in modern businesses than that definition might suggest. On the one hand, the very notion of the free market is founded upon Adam Smith's argument that it is these capitalist mechanisms that produce the greatest social good, although economists ever since have contested the validity of his case. Within organizations, ethics is fundamental since businesses are nothing if not a partnership between people, with endless choices that have to be made that affect all concerned, along with the resources companies use and the capital they deploy. Business ethics is therefore a central element in many decision-making processes, from accounting to advertising. That said, there is little doubt that ethics is placing a greater, more proactive pressure on businesses than it has done in the past. This is due to many complex, sociological factors – not least the failings of businesses themselves – the scope of which can be indicated by considering how business ethics is developing on a number of specific fronts.

Consider the relationship between employee and employer. In many situations, a shift in the balance of power is taking place in favour of the employee which has ethical ramifications. For example, employees today are successfully asserting various rights, notably in the area of discrimination but more recently in relation to issues such as whistleblowing and workplace hazards. Companies, for their part, are at the very least creating clearer guidelines that govern various eventualities. Many are seeking to change the employer/employee relationship more radically, by empowering workers and extending benefits.

The ethical engagement of businesses with customers is also in a state of flux. Advertising is a good case in point, with customer organizations on the one hand pressuring companies to uphold standards of truth, and businesses on the other pressing the ethical limits of advertisements in the interests of reaching an ad-savvy world. Labelling is a particular area in which ethics is informing legislative controls being developed to cover the emergence of such products as health foods. At the time of writing, no discussion could fail to mention the Microsoft court case in the US, and its as-yet-undetermined implications for anticompetitive behaviour and customer relations in the networked economy.

However, the environment is the area in which ethical questioning is currently being turned on capitalist behaviour most profoundly. Scrutiny here extends from global issues such as energy consumption and its relationship to economic growth, to less tangible relationships of cause and effect such as the degree of businesses' complicity in creating demand by manipulating human needs and desires. It is also worth noting that ethics does not always set the interests of the public against the interests of business, if the two can be distinguished at all. Intra-business disputes are a growing concern in this respect, for example the threat posed to agriculture by tourism. The use of animals in research is another lively battleground that is likely to intensify with a booming pharmaceutical industry.

Many other issues could be raised from the responsibility felt by businesses not only to generate profits but to be engaged in the communities around them, to the behaviour of multinational companies in highly fluid capital and labour markets. But it is certainly true that ethics as a subject has risen up the corporate agenda. Apart from anything else, business leaders are often called to account publicly for the actions of their firms and so address specific ethical issues. The tools that can be used to come to ethical decisions are reviewed in most business studies courses.

There are a number of ethical theories that can be brought to bear on particular situations. Utilitarianism is probably the most commonly referenced, that is trying to calculate which outcome brings about the greatest good to the greatest number. However, relativism is probably the most commonly deployed in practice – the idea that there are no moral absolutes but rather different perspectives that may or may not enlighten various predicaments. For example, the boss may believe that it is right for them to do something by virtue of their public role that they would not do as a private individual. Alternatively, a company may feel it is justified in treating employees in one country differently from those in another, as a reflection of the general standards that exist in each place. Various forms of natural law can also be an important source of ethical sense in some parts of the world, notably those where religious beliefs have great influence. Natural law holds that things are right or wrong because of natural design or divine order.

A practical solution, specific to business, that managers might use to think about ethical dilemmas, is stakeholder analysis. It aims to provide a way of structuring different points of view by considering how different stakeholders in the business might analyse the case in point. These interests include those of employers, employees, customers and shareholders, as well as government, non-governmental organizations, the local community, and even future generations. When the full range of views has been laid out a judgement can be reached. Stakeholder analysis also has the value of helping companies to prepare for the reactions of different groups to the ethical decisions they make.

See also: **Accountability, Activism, Advertising, Antitrust law, Culture, Environmental audit, Geocentricism, Industrial relations, Morale, Negligence, Social audit, Stakeholder, Tokenism, Utility, Whistleblowing**

Further reading: Beauchamp, 1999; Bowie and Freeman, 1992; Hosmer, 1991; Post *et al.*, 1999; Quinn and Davies, 1998; Werhane and Freeman, 1997

EVOLUTIONARY CHANGE

A theory of organizational development that stresses gradual, cumulative processes, frequently borrowing from Darwinian ideas.

The concept of evolutionary change is tenable in business not only because of its appeal to common sense, but because, as in nature, it sees the competitive environment as the main driver of change. Some theories draw directly from Darwinian concepts: organizational variations arise spontaneously and are selected by the company according to how they play in the market. Some speak more metaphorically of companies competing for a niche in their different environments and evolving to exploit it optimally.

Other theorists have proposed that organizations typically show periods of evolution punctuated by moments of revolution. Larry Greiner, for example, argued that there are five predictable evolutionary stages that growing businesses must go through, and five revolutionary crises.

See also: **Change management, Diversification, Growth, Organic organization**

Further reading: Abe *et al.*, 1998; Greiner, 1972; Hannan and Freeman, 1989

EXPOSURE

A measure of the financial risk a company is carrying due to factors beyond its control.

Exposure can stem from a number of causes. The most common sources of exposure are financial. Foreign exchange rate risk is one example. Companies may also be tempted to speculate in bull markets in the hope of greater returns, though risking greater losses too.

Other sources of exposure are less tangible. For example, companies operating in markets sensitive to social or political factors may be said to suffer from exposure. Here the risk is that actions or attitudes over which the company has little or no control could turn against it.

Exposure can be offset by various financial products including derivatives and insurance.

See also: **Finance, Foreign exchange risk, Government, Insurance, Risk**

Further reading: Davis, 1992; Munn *et al.*, 1991; Paxson and Wood, 1997

EXTERNALITIES

The incidental impact that a company has on its environment.

Externalities can work for and against a company. A new car assembly line in a run-down part of the country can bring a range of positive externalities, such as local inward investment housing. However, it may also have a negative impact, such as posing an environmental threat to local rivers or countryside.

The problem with externalities usually focuses on their value, if positive, or cost, if negative. With the assembly line again, a foreign investor working with a local government may use positive externalities as part of the justification for the project, especially if subsidies are in the offing. However, negative externalities cannot only cost money, either as a result of fines or to put right, but might damage the company in terms of public relations too.

FACILITIES MANAGEMENT

The administration of plant, computer systems and other support services by a third party.

With the growth of outsourcing and related kinds of partnership between companies has come the emergence of a breed of managers who specialize in ensuring that the various facilities run in these ways are managed to the best advantage of the core company.

Park defines it as 'the structuring of building plant and contents to enhance the creation of the end product'. The point is to attend to the result of running facilities to these greater ends, not to the running of the facilities for themselves, a narrowing of vision that over-specialization can bring. Facilities management looks at how quality control, efficiency and effectiveness measures applied to the task in hand can be related to the overall goals of the company.

See also: **Outsourcing, Quality**

Further reading: Park, 1998

FAMILISM

A business environment that is owned or controlled by a family, or one in which 'family values' have a strong bearing.

There is no strict definition of what constitutes a family firm, and organizational size is no guide. The smallest business may be clearly identified as a family affair according to who owns or controls it. But the largest businesses can market themselves as a family firm, meaning that they strongly uphold the values of a paternal founder, who may or may not be actually present.

Research into family firms, of all sorts, highlights various problems to which they are susceptible. If the company gets caught up in personal issues, detrimental effects such as skills shortages or a lack of delegation can stunt growth or profits. The problem of succession is common too, especially when a business is reliant on a charismatic founder. Motivation amongst non-familial staff can become an issue when nepotism is suspected.

See also: **Paternalism**

Further reading: Anacona *et al.*, 1999; Ellis and Dick, 2000; Leach, 1991

FEEDBACK

Mechanisms by which data can be collected at the end of a process to affect improvements.

The concept of systems that include feedback mechanisms originates in engineering, where it was important that machines could preserve some state of equilibrium by automatically responding to changes. The term has come to be applied much more widely, though it is worth remembering its origins and the concept of automatic adjustments. In general, the best processes are those that can embrace change by acting on their own feedback. For example, the effectiveness of information derived from customer surveys is severely reduced if, as is often the case, there are no or only weak mechanisms in place for reacting to its results. Alternatively, many computer systems now incorporate monitoring tools that constantly assess how an application is being used and adjust it accordingly in order to increase productivity. Another problem is that some of the most valuable sources of feedback can be entirely missed by the organization. For example, complaining customers are often treated as exceptions, since they are regarded as poor sources of profit, and so the content of their complaint is isolated from feedback mechanisms. But it might be that the complaining customer should be regarded as a valuable source of comment on the organization and a potential source of new ideas.

Feedback can also have the more general meaning of staff appraisal. In this sense it is often regarded as an important managerial skill, though one poorly practised.

See also: **BPR, Human resources management, Learning organization, Open and closed systems**

Further reading: Kock, 1999; Schwandt and Marquardt, 2000

FINANCE

The branch of economics that studies the commercial use of capital.

For the purposes of business practitioners, finance can be divided into two broad areas. The first is the general concern of managers who are responsible for financial matters, from budgeting to profitability. The second is the specialist work of financiers acquiring and managing capital.

In the first, capital budgeting deals with long-term investments. It ranges over a number of concerns, including the purchase or sale of fixed assets, product developments, market expansion, or M&As. Clearly, many factors influence the decision to invest, but financial tools are specifically deployed to justify the investment.

The payback period is one of the simplest. It calculates the length of time that it will take to recover the cost of the investment. The great advantage that this tool has is that it is a quantitative calculation, providing companies with a clear indicator of the risk they are taking. The drawback is that it tends to obscure certain elements associated with investing, notably the cash flow implications of a project: the same payback period might carry more risk because the return comes only at the end of the period rather than throughout.

Improving on this point is the net present value tool. It uses a formula that takes account of the higher risk associated with payback which increases as the payback period grows. The analysis derives a present value for future cash flows resulting from the investment that can be directly compared with present costs. However, uncertainty can creep in, since net present value requires a calculation of the risk over the period of the investment. It is represented by so-called discount rates.

Cash flow analysis is another valuable tool, dealt with in the entry under Cash.

Financiers may finance companies from a variety of external sources, though the capital is of two sorts, equity and debt. Equity capital is raised by selling shares in the company. Debt capital is raised by borrowing, either from banks or in the form of bonds.

The most common way of raising equity capital is by selling stocks or shares. In exchange, investors receive ownership rights in the company. Other sources of equity capital include the selling of warrants, guarantees that shares may be bought within a certain time at a specified price. Warrants become tradable securities in their own right, but with the advantage that they do not increase the number of shares in the company and so reduce the power of shareholders. Rights are a kind of warrant security that are limited to existing shareholders alone.

Debt capital in the form of borrowing from financial institutions is a valuable means of cash management. Even the most successful company can experience substantial variations in cash flow, and borrowing on interest through pre-arranged credit lines can be a healthy way of ironing these irregularities out and so avoiding disrupting the activities of the firm. Bonds are a way of borrowing for the longer term. In return for becoming creditors, bond investors receive regular payments of interest called a coupon, the amount of which is related to the term over which the money is lent. When this maturity date is reached, the amount is repaid, called the face value of the bond. Bonds come in different types according to the particularities of the contract. Zero coupon bonds, for example, yield no interest but a lump sum at maturity. Convertible bonds can be traded for stock. Junk bonds are associated with particularly high risk. For companies entering new markets, for example, bonds represent a valuable source of capital since here equity may be harder to come by.

The ratio of debt to equity is called the capital structure of the company. Restructuring is making substantial changes to that ratio. Various models advise whether the ratio should be high or low according to the commercial particularities that the company faces. They seek to account for the importance of various factors to the business, such as competitiveness, risk, cash requirements and business cycles, so that the company can exploit its capital structure and not be hindered by it.

Managers also have to deal with the management of short-term assets and liabilities. For example, they may choose to ask for credit from suppliers as a way of providing temporary financing. Alternatively, leasing items such as computing equipment is another way of financing certain kinds of asset investment. This kind of financing is often best treated as cash budgeting items, dealt with in the entry under Cash.

See also: **Accounting, Asset, Banking, Capital, Cash, Chartism, Equity, Exposure, Forecasting, Foreign exchange risk, Hedging, Income statement, Inflation accounting, M&As, Restructuring, Returns, Risk, Venture capital, Yield**

Further reading: Carroll, 1998; Muckian, 2000; Munn *et al.*, 1991; Paxson and Wood, 1997; Shim *et al.*, 1997; Silbiger, 1994

FLEXIBILITY

The extent to which a company is versatile in its response to changes in the marketplace.

Flexibility was originally used in relation to manufacturing. A flexible manufacturer was one who could produce a variety of products on the same machines, and one who could quickly introduce design changes or new products into the manufacturing process. Flexibility in this sense is still an important source of competitive edge, particularly in relation to customization. The PC industry is a good example of this in terms of making computers to order for individuals. The car industry is an example of a traditional manufacturer that is being revolutionized by the flexibility of being able to make cars to order.

Technology is the key to modern flexibility. In the case of cars, it is the control that computers bring to the supply chain in terms of tracking and delivering parts that enables manufacturers to customize. For other consumer items, it is technology ranging from printers that produce customized packaging, to databases that provide the raw information for customization.

However, as a result of the close relationship between flexibility and computers in the modern world, the concept of flexibility is now often applied to non-manufacturers. Banks, for example, are said to need to be flexible to compete. The marketplace in which they operate has come to reward those firms that can quickly roll out new products to customers, both in response to competitive pressure and in order to build loyalty and profitability. For example, a number of banks saw the ability speedily to launch internet services as a way of building shareholder value. This was only possible because they had adopted a degree of internal flexibility comparable to the manufacturers: staff who are knowledgeable about a number of products, as workers on the assembly line are about a number of processes; or computer systems that can control diverse customized products, as flexible manufacturing systems can control the production of a range of parts.

Some business theorists are seeking to develop the concept of flexibility again by referring to agility. The idea stems from the observation that change in many marketplaces has become continuous, so that competitive edge is no longer gained by being reactively flexible but proactively agile. The agile organization is one that incorporates advanced levels of CRM, entrepreneurship and cooperation.

See also: **Change management, Competition, Product, Technology**

Further reading: Fleidner and Vokurka, 1997; Hamel *et al.*, 1998; Stevenson, 1999

FORDISM

The style of manufacturing exemplified by the Ford Motor Company when Henry Ford invented the Model T car.

Ford brought scientific methods to bear upon the problem of mass production, reversing what he saw as the natural process whereby objects break down into their constituent parts. Fordism is today generally regarded to be out of date, since the emphasis now is not so much on mass production as customized manufacturing.

The term is also associated with the economics of mass markets inasmuch as mass production creates the wealth with which its goods can be bought.

Fordism is sometimes used in a derogatory sense to indicate a resistance to change. Henry Ford notoriously insisted in following his instincts against all market analysis when he continued to make the Model T when competitors had clearly copied and bettered him. The company took years to recover as a result.

See also: **Flexibility, Taylorism**

Further reading: Kipping and Bjarnar, 1998

FORECASTING

The analysis of past and present data in order to plan for trends and developments in the future.

Quantitative forecasting is based upon probability theory and regression analysis. Probability theory assigns a likelihood of something happening in the future according to the number of times it or similar outcomes have occurred in the past. Events are said to have a certain distribution, from those that are most likely to those that are rare. The simplest distribution is the binomial distribution, which represents patterns of events that can be compared to tossing a coin. A more complex and widely used distribution pattern in business is the normal distribution, where outcomes are assigned a statistic chance according to where they fall under the famous bell curve.

Regression analysis works differently by trying to establish a relationship between the variables that have the greatest impact upon determining the outcome. Sales of umbrellas might be closely associated with annual rainfall and with previous sales, for example.

However, even accounting for a few variables makes the equations that regression analysis derives very complex. Graphical means are therefore deployed to predict future events according to the variables to which they are related. Qualitative forecasting is based upon more subjective means. However, since many outcomes are at best only approximated by quantitative analysis, the experienced opinions of those who work closely with the matter concerned can be of enormous value. The Delphi method is a good example of a qualitative approach that includes a degree of the rigour that would otherwise favour quantitative methods.

Even the best forecasts are essentially educated guesses. There is therefore a lot of work that goes into gauging how reliable forecasts might be. Clearly, forecasts of new events, such as in start-up businesses, are likely to be less reliable than established concerns. Start-ups make an interesting case too, since their futures are often themselves based upon forecasts. The best advice is that businesses should treat forecasts as an heuristic device for steering the organization in a certain direction, though one that is readily changed as developments materialize. In practice, it is often the process of forecasting itself which is as valuable as the end result, since gathering the data and thinking about where the business might be going is as useful an exercise.

In the literature, the best advice is to use the appropriate technique for the forecast in hand, and if possible to bring different calculations to bear on the same query. A more radical critique of forecasting is also present. For example, forecasts of profits have become critical indicators to investors in equity markets, especially in America, where the value of a company is most closely associated with its future prospects as opposed to current earnings. Companies are therefore very sensitive to growth predictions, since these have a major impact upon their share price. Many firms, for example, issue profit warnings. This does not mean that the company is not profitable, merely that its earlier forecast needs adjusting. Since forecasts always stand to be corrected, some analysts are beginning to argue that this kind of reactive speculation in financial markets serves little purpose and is simply destabilizing.

Another point that is made follows on from the observation that competitive businesses are today characterized by continuous change. Firms talk of being 'amazoned', for example, a neologism coined after the online bookseller appeared from nowhere to corner a market in only a few months. The point is that no forecasting could have foreseen such an unlikely, though powerful event. So, the emphasis should be not so much on forecasting as experimentation, holding a constantly changing portfolio of commercial options that can be discarded or developed as the market requires.

See also: **Chartism, Delphi method, Game theory, Modelling, Qualitative methods, Quantitative methods, Regression analysis, Risk, Sampling**

Further reading: Bail and Pepper, 1993; Evans and Olson, 2000; Wellings, 1998

FOREIGN EXCHANGE RISK

The cost of the currency of another country.

A number of factors can cause changes to FX rates. High or rising interest rates in one country can cause demand for that currency by investors in another pushing up the price. Alternatively, in times of economic crisis the value of a currency can fall as it poses more of a risk. Countries with hyper-inflation are susceptible to currency volatility as investors try to stave off the erosion of monetary value. Seasonal factors can affect currency prices too, because demand for the currency periodically rises. Confidence in a currency can also dramatically affect its value, although the reasons for the link are generally obscure.

FX risk is the threat that fluctuations in the value of a foreign currency pose to a business. For companies involved in international markets, volatile currency markets can be a significant cost, certainly enough to damage profits. For this reason, a number of financial products bought on futures and options markets are available to hedge against the losses that can result from currency transactions.

Economic and Monetary Union is the European Union's attempt to remove FX risk from the single market.

See also: **Cash, Economic and Monetary Union, Inflation accounting, Risk**

Further reading: Kendall, 1998; Williams, C.A. *et al.*, 1998

FRANCHISE

The right to make or distribute the goods that are owned by another company.

Franchises are often used as efficient ways for companies to enter new markets. For some companies they have provided the basis for phenomenal growth, the obvious example being McDonalds. The franchisee brings local knowledge to the selling and marketing of the products, and an entrepreneurial spirit to encourage growth. In return, they receive the experience of the parent company and help in setting up their business.

The contractual agreement that shapes the franchise might vary enormously, but will generally include expected details such as the fees that the franchisee must pay to the franchiser and assurances of quality compliance, and other particularities such as the geographical region in which the licence can be operated or restrictions on suppliers.

See also: **Joint venture**

Further reading: Deering and Murphy, 1998

GAME THEORY

A process for modelling the outcome of decisions that depend on the decisions of others too.

Game theory is one of the most successful techniques for dealing with complex situations in which intangible factors bear upon the decisions of many participating agents. The optimal action is arrived at by a combination of mathematical modelling based upon the running of scenarios with different starting conditions. These starting conditions can represent any number of variables that need testing. They might represent the external conditions in a market sector or the different strategies that a business can choose to drive its business forward. Game theory can also be used to test the rules that a market itself obeys, since these are also the rules that the game uses. As a group exercise played by management teams, as opposed to being run on computers, game theory also provides qualitative analysis of the situation, since the reasoning of other decision makers has to be taken into account.

An elementary example of the theory is provided by the game in which one by one the characters in a descending balloon must be thrown out on the basis of what the fellow travellers regard as the least important qualities each possesses. The word 'game' itself is also illustrative of the technique, since it derives from its more commonplace use, as in athletic or board games, where different strategies are deployed to beat the other competitors. The main difference in the economic application of game theory is that the competitors also have mutually beneficial goals, such as maintaining the market in which they compete. On the other hand, zero-sum gaming is a variation in which a gain for one player is always a loss for another.

See also: **Forecasting, Zero-sum game**

Further reading: Fudenberg and Tirole, 1991; Rasmusen, 1990

GAP ANALYSIS

A methodology for determining the difference between planned and actual outcomes in business.

Gap analysis seeks to address the problem that a company's objectives are rarely going to be wholly realized in practice. Further, when the vehicle for realizing those objectives is an entity as multifaceted as an organization, closing the gap between the two is complex.

The first stage in gap analysis is to assess how realistic the company's objectives are to start with. They may be revised up if outcomes have exceeded aspirations, or down if the reverse is the case. However, clearly expectations should not coincide precisely with actual performance, otherwise this removes a key motivator. So the second stage of the analysis is to identify the kind of gap the organization is facing. Gaps might arise for a variety of reasons: competitive disadvantage, under exploited markets, or tired products, for example. It is then management's job to devise a strategy to combat it appropriately.

Gap analysis can also refer to the particular marketing issue of identifying new target audiences, that is finding gaps in the market that the company might fill. Gap analysis also carries a generic meaning in scientific research, when the task is to understand why there are differences between experimental results and theoretical predictions.

See also: **Growth**

Further reading: Drucker, 1989

GEOCENTRICISM

A style of management that is blind to local market differences, or conversely, is genuinely global in its attitudes.

Geocentricism carries both a positive and negative meaning. Positively, some global companies do operate more or less consistently wherever their products are to be found on the planet. Coca-Cola and Gillette are two possible examples. In the first case, the brand so dominates that it provides a fixed point around which different markets revolve. In the second case, the core product is generic and the way it is used in different localities is sufficiently similar for the company to use common marketing strategies.

Negatively, geocentricism refers to a certain imperialist attitude which takes no notice of cultural differences, especially in relation to the needs of employees.

See also: **Brand, Culture**

Further reading: Kipping and Bjarnar, 1998; Lane *et al.*, 2000; Mudambi and Ricketts, 1997; Mudambi and Ricketts, 1998; Oddou and Mendenhall, 1998

GEOGRAPHIC INFORMATION SYSTEMS (GIS)

Databases that are designed to handle information on the basis of parameters of location.

GIS technology is a division of object oriented (OO) technology. Object technology has a very flexible approach to defining the relationships between data entities – that is objects. Rather than assuming certain kinds of relationship are determinate, as in DBMS (database management systems), any number of complex relationships can be defined, with greater processing efficiency being the result. GIS is the particular application of OO to the matter of geographical relationships.

The web and the internationalization of even quite small businesses have increased demand for GIS technology. Determining where a resource may be sourced or where a product is to be delivered can prove very tricky, even in countries where the means of determining location, such as postcodes, are well developed. Whereonearth.com is an example of a company that has mapped the globe using GIS techniques to overcome these generic location problems.

See also: **Data, Information and communications technology**

Further reading: Davis, 1997; Shim, 2000; Stair, 1999

GLASS CEILING

The invisible barrier that prevents some groups of people from receiving preferment beyond a certain level.

Shattering the Glass Ceiling, Marilyn Davidson and Cary Cooper's book, is where the expression originates. Here the authors refer specifically to the almost universal hindrances that women in business find once they have achieved a certain level of success, preventing them from rising to the top rungs of the management ladder in particular. The statistics speak for themselves: in Scandinavia, generally regarded as one of the most inclusive commercial cultures, approximately 10 per cent of top jobs are held by women.

Apart from the ethical case, Davidson and Cooper argue that the situation should be addressed because businesses are missing out on the skills resources that these women represent. A number of systemic issues, beyond pure prejudice, might support glass ceilings. For example, if women take time out of their career for family reasons, corporate culture might count this time out against them. Alternatively, management itself might be constructed in a way that favours men, and is favoured by them, so that women are never really in the pipeline.

See also: **Discrimination, Tokenism**

Further reading: Davidson and Cooper, 1992; Maddock, 1999; Thorpe and Homan, 2000

GLOBALIZATION

The theory that cultures and markets from across the planet tend to converge under the impact of worldwide communications infrastructures.

In business, globalization has substantially intensified since the 1950s. Following America's lead, businesses around the world have come to be able to operate on an increasingly international stage, for example, finding investment capital outside their own national borders, or sourcing not only land but labour regardless of location. The globalizing trend that began in manufacturing has extended to other sectors too, notably the service sector. Companies routinely run call centres as international service centres. Alternatively, mergers and acquisition activity in sectors such as banking have been explicitly driven by the desire to realize global economies of scale. The globalizing trend has borne its own institutions too, notably the World Trade Organization and GATT, the General Agreement on Tariffs and Trade. A final phenomenon that has come to be seen as sealing the future of the global village is the rise of the internet. The internet certainly kills distance in terms of data transfer, and potentially reduces the barriers of entry into new, global markets.

Globalization brings a number of benefits to business on top of those already mentioned above. Economies of scale can be realized if R&D and much marketing activity is carried out internationally. The convergence of cultures, notably in terms of consumer lifestyles, means that goods lose their cultural specificity and so can attract much wider audiences.

Whilst globalization is generally regarded to be a good thing for business, there are also signs that it is backfiring on some. The spate of protests at the meetings of the World Bank and IMF, for example, has made some companies with the most successful global brands particular targets, and labelled them as quintessentially imperialistic.

Moreover, globalization itself is a contested term. It is not that some economists argue that globalization is simply not taking place. The point is the more subtle one, made on practical grounds, that the term can hide local differences which persist and, indeed, become more significant because they must be negotiated by alien organizations. Alternatively, whilst global capital markets have greatly facilitated the frictionless transfer of money around the world, they question whether global labour markets operate with similar ease. Again, the case is not to deny that clothes, for example, can be more cheaply sourced in Indonesia. The point is that if the labour market was as efficient as is sometimes made out, why, for example, is there such a dramatic IT skills shortage in the West? Alternatively, others argue that businesses flourish when they are able to behave competitively, that is differentiate, segment and occupy niches. Might there be a kind of 'invisible hand' that resists globalization, if not internationalism?

At the time of writing, the role of national governments in global markets is being hotly debated. One economic argument asserts that nation-states and global markets will collide because the two do not agree about how people should be aggregated. A more practical issue is the inability of governments to legislate for rapidly changing business environments. Self-regulation is the only pragmatic course, it is said. However, others argue that governments have a part to play in business as they have always done, except that it is changing. For example, democratic regimes that combat corruption and promote stability are clearly beneficial to economic growth. Governments also have a determining role in the macro- and microeconomic environments within which businesses operate, and can be more or less friendly to them.

See also: **Culture, E-business, Geocentricism, Government, United Nations trade bodies**

Further reading: Ball and McCulloch, 1999; Birkinshhaw, 2000; Brooks and Weatherston, 2000; Chorafas, 2000; Cohen and Boyd, 2000; Fellenstein and Wood, 2000; Harukiyo and Hook, 1998; Maynard, 1998; Mendenhall *et al.*, 1995; Morosini, 1998; Schniederjans, 1998; Stauble, 2000; Tyndall *et al.*, 1998

GOODWILL

The excess value that a company is deemed to have over and above the value of its assets.

Goodwill arises because a company can clearly be in possession of resources or advantages that represent real financial returns but are not included in its list of assets. For example, it may be dominant in a marketplace, be renowned in a particular part of its operation, or be of particular strategic importance.

It is when it comes to selling the company that goodwill is important. On the one hand, shareholders want to include goodwill in the valuation of the company. Or alternatively, a buyer may be prepared to pay over the odds for the goodwill that the company represents to it. In both cases the problem is to calculate what is a reasonable monetary amount to exchange for goodwill.

In a buying and selling situation, especially if there is more than one potential buyer present, market forces will arrive at a price for goodwill. However, goodwill can also appear in the financial reports of companies, notably those for whom a majority of value is tied up with intangibles, as is the case in the IT sector. Goodwill in this situation is far more controversial. Over-reliance on it, for example, played a significant part in the collapse of the so-called dotcoms, whose value, and therefore ability to borrow, was almost wholly speculative, that is based upon goodwill, but ended up leaving them overexposed.

See also: **Accounting, Finance**

Further reading: Macredie *et al.*, 1998; Morgan, 1998

GOVERNMENT

The administration of a nation, particularly with reference to macroeconomic policy and the regulation of commerce.

There is an argument that because of globalization, economic zones controlled by commercial players today rival the role of nation-states ruled by politicians. However, whilst it is undoubtedly true that international business is a force to be reckoned with, governments still exert considerable power, not least on businesses themselves.

At a global level, politics can open or close markets, ease or confuse international trade. Organizations such as the United Nations contain bodies that aim to look after the international interests of business. It is also the case that multinational corporations play a part in international politics, an obvious example being the oil industry's role in the politics of the Middle East, or differently, those corporations that are being allowed to invest in China and the role they play in unwinding communism.

The local political environment within which a business operates affects it on a number of levels. Political stability is generally preferred by business, since it is essential for long-term planning. Democratic government is often regarded as a key condition for economic growth for this reason, since it tends to minimize the impact on commerce of political change or shock. But it should be added that the strength of a democracy is no intrinsic measure of commercial freedom. The US government is prepared to take on its country's largest companies if it believes it must – witness the Microsoft case, though of course the argument here is that Microsoft is threatening commercial freedom by anticompetitive practices.

Governments may also pursue policies that affect businesses. For example, at the time of writing, the status of the UK within the EU, particularly over the question of whether or not it will join the euro, is important. But the impact it will have on competitiveness and foreign exchange risk is regarded differently by different companies. So, within the same industry – car manufacturing – the UK's ambiguous stance on the single currency has been blamed for plant closure and cited as a reason for fresh inward investment. Governments may also pursue policies to promote business in order to bolster the economies of certain regions. Favourable tax incentives, or matching private money with public investment, are typical tactics.

The legal framework that is defined by government varies enormously, even in the West. Anything from advertising to anti-discrimination will be affected.

Some industries are closer to the political process, and so are more susceptible to involvement with it. The newspaper industry is one such, the so-called 'fourth estate of the realm', as Macaulay put it. Alternatively, industries that are regarded as pivotal to national economies, such as manufacturing or arms, may find themselves under pressure from governments or may be able to exert pressure themselves.

See also: **Economic and Monetary Union, Lobbying, United Nations trade bodies**

Further reading: Buckley, 1998; Coen, 1997; Le Sueur and Sunkin, 1997; Ohmae, 1995; Owens, 1997

GROWTH

The business of increasing profits, market share or company size.

Growth is an aim second only to maximizing shareholder value. Companies adopt many strategies that are designed to enable them to grow, from diversification to increasing efficiency. Forming alliances is a newer and fashionable route to growth. For example, in the IT sector, start-ups often seek to piggy-back their way into larger markets by forming an alliance with one of the larger, global IT players, such as Microsoft. Licensing agreements bring their technology to a far wider audience than they might otherwise hope, although they also risk getting tied into the larger corporation, cannibalizing their own brand or customer base in the process.

So, like a plant that withers and dies if it stops growing, business must move onwards and upwards. A crucial question, then, is what levels of growth are sustainable. This is important, since growth is limited by many factors of which managers need to be conscious. Grow too fast and business failure can be the result.

At a financial level, growth depends on having the capital to invest, though not so much as to not be able to afford the cost of that capital. In this respect it is also interesting to note that economic analysis of how companies finance their growth indicates that debt capital is often a better route than equity because, without dividends to pay, its actual costs are lower in high-growth situations.

Growth also depends upon having the logistical infrastructure to meet the requirements of fulfilment, a major problem say for many fast-growing online retailers. Other factors that need to be considered include the impact of margins upon growth. Many aggressively growing companies operate with low margins, not only to plough profits back into the company, but also to act as a barrier to entry against competitors.

See also: **Change management, Diversification, Joint venture, M&As, Restructuring**

Further reading: Boston Consulting Group, 1971; Harukiyo and Hook, 1998; Lanning, 1998; Pasternack and Visco, 1998; Ramu, 1999

GURU

A management thinker recognized as having expertise and insight into a specific area of business.

Like entrepreneurs, gurus tend to possess certain characteristics or to devise certain strategies that bring a lateral quality to their ideas, exemplified in a selection of 'guru's gurus' below.

Arguably the most famous guru, and the person who has played the largest part in the growth of the 'guru industry', is Peter Drucker. Drucker embodies one of the key attributes of many gurus in that he chose to work outside of the discipline of academic business studies. His ideas, such as the customer-driven business, are in part credited to having this independent view. He has written over twenty books, including *Management: Tasks, Responsibilities, Practices*, *The Practice of Management*, and *Concept of the Corporation*.

Christopher Argyris has brought a multidisciplinary approach to bear upon management, making his name as a behavioural scientist who turned his attention to the mutual workings of individuals and organizations. *Personality and Organization* is probably his most famous book.

Stephen Covey is one of the highest-selling authors amongst gurus with his book, *The Seven Habits of Highly Effective People*, which is surprising since it draws many of its central ideas from the ancient philosopher Aristotle. Business leaders need to nurture practical wisdom, he argues, that is virtues that win them the goals they have identified in life, both at work and at home.

Charles Handy takes spiritual succour to the workplace after a major crisis during his time as a Shell executive. His unconventional ideas, often stressing the importance of the whole individual, are indicated by book titles that include *The Age of Paradox* and *The Age of Unreason.* He is also a useful critic amongst gurus, pointing out that business theory often merely restates the obvious and overstates the unnecessary.

Michael Hammer, famous for business process re-engineering, proves that even gurus cannot escape risk. The backlash against BPR has often focused on him.

Warren Bennis, who made his name writing on leadership in books such as *Leaders: The Strategies for Taking Charge* and *On Becoming a Leader,* has a literary bent. For example, he compares companies to families, which enables him to exploit Tolstoy's comment that happy families are alike, whereas unhappy families are not, as a hook for qualities that leaders need to make their organizations happy.

Manfred Kets de Vries is interesting to followers of Freud, putting organizations on the couch to diagnose *The Neurotic Organization,* as one of his books is called. He has found particular favour with senior management, who find original his ideas that many organizations are dehumanizing.

Michael Porter is arguably the most sought after speaker at present, having made his name in competition, chairing the American President's Commission on Industrial Competitiveness during the boom years of the 1980s.

Gurus receive a mixed reception in the world of academic business studies and actual commerce alike. Like celebrity chefs, managers are wont to wonder whether gurus can actually turn out the results their recipes suggest.

See also: **Hawthorne effect, Maslow's hierarchy, Porter's five forces**

Further reading: Boyett and Boyett, 1998; O'Shea and Madigan, 1998

HAWTHORNE EFFECT

The phenomenon whereby employee productivity increases simply and solely because managers show concern for them.

The social psychologist Elton Mayo performed an experiment at Western Electric's Hawthorne factory that led in 1927 to the identification of the effect. One hundred investigators observed

20,000 workers and noticed that they increased their productivity when the light intensity in the factory went up. The lighting was reduced again, but strangely productivity went up a little more. The researchers concluded that it was the impression of care being taken about the workers' environment that gave rise to the productivity gains, not that lighter or darker conditions *per se* helped them in their work. Another reading of the effect says, more cynically, that workers' productivity increases when they know they are being watched.

See also: **Operations management and strategy**

HEDGING

In general, the act of offsetting risk. In particular, investments made to offset the risk associated with other investments.

Investment risk stems from irreducible future uncertainties. Reductions in the value of an investment can therefore be hedged against by buying an option. For example, a put option allows a buyer of securities to resell them within a specified timeframe at a certain minimum price. The buyer takes out an option's contract with someone who believes that the risk is worth carrying, for a price, or who has other means by which to offset the risk. If the price of the security falls below the minimum agreed, the option is worth the difference at the end of the timeframe. Whilst this amount is unlikely to cover the full loss that the original buyer has to bear, it will reduce it.

This only describes the basic hedging function on financial markets which can become very complex. Options are themselves traded, and are an important means of spreading risk between investors.

See also: **Insurance, Risk**

Further reading: Munn *et al.*, 1991; Paxson and Wood, 1997

HOLDING COMPANY

A company that exists to manage the shares of other companies that it wholly owns or controls.

Holding companies emerged as a result of M&As or other strategies of diversification. They exist to unite a collection of businesses into a single legal entity. Until the 1970s, many holding companies played little or no role in the subsidiary companies they owned. Frequently this was because the effort of integrating new businesses, either by centralizing common business functions or by merging production as a whole, was regarded as too great. However, a number of cases demonstrated that holding companies risked cannibalizing their own business because subsidiaries were in effect competing against one another to their mutual disadvantage. Many holding companies therefore developed skills that could be applied in M&A situations, notably the exercise of financial controls and operational integration. Holding companies have also become important in serving the needs of international business, with little or no organizational involvement in subsidiaries. For example, they provide the means to avoid legal or fiscal demands, and notably when registered in tax havens, the paying of national taxes.

See also: **Corporation, M&As, Transfer pricing**

Further reading: Fraser, 1998; Hopt *et al.*, 1998; Litka, 1991

HOME WORKING

Part- or full-time employment away from the company workplace.

Home working is no new employment phenomenon. Workers carried out tasks at home as employees from the start of the Industrial Revolution. However, home working has become more significant in the modern economy because of the possibilities for working remotely opened up by computer networks. It is for this reason that home working is also known as telecommuting or teleworking: the enabling technologies are the telecommunications network and the PC that allow individuals to connect to corporate networks from any place that has a telephone line or is within range of a wireless mobile network.

Teleworking has become particularly important to travelling salespersons. Being able to file reports, access corporate information, or maintain contact through such technologies as virtual offices on an intranet has led to dramatic increases in productivity.

Many other kinds of employees whose work can be done at the keyboard also home work for at least a part of the time. Benefits include the removal of distractions that are found in offices, cutting out the time wasted as a result of physical commuting, and having greater flexibility to manage personal commitments, notably the raising of children. Home working of this sort is typically carried out on an *ad hoc* basis, with management responsibility informally determined.

The wholesale removal of parts of the working population from the office to the home which had been predicted in some quarters has failed to materialize. The importance of multiple informal opportunities for contact, especially personal, that offices provide was underestimated. It is also the case that, at least for the time being, the formal adoption of extensive systems to support home working is costly both to implement and maintain. The only exceptions occur when local particularities mean the benefits outweigh these disadvantages. One example is the call centre workers in Scandinavia who work from home because of the distances they would have to travel to work, coupled to the fact that the domestic telecommunications infrastructure is more advanced in that part of the world in terms of providing more bandwidth.

This is not to say that home working does not cause increasingly common management problems. In small organizations, reduced personnel in offices can lead to a dramatic increase in the interruptions faced by those who are at their desks, handling phone calls for example. In larger organizations, managers have reported problems with process control because, for example, steps might be ducked to avoid the inconvenience of an individual not being present. Interestingly, the evidence indicates that few home workers are suspected of abusing the system.

Many of these problems are likely to disappear in the near future. With regards to phone interruptions, new technology is rapidly coming to a market that has a far greater capacity for routing calls according to where individuals are. And in terms of process problems, many of the systems that travelling salespersons now deploy, such as the construction of the virtual office based upon an intranet, are likely to be made more widely available to the organization as a whole.

See also: **Human resources management, Intranet, Office management**

Further reading: Smith and McWilliams, 1999; Stredwick and Ellis, 1998

HOSTILE BIDS

The practice of making an offer to buy a company directly to the shareholders and over the heads of managers.

Hostile bids, also known as disciplinary takeovers, arise when a company is sought against the will of its managers because the managers do not believe it is in the shareholders' best interests. However, this virtuous reason might conceal a number of ulterior motives, such as not being prepared to concede the failure of which they are accused. The bidders make a tender offer to shareholders to buy their shares directly.

The managers of the company subject to a hostile bid can deploy a number of strategies in response, short of appealing to shareholders themselves. A common device is to find a so-called white knight, a company that offers an alternative merger plan that managers favour.

See also: **M&As**

Further reading: Cosh and Hughes, 1998

HUMAN RESOURCES MANAGEMENT

The administration and supervision of people within the organization.

HR management is a major organizational activity. It covers every aspect of the relationship between the individual and firm, including recruitment, contractual obligations, individual training and motivation, corporate planning, performance monitoring, grievance handling and general welfare, dismissal and redundancy. The HR function is carried out by all managers with supervisory roles, and in larger organizations by the HR department in particular, where activities can be centralized and advantage can be taken of specialist personnel managers. Different personnel managers possess a variety of skills. Some may specialize in issues such as the human aspects of corporate communications, or in crisis management.

It should be noted at the start that HR is a contested subject in business studies. Various academic debates flourish over psychological, behavioural and cognitive approaches, as well as over how HR might actually be defined in the modern workplace.

There is little doubt, however, that modern HR is characterized by flexibility. During the 1990s there was an increased diversification in patterns of employment, with more and more individuals working temporary and part-time contracts. This is related to a number of wider changes. The number of temporary contracts has risen because companies choose to outsource. The number of part-time contracts has risen as employees share posts or have more than one job. Many firms report that flexible contracts are demanded by employees who recognize that they can dictate terms to a greater degree because of various skills shortages. The proportion of women in the workforce has increased dramatically too: research indicates that for the first time it is approaching half the workforce, up from below 40 per cent less than twenty years ago.

At a deeper level, HR is increasingly seen as a strategic issue for the organization as companies realize that people are a major asset. On the one hand, this means that people should be managed as efficiently and effectively as any other asset, the responsibility for which must be actively borne by management. But a trickier issue of HR concerns liberating employees from the unnecessary constraints of organizational bureaucracy. This is a crucial task for companies trying to become more innovative, as well as for those seeking competitive advantage in the levels of service they offer. HR that stresses these aspects is sometimes unfortunately called soft HR, in contradistinction to hard HR, where the quantitative aspects of HR take precedent over the human.

It should also be noted that contemporary management practice tends to encourage the devolution of HR to line managers. This is partly a cost-cutting exercise and to take advantage of new IT developments, as discussed below. However, it also recognizes the close relationship that exists between the technical and interpersonal aspects of successful management. Having said that, experts also stress the importance of taking an integrated approach to HR, not only so that employees are treated consistently across the enterprise but also so that corporate culture and values can be effectively communicated.

It is not only social and theoretical imperatives that are changing HR practices. Computer applications, notably intranets, are having a major impact too. On one level, online IT systems provide cost-cutting opportunities in HR, removing paperwork by, for example, allowing individual employees to fill in electronic absentee forms or applications for holiday from their desktops. Online HR brings intangible benefits too. Employees can be empowered by, for example, automated training applications that allow them a more proactive role in their personal development. Such facilities can also have a substantial motivational role to play. Alternatively, some HR issues are best dealt with anonymously. Online queries about maternity leave or job opportunities in other offices can be made without embarrassment, indeed increasing the sense of trust that the company has in its staff. Such technology chimes with so-called pluralist approaches to HR: here managers recognize that the personal interests of staff might differ in some respects to the overall aims of the company, but that this need not necessarily be to the detriment of the organization.

See also: **Aptitude test, Discrimination, Home working, Industrial relations, Intellectual capital, Intranet, Labour, Morale, Motivation, Occupational psychology, Office management, Outsourcing, People skills, Training**

Further reading: Analoui, 1998; Baron and Kreps, 1999; Bernardin and Russell, 1998; Betteriss, 1998; Cook, 1999; DeCenzo and Robbins, 1999; Dessler, 2000; Dowling *et al.*, 1999; Flamholtz, 1999; Foot and Hook, 1999; Good, 1998; Hall and Torrington, 1998; Mabey *et al.*, 1998; Peters *et al.*, 1998; Poole, 1999; Walton, 1999

INCOME STATEMENT

A summary of revenues minus expenses over a period of time, often used by non-profit organizations as a way of representing accounts.

Income statements typically include a number of features. The gross margin is the money earned from sales to customers minus the direct costs of producing the goods or services. For a non-profit organization this amount can be taken as an equivalent of profits. The operating profit is the gross margin with a number of other expenses deducted, though notably not fiscal costs. This sidesteps the fact that companies can manage their cash requirements in a number of equally valid ways that could misleadingly affect operating profit. Net income is the figure that the statement derives after all costs, including interest and taxes, have been deducted. This is typically the figure that is reported as the measure of success or failure.

The income statement relates to the balance sheet by showing how changes in net assets occurred over the period.

See also: **Accounting, Non-profit organizations**

Further reading: Gross *et al.*, 2000; Thomas, A., 1999

INDUSTRIAL RELATIONS

A phrase referring to the state of play between employees, unions and management.

In Europe industrial relations have changed substantially since the 1970s. This is partly because the proportion of white collar workers in the total workforce has increased as blue collar jobs have disappeared or gone overseas. Also, the growing importance of the European Union in employment law has tended to disperse power that was formerly in the hands of unions. Having said that, within the EU industrial relations vary substantially, largely as a result of cultural and political differences.

Industrial relations in Japan are traditionally characterized by a spirit of cooperation. Works councils, for example, exist to promote the frictionless exchange of ideas between management and employees so as not to damage international competitiveness. However, it has also been suggested that the over-identification of Japanese workers with their companies has led to rigidity in the job market.

If the Japanese model is cooperative, the American model has tended to be adversarial. This partly stems from the more litigious environment that exists in the US. But it is also an indirect product of the short-termism that tends to be encouraged by the operation of America's equity markets.

A crude measure of industrial relations is often taken to be the number of days lost by businesses to industrial disputes. The figure provides a snapshot of the state of industrial relations in different regions, but little more.

See also: **Ethics**

Further reading: Denning, 1998; Helms, 1999; Thorpe and Homan, 2000; Wooding and Levenstein, 1999

INFLATION ACCOUNTING

The incorporation of measures that are able to deal with the problems faced by businesses working in areas in which monetary values vary significantly.

The problem that inflation causes businesses is obvious, but accounting for inflation has beaten even the best minds. For example, if an asset bought at the start of the year increases in price by 10 per cent over the course of the year as a result of inflation, should the company report a 10 per cent profit on the asset, because that is what it might sell for, or a 10 per cent loss, because the asset now costs 10 per cent more?

Accountants therefore advise a number of strategies to minimize the confusion inflation can cause. Selling prices should be regularly updated or tied to qualificatory clauses; business inputs should be satisfied by means less sensitive to inflation, such as reducing manual labour and increasing automation, or where that is not possible, the inflationary risk should be hedged against with futures options; investments with long-term paybacks or depreciation should be avoided; the debt-equity ratio should be increased in favour of debt capital, since creditors are cheaper to service.

See also: **Accounting**

Further reading: Kaplan and Atkinson, 1998; Muckian, 2000; Rashad Abdel-Khalik, 1998; Thomas, A., 1999

INFORMATION AND COMMUNICATIONS TECHNOLOGY

Equipment that is used to handle data, usually taken to refer to computer systems that process, store, retrieve, transmit and manage information, including voice and video.

Abbreviated to IT, ICT or IS (information systems), information management since the abacus has always been present in business, but it was revolutionized by the production of cheap microelectronics in the 1970s. Computers now pervade every aspect of commercial life.

The benefits of IT are discussed under several other entries, but whilst the exploitation of IT is recognized as essential in sectors as diverse as mining and medicine, the implementation of IT is in general expensive, arduous and challenging, the point that will be pursued here.

IT is expensive not so much because of what it costs up front, but because ongoing project and maintenance costs escalate. Two initiatives are important in terms of tackling the problem. The first is the effort IT vendors put into reducing the so-called total cost of ownership (TCO). For example, research shows that a PC typically costs three or four times its initial cost to keep running. Reducing the number of calls a user has to make to the helpdesk or increasing the resistance of the machine to crashing contributes to cutting TCO. The second initiative concerns the way organizations account for IT. Traditionally, IT has been treated as an unallocated cost because it does not have a direct impact upon revenue generation. However, this makes it hard to calculate investment returns and ensure efficient and effective implementation. Return on investment is now a major concern. Other practices, notably outsourcing to third parties such as ASPs (application service providers), introduces greater controls over IT costs.

IT implementation is arduous because computer systems are complex entities. IT is typically first introduced into organizations only to perform specific tasks; so many companies that have achieved a degree of departmental automation then find themselves lumbered with multiple, incompatible computers, so-called legacy systems, that actually hinder further progress. In some cases, legacy systems can become a severe competitive disadvantage, as traditional banks found in the 1990s when new banks were able to open green field operations that took advantage of fully integrated IT networks. Reducing the effort it takes to implement IT applications has been a major development focus for IT vendors, notably in respect of industry standards that help systems integration. The internet has also eased the situation.

IT is challenging because of the impact it has upon the organization, that is its human ramifications. Since the 1970s, IT has virtually done away with a class of manager whose job it was to push and pull information up and down the organization. To put it another way, IT is deeply associated in people's minds with job losses, and this perception of threat has caused even the best made IT plans to stumble. Even if employees can be assured that IT will help, perhaps even improve, their working lives, subtle issues can cause problems. For example, research shows that many workflow projects meet with resistance because the effect of the technology is to reduce office companionship, even if that is just the chats that people have over the photocopier.

See also: **Artificial intelligence, Automation, Data, E-business, E-commerce, Geographic information systems, Intranet, Network, Outsourcing, Project management, Systems analysis, Technology**

Further reading: Bidgoli, 1999; Compaine and Read, 1999; Currie and Galliers, 1999; Davenport, 1993; Davis, 1997; Galliers and Baets, 1998; Kmetz, 1998; Martin *et al.*, 1999; Parker, 1998; Shim, 2000; Stair, 1999; Thorp, 1998; Ungson and Trudel, 1998

INNOVATION

The strategic development of new products, markets, processes and systems, and the transformation of operations.

Innovation has always been important to many companies. But it is rapidly coming to be seen as critical for survival and growth in the contemporary, fast paced commercial environment. Competitive pressure is forcing firms to move beyond a best practice mindset and become ever more dextrous. The balance of Edison's maxim, that innovation is 1 per cent inspiration and 99 per cent perspiration, is shifting. For management, the challenge is to build practices that, alongside the traditional business objectives of cost efficiency, value creation and revenue growth, encourage the firm to be constantly innovative, to be a learning organization.

Sustaining the ability to create and implement ideas as the company grows is a major organizational hurdle. Typically, small companies that grow rapidly because they are innovative, struggle to maintain the flexibility of their earlier, intimate structures. Other firms simply do not have the processes to channel ideas from the sources of innovation, or there are glass ceilings and vested interests which inhibit the spread of ideas for fear of change. Alternatively, executive lack of self-confidence can prevent growth by missing opportunities.

A number of factors are embodied in the innovative organization.

The organization must have the ability to act more quickly than the competition and then be able to capitalize on the lead before competitors copy or leapfrog ahead. The implementation of plans includes new technologies and corporate structures, as well as new products and markets: that is the company must be able to handle internal pressures on change as well as external.

There is a conscious recognition that value comes from across the entire value chain. Processes are designed to be able to respond to change as well as manage associated risk. Decision making is also empowered to abandon impediments to development, judging success not only on growth but on a whole conception of value.

In an innovative organization, it is also a passion for employees, an attitude that pervades the firm. Research shows that ideas do not come from management itself so much as from customers and staff. Management is prepared to let these ideas question current operations and strategy, and is then equipped with the skills to translate ideas into programmes that can be implemented.

Conversely, employees regard themselves as stakeholders with purchase on the view the company has for its future. In this customer-focused environment, managers need to see their role as managing ideas as opposed to generating them.

Good innovation management is manifest in a number of ways. Employees are given space to develop ideas, as well as structures to maintain ownership of them: talented employees otherwise leave. Collaborative technologies, such as corporate intranets, are proving valuable in this respect.

A flexible attitude towards venture capital or R&D capital is important, again notably in relation to risk. What is culturally acceptable in terms of justifying projects might well need assessing in order to support innovation.

Certain 'kick-start' processes are being developed by consultancies that can be used to test and implement ideas. Other companies have worked on communication, employing managers, for example, who work across traditional company structures. An innovative style has also been shown to be facilitated by altering the physical working environment of the office.

Innovation plays an important role in value creation as well as revenue growth. It is argued that growth should not be regarded as an end in itself but as a means to create value. This way provides the greatest security for the future of the company, in that they do not only depend upon the maintenance or extension of customer markets, but deliver above-average returns for their shareholders too.

See also: **Change management, Competition, Delegation, Entrepreneurship, Learning organization, Risk**

Further reading: Afuah, 1998; Carter, 1999; Galliers and Baets, 1998; Hosking and Anderson, 1992; Jonash and Sommerlatter, 1999; Krogh *et al.*, 2000; Miller and Morris, 1999; Peters, 1998; Sundbo, 1998; Syrett and Lamminman, 1998; Tidd, 2000

INSURANCE

Financial products that protect organizations and individuals from carrying the full liability of a risk.

Businesses seek insurance as a way of hedging against the inevitable uncertainty they face. Operational insurance, that is against the risks associated with running a business – such as natural disaster or criminal activity – is as diverse as the risks that organizations and individuals seek to be insured against. The business has to find a financial institution that is prepared to accept the transfer of the risk in exchange for a premium that represents the average total losses the insurer faces in a given period.

Businesses also seek to insure themselves against commercial risks, that is risks associated with production such as fluctuations in prices or exchange rates. Here the company can turn to financial markets and buy an appropriate derivative product, notably futures and options. In this case, the cost of the insurance is a certain percentage of the reward the business hopes to gain from carrying the risk.

The insurance industry has its own means of protecting itself against the risks it carries. Reinsurance is important, essentially the swapping of insurance contracts since the liabilities of one suit another better.

The industry is also undergoing a substantial amount of change. This is partly a result of research that is being incorporated into the statistical foundations provided by actuaries, such as a deeper understanding of behavioural factors including the impact of insuring itself upon risk. Change is also a result of major losses that have been borne by the industry in recent years, notably at Lloyds of London. The system here, in which risks of unlimited liability were carried by so-called names, has been exposed as antiquated and inadequate. Risks themselves are changing too. For example, crime and fraud are growing in sophistication. Alternatively, there is a growing awareness of potentially major liabilities such as environmental damage and the problems of insuring against them.

See also: **Hedging, Risk**

Further reading: Carter, 1983; Diacon, 1990; Williams, C.A. *et al.*, 1998

INTELLECTUAL CAPITAL

The assets a company has that are bound up in the knowledge it possesses.

Intellectual capital exists in a number of different forms. It is, for example, embodied in organizational structures, practised in processes it might be said, in which case it can be referred to as organizational or structural capital. Alternatively, and more commonly, knowledge is embodied in staff in whom companies themselves have invested, in which case it is referred to as human capital. Intellectual capital can also be said to exist somewhere between the organization and its environment, for example, in the know-how which the company possesses when dealing with the society around it. In this case the organization might be said to possess cultural or social capital.

It is immediately obvious that the concept of intellectual capital is not exact. Sceptics might argue that human capital, for example, is none other than the classical labour factor of production. However, in its defence is a recognition that the assets which intellectual capital seeks to represent are of great importance to commercial performance and profits in the contemporary marketplace. If an organization recognizes the significance of strategic thinking for its future – and which would not – surely, the argument goes, intellectual capital can coherently be called an asset in its own right? It is for this reason that issues such as knowledge management have become so important.

Sullivan defines intellectual capital as 'about the creation of value out of human talent, transforming it through the resources provided by the firm's structure'. It is closely associated in the literature with subjects such as innovation, which is another way of saying that for many organizations intellectual capital is elusive. Unlike financial capital, that can be managed directly on the basis of the profits it can return, intellectual capital requires indirect methods to draw out its value and deliver a return. Intellectual capital management therefore looks at methodologies such as benchmarking and best practice in order to provide the right environment for intellectual capital to grow.

See also: **Learning organization, Value**

Further reading: Haskell, 1998; Klein, 1998; Sullivan, 1998, 2000

INTELLECTUAL PROPERTY

Assets whose ownership is protected by the family of legal entities including patents, copyright and trademarks.

Intellectual property is regarded as a key source of competitive advantage since it embodies the innovations that companies seek to exploit commercially. However, since intellectual property can only be partially protected by lock and key, or password and encryption, the legal rights given to the owners of intellectual property upon registration are important.

Patents exist to protect an invention from being exploited by others, notwithstanding the general details that are inevitably public. The belief is that the owner should have the right to make a return on their investment unheeded by competitors who might otherwise simply adopt the idea, process or know-how themselves.

Copyright is granted to the originator of words, pictures, music, and certain physical objects such as sculptures, to give them the exclusive rights as to their reproduction. Two recent additions to copyright law are particularly significant. The first is the Berne Convention that extends the copyright granted in one country to others signed up to the convention, now a majority of countries in the world. The convention also grants copyright from the moment the intellectual property is completed. The second is the American Digital Millennium Copyright Act of 1999, which as it suggests protects internet service providers from unintended breaches of copyright. This act is one of the first of undoubtedly many acts that will be required to cover copyright on the new medium.

A trademark seeks to address the problems a company can have when its products or services are closely associated with a distinguishing feature, such as a name or brand. Competitors might seek to take advantage of the lead that the feature represents, or simply seek to reduce its impact and confuse customers, by adopting the same or a similar feature themselves. The ™ trademark symbol can be used without registration. The ® symbol indicates registration.

The specifics of the rights protected by these legal entities vary from country to country, a difference that can become a major issue in the case of disputes. The World Intellectual Property Organization (WIPO) is one body that exists to promote the harmonization of international intellectual property laws.

Conversely, the acquisition of competitor knowledge by rival firms is a common, if elusive, commercial activity. For example, it is estimated that technology industries lose up to $100 billion in intellectual property globally per annum. Information might be sought by surreptitious means including industrial espionage. But there now exists a whole category of consultants whose specialty is the interpretation of the public signals that companies emit, voluntarily or otherwise, to gain insights into what is being planned behind closed doors.

Further reading: Helms, 1999; Hussey and Jenster, 1999; Litka, 1991; Pollard, 1999

INTRANET

A secure, internal electronic network used for communications within the organization.

Intranets arose to address a problem that the internet posed to businesses. The power of the internet lies in its openness, that is its ability to provide unlimited access to information. However, in many cases businesses have to ensure that information is secure, not only from third parties such as competitors, but also from unauthorized employees within the organization. Intranets, therefore, use internet technologies to exploit the benefits of the web, but with additional layers of security. Intranets are widely deployed in organizations and are used for purposes from HR to project management.

Virtual private networks (VPNs) are a kind of intranet where the security is provided by protecting the links between computers online, as opposed to the network as a whole. VPNs are particularly applicable to situations in which the intranet has to run over remote locations and so cannot be easily isolated from the outside world.

Extranets are another variant. They can be thought of as intranets that allow controlled access to external third parties too. For example, in investment banking, extranets are used to provide an online interface to serve customers with many kinds of information relevant to the client's portfolio of products. The extranet allows the client to have immediate access to information about their investments without the bank having to provide expensive customer service. More advanced developments of extranets allow customers to execute certain transactions too, since the bank is able to deploy applications online that allow the customer to make decisions for themselves.

See also: **E-business, Home working, Human resources management, Sales management**

Further reading: Lloyd and Boyle, 1998

INVENTORY

Specifically, the stock that a company holds at any given time, including raw materials, work in progress and finished goods. More generally, inventory is used to refer to all the assets a company holds, especially human assets.

Inventory management has become a critical issue for many companies seeking to reduce the overheads inventory represents. The task is to achieve the right balance between too little inventory, which compromises production and sales, and too much inventory, which absorbs cash and other resources that might be put to better use. The trick is often to deploy computer systems that are able to keep track and manage inventory to everyone's best advantage as well as reduce latency in the supply chain.

In manufacturing, materials requirements planning (MRP) is a critical discipline in inventory management. MRP aims to weigh the inventory means and needs of all parties concerned and devise processes to optimize delivery. The economic order quantity (EOQ) is a mathematical formula that might be used as part of MRP to balance the opposing costs of too much and too little inventory.

Just-in-time inventory management is the most widely adopted inventory policy. The idea is that stock is produced and delivered as it is needed all the way along the supply chain. Whilst this has been something of a pipedream, with the weakest members of the supply chain in effect forced to bear a greater proportion of the inventory costs, modern inventory computer systems do provide increased accuracy as to where inventory is in the supply chain, which in turn means that companies can rely on just-in-time deliveries. A good example is the automotive industry: so confident have car manufacturers become in their inventory management that they now make promises of delivery to customers that depend upon the performance of their suppliers rather than factors they can directly control.

However, just-in-time also increases the interdependency of companies, not only between those that trade directly and so might be subjected to service level agreements, but also between those further down the chain with whom there is only indirectly contact, such as the just-in-time suppliers to transport and energy providers. This can make just-in-time economies vulnerable to industrial interruptions, for example.

See also: **Logistics**

Further reading: Schniederjans and Olson, 1999; Toomey, 2000

JOINT VENTURE

A partnership between two or more companies to undertake a commercial project.

Joint ventures take many forms: strategic alliances, outsourcing, licensing agreements and foreign investment. The logic is that complementary partners can generate competitive advantage that they could not alone: a larger company may have cash, a smaller one innovation; one may have developed technology, the other access to cheaper labour markets. Joint ventures also appeal when the risks or costs of a project cannot be justified by one company alone.

In a joint venture there are no rules, only 'horses for courses'. There is therefore a certain additional risk in undertaking the joint venture itself. Experience points to the need for partners to develop mutual trust and commitment in particular. Management structures vary according to the nature of the parties concerned. If one is providing a majority of the financial backing, it is likely to be dominant managerially. If there is close parity of skills, or if one company wishes to protect its intellectual property, a shared management structure might suit. If skills transfer is an important factor, management structures may evolve during the course of the project.

Joint ventures have become more important as the opportunities for international trade have increased. Typically, participants will spread the risk/rewards associated with the project between them, with each bringing particular assets. So, whilst one firm may have the cash for a foreign investment, the other may have the local know-how that can spend it best.

Another area in which joint ventures have proved successful is in relation to innovative computer systems. Here, an IT company will invest substantially in the development of a new application for one company in particular, though with the long-term intention of producing a generic version of the product for wider sale. The advantage to the partner is the committed attention of the IT firm and the chance to steal a march on competitors with the innovation.

See also: **Collaboration, M&As, Outsourcing, Synergy**

Further reading: Geringer, 1998; Morris, 1998

KEYNESIAN ECONOMICS

The macroeconomic theory which holds that market forces of their own accord do not necessarily reduce unemployment to a minimum.

Keynes' theory directly challenges classical economics and its cousins, since the latter assume that a market system is in equilibrium only at full employment, and that should unemployment begin to rise forces within the market automatically strive to reduce it to a minimum again. Keynes, however, believed that the situation described in classical economics was just a special case of the more general situation in which a market can be in equilibrium regardless of unemployment levels. He therefore advocated that governments have a duty to instigate economic policies to reduce unemployment.

One of Keynes' central concepts is that of effective demand. He argued that if national income rises, national consumption also rises, though at a lesser rate. However, Keynes believed that whilst the relation between income and consumption was necessary, there was nothing direct about the relationship between income and the behaviour of businesses that might invest in this expanding market. This is because whilst short-term returns can be predicted, long-term returns are always uncertain. Thus businesses might not generate enough effective demand to compensate for rises in unemployment. So governments should lend money to stimulate investment in the public sector to soak up the surplus unemployment.

The theory takes its name from its founder, John Maynard Keynes, who wrote *The General Theory of Employment, Interest and Money* during the Great Depression of the 1930s. He responded to the apparent laissez-faire attitude of governments at that time to argue that government intervention can have a stabilizing effect upon national economies. Keynes has less of an influence today since, after monetarism, Western governments generally have greater faith in markets, although that faith is somewhat tempered by Keynesian ideas.

See also: **Classical economics, Monetarism, Neoclassical economics**

Further reading: Keynes, 1971–89; Skidelsky, 1983–2000

KILLER APPLICATION

Originally in IT, the software programme that triggers the exponential adoption of a technology. But often used more generally to indicate the product or service that will secure a market.

The IT sector has often witnessed the situation in which a new technology is developed which for all its merits is unable to generate sales because people do not see the need for it. It is a technology in search of an application. However, those technologies that become ubiquitous do so because they become a 'must have'. For example, the internet existed for some time before it achieved the explosive growth rates of the late 1990s. The web browser might be said to be the killer application for the internet, since it transformed the internet from being an inaccessible network to a mass communications media.

A related concept is the network effect. Here, the more individuals that use a technology the more necessary it becomes for others to use it too. The classic example is Microsoft's Windows operating system, which runs over 90 per cent of the world's computers, in part, because its ubiquity massively reduces interoperability and connectivity issues.

See also: **Product**

KNOWLEDGE WORKER

An employee whose most valuable asset is informational, in the form of facts, expertise and erudition.

The term was originally coined by Peter Drucker, who defines knowledge workers as 'high level employees, acquired through formal education, to develop new products or services'. Drucker had in mind professionals with an innovative or entrepreneurial bent. However, since then the term has been more widely applied in the West to refer to the majority of white collar workers. The reason is that in heavily automated industries, an employee's know-how becomes the most important asset that they bring to the organization, for the simple reason that manual tasks disappear. In a knowledge economy, companies increasingly find that present profits and future growth lie in their ability to deal in knowledge too. That is, knowledge becomes a primary asset. It follows that as an economy becomes more advanced, workers in it must become knowledge workers.

Clearly this is not to imply that all knowledge workers carry out identical tasks or processes. Many will be employed in routine and repetitive environments. But the point is that what makes a difference, in terms of the company's competitiveness, is the ability of these individuals to apply their knowledge to various situations as they present themselves. For example, customer service in the call centre improves if agents have a degree of informed flexibility. Alternatively, managers are likely to be more valuable if their responsibilities are not limited, to the detriment of the knowledge they have.

See also: **Learning organization, Training**

Further reading: Alvarez, 1998; Skyrme, 1999; Sparrow, 1998

LABOUR

In economics, the total human effort, mental and physical, that contributes to production. More generally, work performed by individuals.

Labour, alongside land and capital, is one of the three key components of production. Like the other two, a business must assess how much labour it requires, that is how many people it should employ, and at what price. The answers to these questions have a macroeconomic and microeconomic component.

The cost of labour, for example, is set in large part by the macroeconomic climate which determines how much markets are prepared to pay for people who perform certain tasks, or alternatively how much individuals need to be paid to secure them for the purposes of the company concerned. However, at a microeconomic level, companies may be prepared to pay more for labour that is particularly valuable to them or hard to come by. Alternatively, the cost of labour also depends on the cost of living: if this rises, then a balance must be restored at which the company's reluctance to pay more is met by people's reluctance to work for longer hours. The labour market is said to be in equilibrium in this case.

The cost of labour is measured according to productivity, that is the volume of product it can produce over time, and the value of what is produced. Labour is a marginal cost, which means that a company seeks to find the most productive labour available. However, the principle of diminishing marginal productivity says that the output a company gains from more labour does not increase indefinitely, but begins to decrease according to its proportionate relationship with land and capital. This is why, for example, companies tend to hire more labour if wages fall and lay off staff when wages rise.

Companies can manage the diminishing marginal productivity of labour in a number of ways. One is to educate its workforce so that the value the labour represents to the company increases. Another strategy is to automate tasks, notably by the introduction of capital investments such as computer systems, usually in order to reduce the company's reliance on labour.

The relationship between labour and the macroeconomic concern of employment is discussed under Keynesian economics and Monetarism. However, the work of Karl Marx adds an interesting dimension to the discussion of labour. At his funeral, Engels said that Marx had discovered 'surplus value'. This is the difference between what a capitalist pays for labour and what that labour is able to return to him because of its productive capacity. That the labourer can only ever receive the lesser of these two values – the return for his efforts that the market is prepared to pay – is why the capitalist always has the upper hand. This also leads to a critique of the theories of labour as espoused by economists such as Adam Smith. Here, the value of a product is seen as representative of the labour it took to produce it. But Marx says that the value of a product is the sum of the labour it took to produce it and its surplus value, the additional amount that the market places on the product. In general, this surplus value forms the greater part, controlling the labour that produces it, or alienating the individuals who work in a capitalist society.

See also: **Economics, Classical economics, Keynesian economics, Neoclassical economics**

Further reading: Magill, 1997; Marx, 2000; McAuliffe, 1997

LEADERSHIP

The individual qualities and skills that managers need to nurture if they are not only going to control but to direct those committed to their charge.

It is sometimes said that managers solve problems, whereas leaders confront challenges. The point is that leadership is a highly valued ability in business, and becoming a leader is one of its greatest prizes. So-called captains of industry command very high salaries on an international stage, and employing a proven leader is viewed by many boards as a key to competitive success.

The subject is widely discussed in business studies and much is agreed upon; for example, the qualities leaders need to have, which include vision, commitment, integrity and intuition. However, since leadership resides in individuals, and studies of leaders show that these individuals vary enormously in their success, there is little agreement as to the precise formula that makes for leadership, nor the key to teaching it.

Traditional theories of leadership tend to emphasize the role of the leader in directing and motivating others. A common analogy is made with the military, in which the commanding officer issues orders and inspires the respect to be obeyed. This is not to say that leadership is viewed as centralized or dictatorial. The military analogy points out that qualities including mutual trust, motivation and morale, well developed lines of responsibility, and the ability to delegate are important too. However, the great advantage that these theories have is they are task oriented. The leader is someone who gets things done and so can be assessed by their ability to deliver tangible outcomes.

Charismatic theories of leadership emphasize the inspirational qualities of the leader. It is not so much what they tell people to do, as what quality of relationship they have within them that encourages employees to work. Leadership in this mode is therefore much more personal. Leaders set good examples, inspire commitment to themselves on the part of employees, and tend to lead by communicating a vision or set of values that might require others to translate into a tangible business plan. Charismatic leadership has the great advantage of being the sort most likely to be able to carry an organization through a rough patch, or to achieve success against the odds, as say in a start-up situation.

A third category of leadership theories takes a less individual approach. These theories stress the role that the organization plays in leadership. An organization that encourages an entrepreneurial attitude or facilitates delegation is as important as the particular leaders that operate within it. Leadership is also recognized as something that individuals may possess in limited situations, and not universally. For example, some people may emerge as leaders in times of stress. Others are better leaders when routine rules the day. These ideas also discourage the idea that leaders should be treated as a class apart.

In general, leaders may possess these various qualities in different measures. A good leader, therefore, knows him or herself. For example, a leader who is easily threatened, or does not recognize when they are threatened, may become either too weak or too authoritarian. It is also the responsibility of leaders to make sure their leadership style fits the style of the organization. Many a business failure has been caused by a previously successful leader imposing an inappropriate formula.

See also: **Decision making, Entrepreneurship, Paternalism, People skills**

Further reading: Bass, 1990; Bristow *et al.*, 1999; Brown, 1999; Conger and Kanungo, 1998; Fairholm, 1998; Hooper and Potter, 2000; Kraft, 1998; Sadler, 1999; Spears, 1998; Steers *et al.*, 1996; Yukl, 1994

LEARNING ORGANIZATION

A company in which it is not only employees that gain knowledge but where the organization itself can be said to change too. In other words, experience evolves organizational processes.

Peter Senge has described the learning organization as one 'that is continually expanding its capacity to create its future'. However, creating any collective that behaves in a determined way is tricky enough, let alone one so guided. The learning organization therefore represents an advanced stage of organizational development.

At one level, the learning organization can be thought of as one that has overcome the inhibitions that tend to keep others immature. For example, learning organizations do not have an automatic fear of mistakes but have the capacity, either as a result of culture or processes, to incorporate the experience that comes from errors. A related ability concerns change. Organizations that can embrace change will have methods for reflecting on feedback during (not after) decision making. Alternatively, they will be companies that are not defensive in the face of the harsh criticism that follows mistakes.

So there is no magic in the learning organization. It is one that has paid attention to the micromanagement of issues such as efficiency and effectiveness that all companies should pay attention to. Having said that, there is an important cultural dimension to the learning organization too that might be thought of as 'oiling the learning machine'. This can be encouraged in a number of ways. One example is the use of balanced scorecards to measure performance alongside financial indicators. Balanced scorecards simultaneously encourage individuals to consider the long-term view, as well as to think about less tangible qualities that are important for learning.

See also: **Balanced scorecard, Change management, Knowledge worker**

Further reading: Baets, 1998; Chen, 1991; Denton, 1998; Flood, 1999; Kaplan and Norton, 1996; Mailick and Stumpf, 1998; Marksick and Watkins, 1999; Schwandt and Marquardt, 2000; Senge, 1990

LEVERAGE

The process of exploiting inherent advantages.

Leveraging an asset to steal a march on competitors can take many forms. The leveraging of brand is a good example. The company that has high brand recognition in one product area is likely to be more successful at launching a related product if it is able to leverage its brand. This might relate to promoting generic qualities, such as trust, or particular properties, such as quality.

A very different use of the term is as in leveraged firm. This is a company that has high levels of debt. Alternatively, a leverage recapitalization is a restructuring of equity into debt. This can be a useful device for protecting the firm against takeover.

See also: **Restructuring**

LIBERALIZATION

The deregulation of markets that removes restrictions on trade.

Liberalization was a continuous feature of the changing business environment in the second half of the twentieth century. A good ongoing case is that of the telecommunications industry in Europe. Both at a national and international level, state-sponsored monopolies are being actively broken up to encourage new companies to bring in the investment that is needed to cope with rapid technological change. This kind of deregulation can be thought of as a second wave. The first wave, after World War II, was not so concerned with investment as with bureaucracy, in which case deregulation was seen as a means of exposing inefficient organizations to the rigours of the market.

Liberalization clearly requires government intervention. Political regimes embrace deregulation with varying enthusiasm. Governments promote liberalization most strongly when it is part of a political package of privatization or joint ventures between private and public bodies. The deregulation of public utilities is a good case. Conversely, governments can be seen to be dragging their feet when liberalization conflicts with the interests of powerful lobby groups, or when the imperative to liberalize quickly is particularly strong.

Deregulation typically presents opportunities to new players in the markets and poses challenges to vested interests. By reducing entry barriers, the number of firms operating in the market often increases dramatically. Competition also rises, as does the pressure to cut costs. This is because regulated industries find it easier to pass costs onto customers, and so in the deregulated situation there is great pressure to reverse the load. However, as a result of the speed of change, players old and new tend to compete with a short-term view and possibly beyond sustainable means. The early rush of activity that follows liberalization is therefore often followed by a period of consolidation in which the players that have not managed to secure their piece of the cake either go belly-up or are bought out by stronger contenders.

Business culture also changes post-liberalization. Regulated industries are typically reactive, since they are subject to various external authorities. But deregulation favours those with a proactive strategy. This factor tends to favour new, agile players, and it can often take traditional companies many years to adjust to the innovative demands of deregulated markets. Companies that operated before liberalization can also be threatened by critical equity markets that see steep falls in profits. A negative response can develop into a vicious circle as assets critical to success post-liberalization, such as brand, are also detrimentally affected.

See also: **Bureaucracy, Government, Telecommunications**

Further reading: Cox *et al.*, 1999; Mahimi and Turcq, 1993

LIQUIDITY

Liquidity is the measure of an asset's ability to be turned into cash.

Liquid assets are those that are held as cash or can easily be turned into cash. Liquidity can be used as a measure of a company's financial solvency. Typically for a firm, an asset that can be turned into cash within one accounting period, say a year, is regarded as liquid.

To liquidate an organization is to turn its assets into cash, usually with a view to paying back creditors, or paying shareholders a liquidating dividend when a company is being closed down. The process is overseen by a liquidator.

Liquidity preference is a theory of the economist John Maynard Keynes, which says that people prefer savings that have a higher liquidity.

See also: **Banking, Bankruptcy, Cash, Finance, Keynesian economics**

LOBBYING

Campaigning with a view to putting the interests of business to government.

Whilst lobbying in its narrowest sense may be regarded as seeking to achieve nothing more or less than the securing of a favourable competitive environment, the actual practice of lobbying is far more sophisticated. Businesses may employ lobbyists internally or hire a lobbying firm to act as their agent. Networking is at the heart of the lobbyist's work – the term derives from the room outside legislative chambers where lobbyists hope to bend the ear of officials – and so the lobbyist's or lobby firm's greatest asset is the access to power it can secure. Therein lies lobbying's strength and weakness.

For example, many politicians welcome the activities of lobbyists as valuable contributors to the political process, bringing expertise to the business of lawmaking or drawing government's attention to issues that need to be addressed. In the age of the multinational company, lobbying can also be a means whereby the firm expresses its sense of social responsibility, pressing for workable environmental change, for example. Western governments too have, in recent years, tended to seek ways to work more closely with business, partly out of a recognition of the social power they wield. Fundamentally, it is argued, lobbying is one of the mechanisms within a democracy that promotes free speech.

However, lobbying is often viewed with suspicion. And the transparency with which lobbying activities are carried out varies enormously from country to country. The way in which donations are given to political parties is a good measure. In the US, for example, donations are public. In other parts of the world where the activities of lobbyists merge with those of extortionists it would be less easy to determine what money has changed hands. However, even in the US, there exists a sustained critique of the impact of lobbying on the political process when done in conjunction with financial transactions. As one commentator observed, transparent corruption is still corruption.

Negative public perception has been exacerbated by the dramatic growth of the lobbying industry. In the 1960s working lobbyists in any one country could be numbered in the hundreds. Today there are tens of thousands. Advocates, however, claim that this expansion represents an increase in transparency, since previously influence was sought via privilege.

Regulators are continually knocking at the lobbyist's door. The main aim of legislation has been to force lobbyists to register and declare expenditures. These measures have brought a degree of control to the lobbying industry, although in recent years attention has focused on the so-called revolving door, the easy transition that politicians and civil servants seem to take from public work to the private sector, presumably in part because of the access they bring with them.

See also: **Government, Public sector**

Further reading: Coen, 1997; Mack, 1989; Randall, 1996

LOGISTICS

The management of the flow of goods and services from origin to the point of delivery.

The term originates in the military, referring to the movement of troops and supplies to and from the front line. In commerce, logistics covers everything from inventory holding to product distribution, as well as the financial and human resource aspects that are required for a successfully functioning business. For larger organizations logistics is a major management task. Failure in logistics leads to productivity and profit loss, and in extreme situations to the collapse of the business. In order to drive logistical efficiency and effectiveness, many organizations outsource logistical functions to firms that specialize in tasks or can share economies of scale in terms of reduced charges. Logistics is also a key issue in international business, though in this case often more so for smaller organizations looking for logistical support as they move into global markets.

See also: **Inventory**

Further reading: Arnold, 1998; Christopher, 1998; Schönsleben, 2000

LOSS LEADER

A product or service that does not make a profit itself but increases the profitability of other products or services.

Loss leaders can be used in a wide variety of ways, although the strategy is always to increase profits. For example, retailers may carry goods that they know will not sell well but the presence of which encourages other sales. In men's shirt retailing, for example, the volumes and therefore the profits are in white and blue shirts, though red and green shirts are carried too since they are seen to enhance choice. Another kind of retailing loss leader expects the goods to sell if at a loss, but it is worthwhile because it brings customers into the shop who buy other profitable products. Supermarkets discount brands for this purpose.

The use of loss leaders can lead to tension between manufacturers and retailers, since the former may believe their brand is being eroded in the process.

See also: **Retailing, Sales management**

LOYALTY

A measure of the commitment a customer has to buying the products of a particular brand.

The loyalty a customer has to a brand stems from many complex issues. However, increasing loyalty is a particular goal of brand marketing. Customers are also segmented according to loyalty. According to Kotler, hard-core loyals never veer from the brand, soft-core loyals are committed to two or more brands, shifting loyals readily switch but are committed for a time, and switchers show no commitment to brand at all. Different customer segments will be attracted to the product in different ways. Hard-core loyals need their commitment reinforcing by advertising. Soft-core loyals will respond to promotions. Switchers may be attracted by price reductions. Shifting loyals can be particularly valuable, since they may tell the company about inadequacies in its product.

Customer loyalty becomes a critical issue in saturated markets. Loyal customers are perceived as especially profitable customers in these competitive environments, since they are susceptible to cross-selling and up-selling, which is far more cost effective than trying to win new customers, and have the effect of increasing loyalty.

Loyalty has also become an issue in online retailing. Here the problem is that of a lack of loyalty. In a business environment where the competitor is 'only a click away' loyalty is much harder to secure.

Another occasional use of the word loyalty refers to the commitment an employee has to the company, especially when they receive little or no tangible return.

See also: **Brand, CRM, Relationship marketing**

Further reading: Fletcher, 1993; Hill and Alexander, 2000; Kotler, 1994; Stone *et al.*, 2000

MANAGEMENT

The administration of capital, labour and land within an organization to achieve its aims.

The management task may be variously described. In financial terms it is to optimize the relationship between inputs and outputs, so that the highest returns are generated from the least means of production. In economic terms it is to satisfy the needs and desires of markets with whatever resources are available. In business terms it is to improve the productivity and profitability of a company to increase shareholder value, cut costs, manage risk, or improve growth.

The verb 'to manage' is ancient, possibly originating in the Italian *manneggiare*, which usually referred to the exercise of horsemanship. But the study of management is modern, beginning after the Industrial Revolution. Today management is one of the fastest growing applied sciences in education.

But whilst certain premises may be held in common, management is a highly contested area of study. Fundamental divisions are held between neoclassical economists, who believe that management should be free of ownership, the bureaucratic theorists who believe that owners should control businesses, and those managers who look only to the interests of shareholders.

Management theories also change dramatically over time. In the last one hundred years alone, a rejection of a mechanistic approach, exemplified in Fordism, first led to an emphasis on the management of human relations. This was in turn eclipsed by a belief in contingency management in response to the economic turmoil of the war years, which has now evolved into a more optimistic and strategic approach, popular today.

International management is another growing dimension, and it is far from the case that norms in the West are spreading elsewhere. Japan's system of *ringi* decision making, based upon consensus, and the presence of *nemawashi*, that brings cultural and organizational cohesion, are receiving renewed attention in the West. Management has specialized too, so that the subject boasts experts in everything from crisis to customer management. Management journals provide more evidence that the subject is booming. In 1956 the *Harvard Business Review* became the first. Now there are hundreds.

Thomas points out that management theory suffers from a double challenge to its quality and its relevance. He believes along with many others that management researchers and practitioners are subject to whims of fashion. They become influential because they initially address a management need that is current, but then often take on a life of their own, becoming popular through a process of mimesis. Perhaps this is the only way of bringing a sense of discipline and rigour to a matter that is not so much a science as an art.

This aesthetic turn is one of the current trends. As articulated by Dobson, it recognizes that the activities of business are closely intertwined with the values of society, and so management needs to be sensitive to changes in culture. Aesthetic management is timely. There is a broad dissatisfaction in business studies with management's scientific basis, a feeling not that scientific methods are not necessary but that they are not sufficient, because of a developing recognition that the good manager is one who is intuitively in step with cultural moods, financial and ethical. Senior management must steer the company with the prevailing winds. And middle management needs to be sensitive to a changing workforce. Business, as Dobson puts it, is an indeterminate aesthetic activity, not a deterministic technical enterprise, as it might have been held to be before.

See also: **Category management, Change management, Crisis management, CRM, Decision making, Ethics, Facilities management, Familism, Glass ceiling, Human resources management, Leadership, Office management, Operations management and strategy, Paradox management, Paternalism, People skills, Portfolio management, Project management, Sales management, Taylorism, Total capacity management, Total quality management, Training**

Further reading: Ackoff, 1999a; Bartlett and Ghoshal, 2000; Beechler and Stucker, 1998; Boddy and Paton, 1998; Callaway, 1999; Channon, 1997; Cooper and Argyris, 1998; Crainer, 1998; Cronje *et al.*, 2000; Danford, 1999; Dawson, 1998; Dessler, 2001; Dobson, 1999; Forrest, 1996; Glass, 1998; Hannagan, 1998; Harding and Long, 1998; Helliegel *et al.*, 1999; Helms, 1999; Hussey, 1998; Johnson, 1999; Johnson and Duberley, 2000; Keuning, 1998; Kuhn, 1988; Lane *et al.*, 2000; Lock, 1998; Mendenhall *et al.*, 1995; Mockler and Dologite, 1997; O'Connell, 1997; Ramsden, 1998; Remenyi *et al.*, 1998; Roth, 2000; Statt, 1999; Stewart, 1998; Thomas, P., 1999; Wallace, 1998; Warner, 2000; Wren and Greenwood, 1998

MARKETING

The process by which a company tries to identify, inform and satisfy customer needs and desires, efficiently and profitably.

Marketing has existed in many forms since the Industrial Revolution, and has played a central part in the emergence of mass markets and the modern consumer in particular. Marketing connects the business to the customer. It seeks to connect the means of production with its ends, that is consumption. It therefore covers a multitude of activities that Lancaster and Massingham summarize in eight points:

- Marketing focuses the firm's or individual's attention towards the needs and wants of the marketplace.
- Marketing is concerned with satisfying the genuine needs and wants of specifically defined target markets by creating products or services that satisfy customer requirements.
- Marketing involves analysis, planning and control.
- The principle of marketing states that all business decisions should be made with a careful and systematic consideration of the user.
- The distinguishing feature of a market-orientated organization is the way in which it strives to provide customer satisfaction as a way of achieving its own business objectives.
- Marketing is dynamic and operational, requiring action as well as planning.
- Marketing requires an improved form of business organization in order for it to be able to lead and catalyse the application of the marketing approach.
- Marketing is both an important functional area of management and an overall business philosophy which recognizes that the identification, satisfaction and retention of customers is the key to prosperity.

Successful marketing rests on communication. It aims to get its message out to the intended audience by concentrating on its subject matter, summed up as the four Ps of marketing: product, place, price and promotion. Marketing has in common with other kinds of management the four key ingredients of analysis, planning, implementation and control. But it incorporates more business functions than most, called the marketing mix, which includes advertising, research, promotion, PR and organizational management. In fact, in terms of function, marketing impacts many if not all parts of the enterprise, which is reflected in the phrase 'integrated marketing communication'. The aim here is that the different activities of marketing should not conflict but that a consistent message and offer should reach the customer.

Marketing differs at a deeper level too. Marketing, it is argued, is an attitude that should permeate the enterprise to bring customer focus. In other words marketing is the defining business function, much to the marketing department's delight and everyone else's chagrin.

This is called the marketing concept, although customer-orientation as *the* management goal is a relatively modern principle. Having said that, the concept itself has been around since the time of Adam Smith. He wrote, in the *Wealth of Nations*, 'Consumption is the sole end and purpose of all production and the interests of the producer ought to be attended to, only so far as it may be necessary for promoting that of the consumer'. Smith's use of the verb 'promote' is decisive. A product philosophy of business would promote the business's specialist knowledge of what it produces. A selling philosophy of business would promote the business's specialist knowledge of how to sell what it produces. However, the argument is that both of these strategies miss the crucial link to the consumer. The customer is always right in respect of what products a business should make and how it should sell them. Critics of the marketing concept point out that customers do not always know what they want, and that a doctrinaire application of the marketing concept would stifle innovation.

At the time of writing, marketing is being profoundly affected on two fronts as a result of technology and environmentalism. The technology comes in two guises, the database and the internet. The power of modern databases to handle vast amounts of market information and the customizability of the internet is what is significant. Combined, they suggest that ultimately marketing will whittle down its mass audiences to communicate directly with audiences of one. This is a trend that is well under way in many organizations, and it is having a major impact on the way businesses function, notably by reinforcing the marketing concept.

Environmentalism is less significant, though it is an influence that seems likely to increase. The problem here is marketing's role in creating consumptive behaviour. The environmental argument is that modern patterns of consumption are not sustainable, since resources are limited – a point that any economist would also make.

So environmental marketing seeks to alter the blind promotion of the consumption of goods, in favour of one that is informed and aware of its responsibilities.

See also: **Advertising, Brand, Brand extension, Communication, Consumer, CRM, Direct operations, E-business, Ethics, Gap analysis, Merchandising, Positioning, Price, Product, Public relations, Relationship marketing, Retailing, Sales management, Segmentation, Soft sell, Subliminal advertising, Value**

Further reading: Aaker *et al.*, 1998; Allen *et al.*, 1998; Belch and Belch, 1998; Berry, 1998; Davies, 1998; Doyle, 1998; Evans and Moutinho, 1999; Foxall *et al.*, 1998; Fuller, 1999; Gronstedt, 2000; Hartley, 1998; Hill and O'Sullivan, 1999; Kotler and Armstrong, 1999; Lancaster and Massingham, 1999; Macchiette and Roy, 2001; McDonald, 1998; O'Malley *et al.*, 1999; Palmer and Hartley, 1999; Phillips *et al.*, 2000; Rook, 1999; Stauble, 2000; Steinbock, 2000; Sterne and Priore, 2000; Weinreich, 1999; Zyman, 1999

MARKET PENETRATION

The proportion of sales, or some other measure of presence, that a company enjoys in a particular sector.

Market penetration is a dynamic concept that is usually used in conjunction with market entry. So, a company seeking to enter a market for the first time will set targets as to the penetration it hopes to achieve within a certain timeframe. Once a company has become established in the field it is said to have a certain share of the market. Market entry can be gained in a number of ways, not least by penetration or predatory pricing in which the new player seeks to undercut competitors by selling a product at a lower price. This short-term strategy can also be combined with a longer-term approach by, for example, attaching penetration prices to a budget brand. In this way the initially low price can be sustained over time.

See also: **Barrier to market, Growth, Price**

MASLOW'S HIERARCHY

A behavioural theory that categorizes needs so that when one is fulfilled another becomes the focus of attention.

Maslow's hierarchy of needs is a useful indicator when it comes to understanding consumer motivation. According to psychologist Abraham Maslow, people prioritize their needs so that when basic ones are satisfied more complex desires come to the fore. In ascending order, needs are: physiological needs, notably food, housing and sex; security needs, associated with safety and stability; social needs, notably human relationships and a sense of place; individual needs, that is self-esteem, power and recognition; and finally self-actualization needs, to exercise creativity and find fulfilment.

Maslow's ideas can be used with varying degrees of sophistication in marketing. It explains on one level why 'free', 'chocolate', 'sex' and 'new' are such powerful selling points. But on another level, products may be marketed to appeal to the sense of satisfaction that comes from ascending the hierarchy: a single good will meet physiological needs, bring the benefits of security and social needs, and represent the values that contribute to individual self-actualization.

See also: **Economics, Marketing**

Further reading: Maslow, 1970

MBA

The Master of Business Administration degree, often seen as the definitive qualification for aspiring managers.

MBAs have developed out of the demand from usually experienced business practitioners for a postgraduate academic course that teaches the assorted disciplines which together make the science of management. Courses typically take between one and two years, depending on whether they are full- or part-time. Entry qualification in the US, at least, is based upon GMAT (Graduate Management Admission Test), a written test in English of over three hours that assesses comprehension, arithmetic and analytical skills.

Hindle reports that the growth of MBAs stems from a change in the belief that managers are born to the conviction that they can be made. The number of MBA courses grew fast: in the UK there are over 100 to date. And the number of MBAs, as graduates of the courses are called, has exploded too: in the US tens of thousands are produced every year. However, the status of the MBA is changing. It is no longer seen as a guaranteed ticket to a highly paid job as it was in the 1980s. Research shows that businesses are increasingly looking not for learnt skills sets in their managers, but for an ability to learn how to cope with rapidly changing, globally competitive markets. MBA courses are changing as a result.

Even in their boom years, MBAs did not have a monopoly in business education. In Japan there is no such thing as an MBA and neither do they carry the kudos that a graduate from the UK or America would hope. In many parts of Europe, business studies can be taken at many levels too, though academic MBA equivalents are rare. Here, industry-based education is preferred.

See also: **Management**

Further reading: Hindle, 2000; Muckian, 2000; Shim *et al.*, 1997; Silbiger, 1994

MERCHANDISING

The various elements that come together in the selling of consumer goods.

Merchandising can be used in a more or less precise sense. Its specific meaning refers to high street retailing in particular, that is the location and layout of the store and the goods that are displayed within it – the so-called merchandising mix. A more general use describes the whole process of retailing, from developing goods through to securing sales. It is often used in this wider sense in America, and more narrowly in Europe.

This is not to say, of course, that merchandising in the narrower sense is not important everywhere. Store design is a major weapon on the competitive high street and has, in recent years, been subject to the scientific eye of retail studies, examining every aspect from the shopfront to the smells inside.

See also: **Retailing**

Further reading: Levy and Weitz, 1995; McGoldrick, 1990

M&As

The two ways – mergers and acquisitions – that companies join to become a single commercial entity. In mergers, the assets are combined to create a new firm. In acquisitions, the assets of one are bought by another with the identity of the former usually remaining intact, though not necessarily that of the latter.

M&As occur for a number of reasons. The achievement of economies of scale is commonly cited. For example, the companies may be in the same business and so be able to reduce unit costs by merging. Alternatively, the greater market share that follows from a merger can buy the company greater power in the market, notably in terms of competitive advantage.

M&As also take place in industries undergoing change. For example, they have been popular in the banking sector in recent years as a way of diversifying quickly, following the deregulation that has led to the opportunities of offering many different financial services under one brand.

However, companies involved in very different kinds of business may also merge. For example, one may be cash-rich and profitable but with few investment opportunities and little prospect of growth. This company may acquire one with exactly the opposite commercial profile. M&As also sometimes take place simply to increase share price.

In use, M&A activity is usually differentiated from takeovers since this term carries a hostile connotation.

The financial justification for M&As is complex. It hinges on the relative value of the companies before and after merger, and the cost of merging both in terms of buying equity and integrating organizations. A calculation that involves stock market value, cash flow, expected earnings and the value of likely synergies post-merger is typical.

M&As are often risky undertakings. Not only can they be questionable as a commercial strategy, but the matter of integrating companies post-merger can even cause the merger to fail. Cultural incompatibilities are a common complaint, as are the unworkable management structures that can be the result of trying to merge boards. Another issue is the cost of integrating heterogeneous IT infrastructures, a necessary task since it is often only then that economies of scale can be realized.

See also: **Diversification, Goodwill, Growth, Holding company, Joint venture, Synergy**

Further reading: Clemente and Greenspan, 1998; Cosh and Hughes, 1998

MISSION STATEMENT

A written summary of a company's broad aims and goals.

Mission statements are also known as the corporate philosophy or creed. Their aim is to bring a consistent focus on objectives and values across the enterprise that can inform decision making at many levels as well as build a certain attitude in general.

Research indicates that mission statements are effective. For example, in the 1980s Bill Gates saw Microsoft's goal as putting a 'computer on every desk in every home' – remarkable then, but the success of which can be judged by the fact that it is commonplace now. Ideally, the mission statement will relate directly to strategic, tactical and operational goals, and it can provide a powerful means of drawing these elements together when they could otherwise easily drift apart. Since achieving this collective vision in one short statement is often not possible, some companies develop several statements that have a visionary phrase in common but different applications of it for the various parts of the organization.

For mission statements to work throughout the organization, the whole enterprise must be able to take ownership of it. This means that the mission statement must be arrived at by a process of consultation. It needs to be memorable and preferably memorizable. It needs to have the right balance between aspirational and achievable goals. Avoidance of jargon is also advisable, since a predominance of buzzwords will lessen the impact of the mission statement in terms of focus. Jargon also increases its generic quality, undermining the aim to give individuality and character to the company. And of course, the process of writing a mission statement can often be as valuable to an organization as the actual product itself.

Further reading: Helms, 1999; Schuler and Van de Ven, 1997; Trout, 1999

MIXED ECONOMY

An environment in which more than one economic theory can be seen in operation.

Usually a mixed economy is taken to mean that elements of socialism are present alongside a dominant capitalism, particularly in relation to the public sector, where government spending is sanctioned. However, a mixed economy can also refer to more diverse economic methods being present simultaneously, notably in the countries of former or reforming communist countries, in which capitalism may not be nearly so dominant as in the West.

In its milder form, a mixed economy includes policies to redistribute wealth through taxation and the maintenance of a welfare state. A socialist presence may be felt more substantially in economies that adopt incomes policies or favour state-owned over private firms in certain sectors. Government planning of the economy, as advocated by socialism proper, has been all but abandoned in the West, and only remains in varying degrees in the former Soviet Union and China in particular.

See also: **Keynesian economics**

Further reading: McAuliffe, 1997

MODELLING

The creation of computer simulations to show the impact of variable inputs and outputs.

Modelling is an important advance in quantitative analysis. It differs from traditional statistical analysis in that computer models are typically able to include many variables and produce dynamic results that incorporate feedback effects. In this last respect, artificial intelligence systems also help the programmer to construct the model to start with, either by applying mathematical solutions to a problem described or by using models already developed for similar analyses.

Modelling techniques are also useful for interpreting anomalies. For example, in decision support systems that draw on large customer databases, there may be many customers who do not fall into previously defined market segments, and would, unless interpreted by an appropriate model, tend to fall by the wayside.

See also: **Artificial intelligence, Forecasting, Quantitative methods, Regression analysis**

Further reading: Dyson and O'Brien, 1998; Evans and Olson, 2000; Ilgen and Hulin, 2000

MONETARISM

A macroeconomic theory that stresses the importance of controlling the money supply to manage the economy.

Monetarists believe that markets work best when left alone. Competition produces the greatest market stability and is sufficient to deal even with the social ill of unemployment. If unemployment does rise, monetarists believe that labour costs fall, along with price, stimulating new demand that in term generates new jobs. The one factor that stymies the mechanism is inflation, and so monetarists seek to control inflation by controlling the money supply, since inflation is caused by 'too much money chasing too few goods'. Milton Friedman is the Nobel prize winning economist most closely associated with this theory today, although his ideas are born of a long tradition. He restated confidence in the ability of markets to generate social goods after a critique of Keynes. For example, he argued that Keynes' interventionism is too risky, even if desirable, since economic data is always partial and comes too late. The result is that the artificial manipulation of markets by governments is rarely successful and blunts the efficiency of private entrepreneurialism. This led to Friedman's argument that governments should in general not intervene in markets and that a policy of deregulation is a good one.

Monetarism gained favour during the 1970s when inflation rose dramatically in many Western countries. The Thatcher 'revolution' of the 1980s in Great Britain represents the most consistent attempt to run a macroeconomy along monetarist lines. The extent to which the market instability of those years discredits monetarism is a matter for debate, although many governments now follow a policy that borrows from pure monetarism, for example implementing monetary targets to keep inflation low and promote economic stability.

See also: **Classical economics, Keynesian economics, Neoclassical economics**

Further reading: Boaz, 1998; Magill, 1997; McAuliffe, 1997

MONOPOLY

A situation in which only one producer commands a market of many buyers.

In economic theory, a monopoly is taken to be the extreme opposite of pure competition, because in a monopoly complete control over all aspects of output resides with the producer rather than being determined by many, perfectly coordinated buyers. However, in practice effective monopolies can exist when the producer is not alone but merely dominant. Also, duopolies or oligopolies can exercise anticompetitive control, notably in the form of cartels.

The monopolist is usually taken to abuse their power in a market by optimizing their profits through the illegitimate means of controlling the quantity of goods that is produced and their price. Usually, it is in the monopolist's interests to keep prices high and volumes low. This represents an inefficient use of economic resources, and so capitalist governments devise policies to prevent monopolistic practices, in the shape of laws against anticompetitive behaviour. Having said that, monopolies are often very difficult to penetrate, since the barriers to entry for competitors are so high, and so when monopolistic advantage is proven, often the only way to open the market up to competition is by the break-up of the monopolistic company.

The only monopolies that are sanctioned by capitalist governments are so-called natural monopolies, that is businesses which run services that are deemed best produced by a single operator. The argument here is that the monopoly is efficient because it would be disadvantageous for society as a whole if the service was subjected to competitive pressure, or perhaps because the risk associated with running the service along free market lines would be too great.

See also: **Antitrust law, Barrier to market, Cartel, Competition**

Further reading: Howard, 1983; Magill, 1997; McAuliffe, 1997

MORALE

The psychological well being of the organization, particularly in relation to work attitudes.

Morale was recognized as a factor that contributes to productivity following the work of the behaviourist school in the 1930s, notably the Hawthorne experiments. These and later studies showed that the satisfaction, confidence and willingness of individuals in relation to their work was as important a motivating force as the details of their pay, benefits or environment.

Scientific measures of morale are at best ambiguous since morale, especially on a day-to-day basis, is linked to a whole range of intangible factors which may easily be missed by tests. For this reason many companies take a proactive attitude towards morale and engage in activities from team building exercises to office parties in order to keep morale up.

See also: **Behavioural theory, Hawthorne effect, Productivity**

Further reading: Anacona *et al.*, 1999; Ellis and Dick, 2000; Greenberg, 1999; Greenberg and Baron, 2000; Handy, 1999; Hosking and Anderson, 1992; Rollins and Roberts, 1998

MOTIVATION

The psychological factors which determine whether employees will satisfactorily complete the tasks allotted to them.

Motivation is a complex issue in the organization, since, as Kanfer points out, it is not something that is directly observable but is felt in terms of people's behaviour or the results of their work. It is also the case that, at least potentially, motivation varies much more than say an individual's reason or intention. Motivation is effected by a range of constantly evolving factors that originate internally and externally, both in relation to the organization and the individual. Kanfer also believes that motivation is mistakenly related directly to performance. Rather motivation affects behaviour which then in turn may or may not affect the way an individual works. This implies, for example, that programmes to increase motivation may have little or no impact upon productivity since employee behaviour, whilst it might be improved, is not changed in a way that relates to their output.

Whilst motivation will then be affected by a range of factors that vary according to temperament and culture, most studies indicate that management is a common issue. To put it another way, managers play a key role in motivating their staff, notably in the sense that there is always some kind of personal relationship between the two. Motivation can be maintained by respecting that dynamism. Good communication is key, as is exemplary, consistent and fair behaviour, an ability to delegate, and empowering individuals. In short, good management.

See also: **Management**

Further reading: Kanfer, 1992; Maslow, 1970; Parkinson, 1999; Steers *et al.*, 1996

NEGLIGENCE

The failure to take reasonable care or precautions in relation to a business function.

Negligence is usually taken to mean an ethical omission on the part of a company, that might result in anything as diverse as a personal injury, reduced service levels, or environmental damage. However, shareholders may also hold directors negligent, if for example a firm is proven to have been badly managed or to have failed its customers. In all these cases, individuals may be subject to legal sanction as a result.

E-business is providing new areas in which negligence is a legal concern. For example, the extent to which companies are responsible for the electronic communications of employees is greatly reduced if firms have taken reasonable precautions to ensure that e-mails, say, do not contain defamatory material.

See also: **Environmental audit, Social audit**

Further reading: Le Sueur and Sunkin, 1997; Owens, 1997; Wolkinson and Block, 1996

NEOCLASSICAL ECONOMICS

The school of economic theory that developed in the late nineteenth century following the work of economists such as Alfred Marshall, and which has remained dominant ever since, at least in the West.

Neoclassical economics departed from its classical roots with the systematic integration of demand-side factors into the established focus on supply-side economics. Marshall's famous analogy argued that to ask whether supply or demand is dominant in economics was as meaningless as asking whether one blade of a pair of scissors or the other is responsible for the cutting. He was able to link supply and demand by considering the effect that time has on the value of a product or service, pointing out that over longer time periods, supply-side factors such as cost of production have a greater significance, whereas in the short term demand-side factors such as utility dominate.

Perhaps the single most important result was the idea of the equilibrium price: this is the price that is arrived at when the quantity of a product demanded by customers matches the quantity of the product supplied by producers. Similarly, the price of elements in the production of goods, notably capital, land and labour – so-called factors – is determined both by supply and demand. Factor price distribution is the neoclassical theory that covers this aspect.

Other features of neoclassical economic development include a greater theoretical sophistication in relation to the operation of markets. For example, the theory has a reduced dependency upon the concept of pure competition to account for mixed markets where monopolistic and competitive features coexist. Marshall is credited with discovering the concept of market elasticity that measures the effect of price changes. Products or factors are elastic if even a small price rise results in a substantial fall in demand. Other products or factors for which marginal changes in price make little difference are termed inelastic.

In terms of understanding the way that organizations work, neoclassical economics offers greater subtlety too. For example, the concept of returns to scale accounts for the fact that size is not the only factor that has a bearing on organizational efficiency: a firm may gain economies of scale by growing, but many factors in addition to the classical law of diminishing returns means that efficiency does not increase inexorably. In the neoclassical model, organizations tend to the size that maximizes efficiency.

One common governmental policy application of neoclassical economics is in the setting of the level of minimum wages. The factor price of labour is determined in the market by the principle of equilibrium, where the marginal cost of labour to the company is matched by the cost to the household supplying it. If minimum wages are set above this value unemployment is the result, and vice-versa, although the sensitivity of this relationship varies since labour markets can be more or less elastic.

See also: **Classical economics, Keynesian economics, Monetarism, Price, Supply and demand**

Further reading: Ekelund and Herbert, 1996; Magill, 1997; Marshall, 1999; McAuliffe, 1997; Rima, 1996

NETWORK

A collection of connected but discrete objects, in business referring to organizations linked by lines of communication, and in computing referring to a system of many computers that functions as a whole.

The concept of the network is seen by some as the defining feature of the current age. Manuel Castells, for example, has described how the defining feature of individuality, commerce or even nationhood can now only be thought of in relation to their integration into the multiple and diverse networks that crisscross the planet. In relation to commerce, the rise of the network has many related effects. At the macro level, it is the network that lies at the heart of globalization and the information economy. At a micro level, the networked organization is one that is able to exploit the power of the network to become more productive, refining the division of labour notably by information sharing. The network effect is a related concept: here the growth of networks is linked to a virtuous circle of growth. The network effect is either meant in terms of how networked individuals can achieve more than they would be able to if not so connected, or it can refer to the network itself, in the sense that networks of a certain critical size tend to then experience exponential growth. The most obvious case here is the computer network.

Having said that, whilst the contemporary manifestations of networks have undoubtedly grown in their importance to businesses, commerce since the Industrial Revolution would be nothing without many, older kinds of network too, be it the railways or the legal frameworks that sustain commercial relationships. So, dramatic accounts of the departure that the modern network represents should probably be moderated to some extent.

In terms of organizational behaviour, network analysis is an important analytical tool. It applies critical path analysis to organizations. Critical path analysis looks at organizations according to their processes, listing the discrete activities within a process along with their attributes such as time or resource requirements. Network analysis looks at organizations as systems of interacting players with various attributes, such as the position they hold in the organization or the kind of relationship that links them. In this way the wide variety of issues that affect the successful functioning of the network can be analysed, from the existence of groups in the network to the role that status and structure plays. Network analysis can be particularly useful when an organization is undergoing change that is likely to impact parts of the organization differently.

The concept of the network is present in many different business disciplines. For example, it is central to relationship marketing, where the idea is to exploit the realization that alongside purely commercial factors in decision making, buyers and sellers relate through informal networks of contacts. The same can be said of organizations themselves: some researchers prefer to describe markets according to the family resemblances that group different businesses, rather than solely in relation to the products or services they sell. In this way of seeing things, cultural similarity, for example, is a critical issue when it comes to collaboration, rather than the mere fact that one organization has something another requires. The ability of organizations to work together as a unified, networked whole is certainly vital when it is deployed as a strategy for achieving global cover, as is commonly the case in service industries that would otherwise be unable to provide the kind of service that their multinational, perhaps similarly networked, clients demand.

See also: **Collaboration, E-business, Information and communications technology, Joint venture, Killer application, Organization, Relationship marketing, Value**

Further reading: Birkinshaw and Hagström, 2000; Castells, 1998; Galegher *et al.*, 1990; Gemünden *et al.*, 1997; Grandori, 1999; Juliff *et al.*, 1999; McKenna, 1991; Nohria and Eccles, 1992

NON-PROFIT ORGANIZATIONS

Companies that deliver a product or service without the requirement of generating profits in return. Also called not-for-profit organizations.

The non-profit sector is expanding rapidly in many parts of the West at the same time as it is changing fast too, notably in terms of becoming more subject to certain commercial disciplines. However, non-profit organizations are frequently only given marginal treatment in business studies, partly because they are not subject to the full demands of conventional market economics and so defy easy classification. However, in many respects they do operate and look like profit-making organizations, which provides a starting point for understanding them and their differences.

The efficiency and effectiveness of non-profit organizations has been a subject of scrutiny in recent years. The concern is that by not being exposed to the full rigours of competition, non-profit organizations will inevitably become bureaucratic or slack. However, many non-profit organizations recognize both the implicit dangers of operating in non-competitive environments and the damage which can be done to their brand if they are perceived badly in this respect. They therefore seek to impose competitive-like disciplines on themselves. For example, a charity may come to regard its donors as shareholders and the people it helps as clients. Donors too are encouraged to expect a good return on their money, the difference being that the benefit comes not to them but to those who receive the charity's services. To put the business-like emphasis a different way, non-profit organizations are encouraged by professional managers to put as much effort into optimizing the outputs gained from inputs, as into merely providing services. Thinking in this way can lead to substantial organizational change, typically moving away from centralized and bureaucratic structures to those that are proven in the commercial environment, such as process- or project-orientated ways of operating.

This tripartite relationship, between donor, organization and receiver, is frequently referred to as the gift relationship, which points to perhaps the most obvious difference between a non-profit and profit-making organization, that is the relationship with staff. In a non-profit organization, individuals are of course employed to perform certain functions. However, most companies of this type depend to a high degree on volunteers. Using commercial language, volunteers can be thought of as suppliers, though with the critical difference that they are not bound by the usual contractual terms of the profit-making case. Therein lies another source of problems for non-profit organizations, an issue that can compound when the professional manager tries to impose commercial rigour: part of the pleasure that volunteers often receive from working for a charity is that very lack of managerial discipline which they are used to in their employment. In general, then, internal control is a major issue for non-profit organizations.

On the other hand, paid staff may be expected to approach their work vocationally, that is looking for returns in addition to financial remuneration. Issues such as goodwill and self-help are therefore not only desirable, as in conventional firms because they increase productivity, but necessary in non-profit organizations since without them the whole enterprise would collapse.

Managing the gift relationship is tending to become more complex for other reasons too. For example, funding bodies that give money to the voluntary sector, notably government agencies, are expecting greater commercial rigour. In many European countries and America, money is increasingly granted for particular purposes only, and then has to be seen to be properly utilized. Alternatively, the kind of services that non-profit organizations provide must now be justified on more grounds than altruism alone. The 1990s also saw an extension of contractual relationships between non-profit organizations and funding bodies. This again adds another dimension to the task of non-profit organizational management.

Further reading: Billis and Harris, 1996; Butler and Wilson, 1989; Gross *et al.*, 2000; Handy, 1988; Mauss, 1954

OCCUPATIONAL PSYCHOLOGY

The branch of psychology that researches the way people react in the workplace.

Occupational psychology, taken here to cover all aspects of psychological research into the workplace including industrial and organizational psychology, originates with the genesis of psychoanalysis itself. For example, Freud, in *Civilization and Its Discontents*, discusses the psychoanalytic impact of the modern workplace upon individuals, notably in terms of the psychological price that must be paid for the voluntaristic, regulated behaviour that capitalism demands. Books such as Scott's *Psychology of Advertising* and Munsterberg's *The Psychology of Industrial Efficiency* were published as early as 1908 and 1913 respectively.

However, it was not until the advent of what is sometimes called second generation psychology that the subject formed a strand that departed from its psychoanalytical roots and developed a scientific element that could be practically utilized by businesses. Advances accelerated during the war years as psychologists' work in areas such as intelligence testing were mobilized for the war effort. This established occupational psychology as a branch of social psychology firmly rooted in the scientific method that applies statistical tools to illuminate the broad range of issues that the subject embraces today, including various forms of testing such as intelligence, performance and personality, as well as commercial concerns such as motivation, process design, and the various sorts of decision making.

One area growing today is that of clinical occupational psychology. In conjunction with cognitive approaches to organizational behaviour and the sophistication of human resource management, this division of the subject seeks to promote the health and well being of the individual in the workplace for the benefit of the organization, as well as deal with what are increasingly recognized as the significant effects of mental illness. Common issues that may be addressed in groups include the psychological impact of change or problems with management. And issues that may be addressed on an individual basis include domestic problems or drug abuse.

Partly as a result of this development, various attempts have been made to regulate the exercise of clinical occupational psychology.

Privacy and confidentiality are the key concerns. One example of the codes of conduct that are being drawn up comes from the work of the New York State Psychological Association's Occupational Clinical Psychology Committee. This kind of body is frequently continuing the earlier work that was begun by unions and labour relations organizations. Occupational psychology also has an important part to play in making organizations less discriminatory, pointing out, for example, where prejudice occurs and suggesting ways of dealing with it.

See also: **Aptitude test, Behavioural theory, Morale, Motivation**

Further reading: Cooper and Robertson, 1990; Dunnette, 1990; Parkinson, 1999; Schmidt, 1994; Tiemann, 1996

OFFICE MANAGEMENT

The planning, administration and resourcing of the workplace.

Many employees will testify to the importance of the workplace and the disruption that changes to it can cause. It is therefore perhaps a failure of many management courses that the subject barely appears on the curriculum. The irony is compounded by the fact that new offices are a common source of corporate pride, though whether the architects pay as much attention to interior details as they do to external impact might be questioned again.

Office management concerns everything from location, through layout, to look and feel. For employees, location matters for reasons varying from how far it is to travel to work to where is the best place to buy lunch – non-trivial matters in many instances when it comes to recruitment.

The layout of an office conveys much as to the hierarchical nature of the organization. It also has an impact upon cost: in the business centres of major cities the price of floor space is so high that significant savings can be generated simply by cutting the number of filing cabinets in use. Look and feel is no less critical, especially when it is wrong. A more rigorous approach that takes this seriously is commonly found in Japan's '5 Ss' system. The five Ss refer, in Japanese, to the factors that make for the best workplace: organization, notably in terms of constantly reviewing the way the office is organized; neatness, meaning not so much that the place is tidy as that things in the office are in the right place; cleaning, which can sometimes appear obsessive to Western eyes but is intended to promote quality; standardization, so that wherever possible the office makes intuitive sense to those who use it; and discipline, an almost virtuous approach that aims to instill good habits and best practices.

Office management also concerns such issues as dress. It has long been received wisdom that an efficient office requires a professional style of dress, though taking a lead from the IT sector, in which informality is regarded as indicative of innovation, many service industries now encourage employees to 'dress down' on at least some days of the week. A related culture of ease is seen in open-plan offices.

Deciding when to move offices can be a major management decision for growing businesses, small and large. For multinational companies, the move is often connected to M&As and forms an important if intangible element in the success of the evolution, since it affects the workforce so profoundly. In small organizations, careful planning is required to minimize the disruption a move can cause, logistically and financially.

In extreme cases an office move might be construed as constructive dismissal if the new location makes it effectively impossible for individuals to continue working for the company. This has been a problem in some outsourcing contracts when the IT department, for example, is moved to a new location for the convenience of the computer services firm but to the great inconvenience of internal IT staff.

See also: **Ergonomics, Small office-home office**

Further reading: Clements-Croome, 2000; Forsyth, 1999; Horgen *et al.*, 1999; James and Arroba, 1999; Lacey, 2000; Takashi, 1991

OPEN AND CLOSED SYSTEMS

Organized units that operate by interacting with their environments, if they are open systems, or operating in isolation, if they are closed systems.

The concept of open and closed systems is applied to the workings of organizations. Generally speaking, traditional approaches to the organization viewed it as a closed system. This meant it operated in a way synonymous, say, to a watch: once the system had been assembled with the appropriate materials and technology it would continue to run of its own accord. However, especially following the work of theorists such as Katz, Kahn and

Adams, the open system model came to be seen as more realistic. Here the organization might be thought of as a television, since its outputs depend upon its inputs, notably the right programming, a receivable signal and an electricity supply. The general point is that organizational outputs need to be responsive to external factors from customers or suppliers for the business to be successful. An open systems approach allows for a more dynamic model of the organization in terms of its interaction with its environment.

Although open systems have gained the upper hand in organizational theory, management styles can still be seen to be more closely associated with closed systems. This explains why centralized, bureaucratic or mechanistic managers are often resistant to change. The threat stems from the fact that they are being asked to expose themselves to external factors that are beyond their control.

See also: **Feedback, Organization**

Further reading: Bertalanffy, 1975; Katz *et al.*, 1980

OPERATIONS MANAGEMENT AND STRATEGY

The management of production processes. Operations strategy ensures that operational results coincide with company objectives.

Slack defines operations management as 'the set of tasks which manages the arrangement of resources in an organization which is devoted to the production of goods and services'. The subject, he believes, has been radically transformed over the last twenty or more years, because in that time it has been freed from its relatively constrained scientific roots that concentrated on techniques for problem solving in manufacturing. Operations management has widened its scope because organizations today operate within networks of supply and demand that extend beyond conventional boundaries. Operations has come to be seen as a strategic issue, and operations strategy is no longer an oxymoron. The point here is that organizations have spent a long time focusing on issues such as their effectiveness which, coinciding with developments such as outsourcing, has led to an examination and tightening of operational concerns such as resource management and logistics. Operations has also had to take account of the production of services as opposed to the manufacture of products, since the service economy not only continues to grow, but through modern processes and innovations is increasingly the source of profits and growth.

Slack also points out that many of the skills deployed in operations management have been more closely studied in recent years, and so defined as subject areas in their own right. Just-in-time and total quality management are two obvious cases. This is related to a change of attitude in management that sees most if not all commercial disciplines containing an operational element. The point is that all decisions made must then be made manifest in order to benefit the company, and this requires adherence to operational standards of quality, cost, reliability and so on. It is for this reason that certain management techniques, such as business process re-engineering, regard all business functions as operational, from manufacturing to marketing.

The strategic dimension can be seen in the changing role of the chief operating officer or COO. The COO's job is not just about responding to market changes but involves the proactive attitude usually associated with such functions as marketing and development. The COO also has a part to play in such strategic moves as M&As, since operational flexibility is recognized as key to making these projects successful.

With the widening scope of operations management there is also a view developing that it can no longer be usefully considered a subject in its own right, but rather must devolve into a number of discrete areas such as supply-chain management or resource-based management. This move chimes with the strategic emphasis, since it demands a closer examination of constituent parts than is provided by the traditional operations management techniques of high-level price/cost analysis, quality control and factors such as flexibility.

See also: **BPR, Facilities management, Fordism, Inventory, Logistics, Product, Resources, Supply and demand, Taylorism, Total capacity management, Total quality management**

Further reading: Aronson and Zionts, 1998; Chase *et al.*, 1998; Dilworth, 2000; Meredith and Shafer, 1999; Russell and Taylor, 1998; Schniederjans, 1998; Slack, 1997; Stevenson, 1999; Summers, 1998

OPPORTUNITY COST

The profit that is lost because an investment prospect is missed.

The idea of accounting for a profit that was never made may seem a strange one. And indeed, opportunity cost is not an entry that will be seen in an accountant's books. But the concept is important economically, particularly in relation to decision making. Businesses are constantly having to make choices about which investments to make or which market opportunities to pursue. Assessing which are the right decisions requires a measure not only of the opportunity in a positive sense but also in the sense of the cost to the company if it does not invest in that way. For example, not capitalizing upon an opportunity may leave a market open to a competitor that could threaten future business. Alternatively, many companies today try to work with a portfolio of investment and development opportunities that can be discarded or pursued with a high degree of flexibility, as a way of coping with rapidly changing markets. Opportunity cost is a valuable tool in this context.

Having said that, as with all future costs, opportunity costs are intrinsically hard to calculate accurately.

See also: **Accounting, Decision making, Finance, Portfolio management**

ORGANIC ORGANIZATION

A company that is structured to mimic certain aspects of social or biological systems.

Organic systems are very good at responding to their environment, notably its uncertainties, and so this organizational theory tries to apply the characteristics of organic systems to companies. For example, biological systems consist of relatively autonomous parts in the sense that each organ in the body fulfils its role independently, though contributing to the whole. This allows the system to specialize in certain tasks and be flexible in response to external change. Decentralization is the corresponding feature in the organization, encouraging the division of labour and the devolution of responsibility, for example. Alternatively, social groups that function well are characterized by such features as appropriate levels of personal interactivity and the capacity for individuals to switch roles as needs change. The organic organization in this respect is therefore one that encourages employees to mix widely with colleagues, as well as empowering them to show initiative and make decisions.

There is an increasingly important technological role in the organic organization, again trying to mimic a characteristic of the biological system, this time feedback. Plants, for example, respond dynamically to changing factors in the environment, such as weather changes, and the idea is that organizations should also embody systems that not only allow them to be aware of external change but respond dynamically too.

See also: **Organization, Rationalization**

Further reading: Abe *et al.*, 1998; Hannan and Freeman, 1989; Scott, 1992

ORGANIZATION

The system or collective that works for the ends of the business. The practical management of organizations and academic research into the way they function is a major subject in business studies. It embraces a wide variety of concerns, including organizational behaviour, organizational culture, individual behaviour, motivation and performance in the organization, leadership, communication, decision making, and design. In this book the subject is therefore covered under a number of headings. Here we will attempt to highlight some important current developments in the study of organizations.

An obvious one to start with is the global context within which many organizations operate. The point is that as organizations are social entities set within societies, an international perspective complicates the matter. For example, the stakeholder model of organizations sees them as composed of different interest groups, beginning with employees and shareholders and extending to customers and the media. A multinational business therefore has to be able to handle an enormous variety of stakeholder expectations: it is not unusual for even quite modest companies to have to deal with elements as distinct as Indian employee contracts, Far Eastern media peculiarities, and Western market pressures.

A related issue is the increasingly diverse nature of the workforce itself. As a result, modern organizations inevitably consist of individuals who differ widely according to gender, race, religion, sexual orientation and physicality, all of which may have a bearing upon organizations' behaviour. Issues that arise include having to develop language skills within the organization, or learning to deal with cultural differences that, say, need valuing in different ways or that look for different rewards in a career.

Proactive companies learn to treat their inherent diversity as a strategic asset. The logic is that a diverse organization is better able to serve a diverse market. Alternatively, organizations are able to turn socialization programmes into projects for deepening overall organizational cohesion.

The impact of the internet and e-business on organizations is an emerging area. There are numerous ways that it might affect the organization, but the matter can be approached by considering the core principles that derive from the spread of online networks. For example, consider the so-called 'death of distance'. This is a powerful idea for organizations, since it potentially removes one of the limiting factors with which they have traditionally had to grapple. It suggests that organizations do not have to aggregate individuals in the way they had to previously simply to function – employees can work remotely.

Another principle of the internet is 'instant communication'. This possibility might overcome some of the traditional barriers to communication, such as selective listening that stems from information that is impersonal.

However, the internet also introduces new organizational problems, such as 'communication overload': many e-mail systems now incorporate filtering or sorting facilities as a first step to coping with the deluge. 'Open access' is another internet principle that carries positive and negative possibilities for the organization. On the one hand it might work to transcend organizational hierarchies when, for example, the CEO sends regular messages to staff or when the individual is able to access their HR records. Negatively, many organizations are having to learn to cope with various new kinds of security threat.

See also: **Centralization, Communication, Company, Corporation, Culture, Decision making, Enterprise, Familism, Glass ceiling, Holding company, Home working, Human resources management, Intranet, Learning organization, Mission statement, Morale, Motivation, Office management, Stakeholder, Vertical integration, Virtual corporation**

Further reading: Ackoff, 1999b; Anacona *et al.*, 1999; Cameron and Whetten, 1983; Ellis and Dick, 2000; Francesco and Gold, 1998; Greenberg, 1999; Ivancevich and Matteson, 1999; Jablin *et al.*, 2001; Jackson, 1999; Katz *et al.*, 1980; McMahan and Woodman, 1992; Nohria and Eccles, 1992; Ostroff, 1999; Pfeffer, 1981; Rosenfeld and Wilson, 1999

OUTSOURCING

Contracting work out of the organization instead of having it completed within.

Outsourcing is a method whereby companies control costs. For example, consider IT. Organizations have long had a problem accounting for their investment here since, though clearly strategic, IT is an unallocated cost that does not have a direct impact upon revenue generation. Outsourcing IT therefore provides a way of running IT as a fixed cost.

Other benefits accrue. Again sticking with IT, implementing and managing computer systems requires specialist knowledge, not only of networks in general but of products in particular. An outsourcing relationship provides the firm with access to the expertise that it requires without having the cost of developing those skills in-house. Another dimension is added when it comes to economies of scale. For many, even quite large organizations, their reliance on computers means that they have to carry substantial amounts of redundancy in case of system failure. Typically an organization will have to run at least one mirror image of its network that can be switched over in an instant to avoid disruption to business. However, an outsourcing partner is able to provide this redundancy for many clients at the same time, on the basis that the chances of simultaneous failure are vanishingly small.

The latest wave in outsourcing carries these benefits a stage further. As computers have automated more and more business functions, including treasury, HR, supply chain, fulfilment and even customer management, firms realize that these are not core competencies for themselves and so can be outsourced to a very large extent. This possibility coincides with the emergence of effectively infinite connectivity that modern networks provide so that the actual location of a computer is irrelevant. Application Service Providers (ASPs) are aggregates of IT suppliers that deliver a package of IT functions to the client by exploiting precisely this fact. The logical endpoint of this trend is the virtual organization, one that actually consists of a network of partnered companies operating under the brand of one of them.

Whilst IT typically represents the most complex outsourcing arrangements, many other business functions can be outsourced too. For example, staff are increasingly outsourced, meaning that they are not on the permanent payroll of the organization. Staff may be individually leased from an agency or only employed temporarily. Alternatively, they may work as independent contractors. In this latter case, a specialist company will often be brought in to carry out a function, such as maintenance or security. The extent of this practice is indicated by one statistic from the US: the Bureau of Labor Statistics showed that in 1997 nearly 10 per cent of the workforce was outsourced. Outsourcing staff in this way brings benefits that are similar to those associated with outsourced IT. It helps control costs, helps the company work more efficiently and effectively, and gives the company flexible access to skills. In this case it also reduces the HR burden it would otherwise have to carry.

Outsourcing does of course present its own set of problems alongside the advantages. One of the most significant is an inevitable loss of control. Outsourcing tends to distance a business function from corporate goals and aims. Whilst in many cases this may have no impact upon performance, there is an increasing concern in research on the matter that companies can outsource too far and lose vital control on mission-critical functions, that is those upon which commercial success directly depends. A related concern is that outsourcing increases company dependency. If something happens to the outsourcing partner it could carry operational ramifications and perhaps be damaging to reputation. Another issue is that outsourcing is no quick fix, since partners can take time to acclimatize to the internal workings of their client company. A further issue concerns what happens when things go wrong. Service level agreements (SLAs) should govern the quality of the work, but as outsourcing relates more closely to mission-critical functions, recourse after a failure may prove poor compensation indeed. And as IT contracts have shown, an SLA is no guarantee itself, once the lawyers have been at it.

See also: **Core competency, Virtual corporation**

Further reading: Burnett, 1998; Cook, 1999; Domberger, 1998; Gay and Essinger, 2000; Lonsdale and Cox, 1998

OVERCAPITALIZE

To overestimate the value of an asset or to invest too highly in one area.

Overcapitalizing is essentially a waste that can lead to profit losses and in extreme cases perhaps even the collapse of the business. It is the job of accountants to ensure that capital assets are used effectively.

However, the business of monitoring capitalization is increasingly seen as strategic as well as remedial. The connection here is with modern asset management techniques. On the one hand advanced computer systems such as enterprise resource management (ERP) applications are able to tell managers much more about how a business in its multiple activities is capitalized, as well as predict likely future demands. In conjunction with the ability to move capital quickly, just-in-time-type concepts can be applied to capitalization.

See also: **Asset**

PARADOX MANAGEMENT

An attitude in management which acknowledges that apparently conflicting ideas will often be present at the same time in a successful company.

Paradox management stems from resignation in the face of the world's irreducible complexity. These managers know that they must be close to staff and yet maintain a distance, be able to lead and yet stay in the background, be visionary but keep their feet on the ground, or be innovative and yet provide commercial surety – as Lego managers put it on the walls of their offices. Alternatively, companies have to deal with the paradoxes of thinking global and acting locally, having centralized structures which devolve power, having the fresh approach of the new and the maturity of the experienced, or encouraging autonomous responsibility amongst staff who must also work together as a team. The point is that both attitudes or stances must exist within the organization for it to be truly effective, if not always at exactly the same time and place.

See also: **Management**

Further reading: Evans and Olson, 2000

PARETO EFFECT

The apparently irreducible 80–20 rule. For example, that 80 per cent of a company's profits stem from only 20 per cent of its products.

The 'law' actually derives from the empirical observations of the nineteenth-century economist Vilfredo Pareto. He complicated matters further, first of all by realizing that in many cases the question 'which 20 per cent?' was very difficult to answer; but also by concluding that markets tend to revert to the 80–20 rule even when efforts are made to redress the situation. One macroeconomic result is a wariness of redistributive policies in government. To put it another way, the only way of increasing the wealth of the poorest members of a society is to increase GDP overall.

Further reading: Kock, 1998

PARTICIPATION

A management style that seeks to involve everyone in organizational processes.

A participatory approach to management is closely related to other styles that seek the contribution of all concerned, such as those that are decentralized or democratic. However, it can be differentiated in the sense that participatory approaches not only seek to empower individuals in the decisions they can make or the responsibilities they hold, but that they also try to widen the employee's sense of belonging to the organization. Participation will therefore not only include indicative planning that incorporates a consultative process to reach broad agreements before acting, but will also try to involve the individual in extracurricular activities that build a stronger sense of the mutual relationship that exists between manager and employee.

See also: **Management**

Further reading: Parsons, 1997

PATERNALISM

The policy or practice of managing in a father-like way in relation to associates or subordinates.

Paternal attitudes combine a strong sense of authority with a moral sense of responsibility. Perhaps the greatest period of paternal management style came in the Victorian period soon after the Industrial Revolution, when aristocratic managers inherited the old attitudes of class in relation to their employees that could be both altruistic and demanding. However, this association with class has led paternal attitudes to be seen as merely patronizing. Further, the modern mind strongly associates paternalism with 'old boy networks' that are inherently unfair, hierarchical or discriminatory. So, apart from the exceptional case of firms with a strong family ethos, paternalism has fallen out of fashion and would usually be used in a derogatory sense.

See also: **Familism, Management**

PEOPLE SKILLS

The capacity individuals possess of relating to others.

The concept of people skills is often used passively, in the sense that some people are taken to possess people skills whereas others do not, and whilst this latter group can compensate to a certain degree, they are unlikely ever to achieve the ease of one-to-one communication possessed by the former. Managers with good people skills are therefore highly valued.

However, because people skills are recognized as an important constituent in the overall communicative effort of a successful, modern organization, they are taught on management courses and can be learned to a high degree. These courses develop the individual's ability to listen and to be sensitive to others, often borrowing from counselling techniques. Managers are taught that good people skills depend upon gaining respect which comes with good planning, decisiveness, and related skills such as analytical and motivational ability. Finally, there is a need for personal integrity, without which interpersonal trust will always be limited.

See also: **Management, Occupational psychology**

Further reading: Maister, 1997; Parkinson, 1999

PERFORMANCE

A word that has a number of meanings in business, though usually meant in relation to an individual's achievement. However, performance is also a measure of a piece of machinery or a process's productive capacity. And in economics, performance is the measure of return on an investment.

Whilst clearly always being an organizational issue, performance has come to the fore in recent years with the rise of performance management techniques. Armstrong and Baron define performance management as 'a strategic and integrated approach to delivering sustained success into organizations by improving the performance of the people who work in them and by developing the capabilities of teams and individual contributors'.

This definition seeks to differentiate performance management from older ideas on a number of fronts: it is strategic in that it has an eye to longer-term goals and so, for example, invests in individuals; it is integrated in that the needs of individuals and different parts of the business are aligned whenever possible; it is concerned with improvement, as well as capability, since the question is how and not only what is achieved; and it is concerned with development, since performance management is a continuous process rather than an imposed rigid structure, that seeks a contributory attitude from both individuals and the organization.

Whilst performance management can be differentiated in such ways, it uses many familiar management techniques, if seeking to orientate them in a different way. For example, individual and collective targets are central, though performance management asks questions about effectiveness as well as efficiency, development as well as reward (such as performance-related pay). Alternatively, performance management places a great stress on measurement, though in conjunction with analysis too, since it is only with both aspects that improvements can be made.

See also: **Activity-based costing, Balanced scorecard, Benchmarking, Effectiveness, Efficiency, Management, Motivation, Training**

Further reading: Armstrong and Baron, 1998; Donaldson, 1999; Dutta and Manzoni, 1999; Hale and Whitlam, 2000; Harrington *et al.*, 2000; Hennell and Warner, 1998; Rollins and Roberts, 1998

PLANNED OBSOLESCENCE

The design of a product so that it will become outmoded after a period of time.

Planned obsolescence is used by businesses to keep markets active. It can be thought of as having active and passive forms, and the IT industry provides good examples of both cases.

Actively, companies may plan for a technology to become obsolete in order that consumers can be migrated from one kind of product to another. For example, at the time of writing WAP mobile phones are being heavily promoted although the industry acknowledges that it represents a transitional technology, a step before wireless broadband becomes available. However, WAP companies invest in devices that will become obsolete in order to keep the market moving forward before the technology in which they truly expect to make profits arrives.

Passively, other companies, notably manufacturers of computers, expect products to become obsolete, since the technology upon which it is based will both fall in price and increase in power. The release of new PCs to the market, for example, is therefore staged to match the rate at which consumers are either likely to replace obsolete products or enter the market for the first time.

See also: **Marketing, Product**

Further reading: Channon, 1997; Costin, 1998

PORTER'S FIVE FORCES

A model developed by Michael Porter to describe the forces of competition.

Porter's five forces attack the problem of competition by finding a strategic position that a company can adopt when approaching a new market according to how his five forces act upon it.

The first competitive force is the threat of entry. This determines the ease or difficulty that a company first faces in the new market. It depends upon a number of factors including economies of scale, product differentiation, capital requirements, switching costs and access to distribution channels.

The second competitive force is pressure from substitute products, that is the ease with which one product renders another redundant by providing the same utility more effectively or efficiently. A product that increases effectiveness and efficiency is at great competitive advantage.

The third force is the bargaining power of buyers. Buyers have more or less power in a market according to factors such as the volumes in which they deal, the availability of the product they want to buy, the margins to which they work, and the control they have over manufacture of the product. If buyers are more powerful, competitive pressures increase for producers.

The fourth force is the bargaining power of suppliers. Similarly to buyers, suppliers can exert competitive pressure if they control the market for a resource, hold the balance of power in the supply and demand relationship, or could themselves produce the products the buyer does.

The fifth force resides in the rivalry among existing competitors. Competition is more intense if certain conditions prevail, such as numerous competing firms, slow growth, high logistical costs, seasonal or fluctuating sales cycles, high exit barriers, and if competitors are not easily differentiated.

See also: **Competition**

Further reading: Porter, 1998a, 1998b

PORTFOLIO MANAGEMENT

The administration of a diverse number of assets. Financially, portfolio management means investing in a number of different assets to offset the risk of any one. Managerially, portfolio management means attending to core competencies and building the business around this portfolio of skills.

In both cases portfolio managers assess what is available for investment and then decide how capital should be distributed across these possibilities. Complexity arises because potential investments can only rarely be compared directly. Portfolio management therefore requires mathematical tools for making such comparisons. The economist Harry Markowitz devised such a methodology based upon calculating the utility of the investment: this is proportional to the expected return and inversely proportional to the risk. The utility of any given portfolio is then the mean of all returns and the variance of all risks.

See also: **Core competency, Finance**

Further reading: Elton and Gruber, 1995; Markowitz, 1959

POSITIONING

The identification of a product with a certain place in the market.

Positioning is a marketing technique for reaching a desired audience of consumers or for enabling a product to compete in a crowded market. It aims to give the product a unique feature, or unique selling proposition (USP) by which it can be distinguished and with which it can dominate the associated place in the market. For example, toothpastes are variously marketed according to their different properties, powers, price and brand. In this way, a number of products, whose utility is virtually identical, can coexist to the benefit of all concerned: in this case, because a consumer wants say a cheap toothpaste that tastes of mint, and because the manufacturer wants to maximize their sales.

See also: **Brand extension, Category management, Marketing, Segmentation**

Further reading: Hooley, 1998

PREFERRED SUPPLIER

A provider of certain services or materials that a company has determined should be used in procurement.

The practice of identifying preferred suppliers stems from large manufacturing companies. The problem is that although these firms seek to source materials from the best supplier, the suppliers they deal with, and those dealing with them, number into the thousands. It is therefore hard to ensure that economies of scale are optimized, that quality standards are adhered to, and so on. Further, such procurement activity generates enormous amounts of bureaucracy. Companies therefore identify preferred suppliers for different products so that they can negotiate deals with them and so that managers can be encouraged, though typically not enforced, to use them.

The concept has become widely applicable in many business sectors, particularly with the implementation of electronic procurement systems. A key benefit of these applications is the rationalization of procurement practices, in part because they manage the use of preferred suppliers.

See also: **Buyer, Inventory, Network, Operations management and strategy, Supply and demand**

PRICE

The means by which prices are derived and the role they play in markets vary according to different economic theories. However, neoclassical economics provides the basic concept of the equilibrium price: this is the price that is arrived at when the quantity of a product demanded by customers matches the quantity of the product supplied by producers. In other words prices represent the point at which demand meets supply. Most economists believe that competitive markets alone arrive at the best prices, though certain interventions might be necessary to ensure equilibrium is reached. For example, monetarists believe that the one factor that stymies the mechanism is inflation, and so they seek to control inflation by controlling the money supply.

Businesses devise pricing mechanisms in order to determine what the market rate for a product should be, although amounts are commonly set by financial managers who have more of an eye to manufacturing costs than market values. Price is also one of the so-called four Ps of marketing.

Pricing strategy is a slightly different activity. It uses pricing to achieve business goals. For example, a new product may initially be priced more highly, since this is seen to represent the novelty value of the product to early adopters. As early majority consumers become interested the price may be reduced to encourage larger sales. As a product ages price may be reduced again, not only to encourage new purchasers but also since the development costs of the product may have long been recovered and the product has to a large degree become a commodity.

Occasionally companies find themselves in the bizarre position of having to increase prices in order to stimulate sales, since the value of the product is not perceived by the consumer to be accurately reflected in its price. Alternatively, firms may engage in short-term competitive or predatory pricing strategies. Competitive pricing may be involved in the use of loss leaders; predatory pricing to achieve market penetration.

Businesses may also artificially alter price for other reasons. For example, price discrimination may be introduced when the company can sell the same product in markets at different prices. Price discrimination has been a major issue in the formation of the European common market, for example, where increased price transparency has exposed the practice and firms have been forced to reduce prices by governmental and consumer pressure. Price discrimination is also commonly deployed when the same product is sold to different groups of buyers. Some justification for this may be given, such as services added or quantities sold. However, economists tend to discourage this too, since it reduces the operation of market competition.

An invasive form of price determination is the setting of price ceilings. This occurs when governments set the maximum legal price for a product below that which would be arrived at by the competitive matching of supply and demand. It is an instrument that can be used when the economy is in some kind of crisis, notably during periods of high inflation or during wartime, as a policy to reintegrate a poor underclass back into the economy, or when the competitive operations of supply and demand are interrupted for some reason, say by monopolistic practices. The problem that follows from the fixing of price ceilings is how to return to normal market conditions. They can also create shortages or encourage a black market.

See also: **Economics, Loss leader, Marketing, Product, Supply and demand, Value**

Further reading: Nagle and Holden, 1995; Scherer, 1990; Shepherd, 1996

PROCESSES

The tasks that must be carried out to complete a business transaction.

Organizational activity can be thought of in two dimensions: vertically, since certain departments perform certain functions; and horizontally, since the goals of the organization are achieved by these vertical functions being integrated together by processes. The design, management, and development of processes are therefore essential for successful commerce, and it is for this reason that processes are never far from the focus of a business's efforts.

For example, business process re-engineering is 'the radical redesign of business processes to achieve dramatic improvements in performance'. Alternatively, businesses attend to processes in order to add value to their products. At each stage something may be altered, added to or omitted in order to increase the marginal value of the product or reduce its marginal cost. The sum total of processes is therefore called the value chain.

See also: **BPR, Management, Organization, Quality, Total quality management, Value**

Further reading: Anacona *et al.*, 1999; Harrington, 1991; Lee *et al.*, 1998

PRODUCT

The end result of the manufacturing process for purchase by the customer. A product only sometimes refers to a physical good as opposed to a service.

Many of the company's activities will be oriented towards the products it produces, although current management theories recommend keeping as much of an eye on processes and customers. The different viewpoints meet in product development.

Product development is not so much to do with entirely new products, that incur very high costs, as to do with the evolution of old products for changing market tastes. For example, strawberry jam has probably not changed that much in the course of retail history, but the way it is packaged, marketed, priced and sold has. So, the processes by which jam reaches its market have changed dramatically: from corner shop to high street supermarket, for example, just to consider the last stage of the value chain. Customer needs have altered substantially too: jam might now be marketed as a health food with high fruit content, for example, whereas just a few years previously it was sold as a valuable source of energy because of its high sugar content.

The ability of companies to evolve products in this way is in large part responsible for the surprising longevity of a majority of products.

See also: **Brand extension, Category management, Marketing, R&D, Time to market, Value**

Further reading: Klostermann and Tukker, 1998; Morse, 1998; Trott, 1998

PRODUCTIVITY

The ratio of output to input.

Economists and managers monitor the productivity of resources or assets according to type. So, labour productivity is a measure of what employees achieve, land productivity is a measure of how material resources can be exploited, and capital productivity is a measure of the return on investments. Thus improving productivity is a complicated process. However, step improvements can be achieved by attending to a variety of areas that compromise productivity. For example, the company may not be very efficient or effective in certain respects.

Occasionally, productivity increases dramatically. This, it is argued, is at the heart of the information revolution, since the automation that comes with computers and the network effects that they introduce when online introduces a dramatic, though one-off, opportunity for companies to increase their productivity. Similarly, the Industrial Revolution impacted on productivity by increasing the division of labour through such techniques as factory-based manufacturing.

Macroeconomic limitations on productivity have become a subject of discussion with the growth of international markets. The level of bureaucracy that governments impose upon organizations is exposed on the global stage, as is the effect of different cultural biases. In the West at least, there is pressure to decrease the former and analyse the latter to see how laws can be changed to increase the productivity of national economies.

See also: **Automation, Economics, Effectiveness, Efficiency, Performance, Technology**

PROFIT

The revenue that remains after all costs over a given timeframe have been deducted.

As Bishop *et al.* point out, this definition of profit fits well with the accounting equation where 'the opening capital plus profit less drawings equals the closing capital'. The profit and loss account (or P&L) aims to represent the company's activities over the course of the accounting period, as opposed to the balance sheet that merely provides a snapshot at the end of the accounting period.

Profits can be accounted for in a potentially endless variety of ways. Thus national regulations provide standards that are legally enforceable so that a certain degree of transparency is maintained with regard to profit reporting. For example, the UK's Companies Act gives four profit and loss account formats. Profit is based upon revenue minus costs, although since sales, distribution and administrative costs are not precisely defined there is already some scope for interpretation. The law only insists that a company's profit or loss on 'ordinary activities before taxation' must be shown and that definitions must be consistently applied from year to year. The same principle requires comparisons to be made on the profit and loss account with previous years.

Profit and loss accounting therefore leads to a number of different kinds of profit: gross profit is the total revenue minus costs associated with sales alone; operating profit or accounting profit is the profit derived including the costs of normal business operations, that is deducting costs such as depreciation, hire of plant and directors' remuneration; net profit or profit for the financial year is the final figure that includes all other costs such as capital costs, taxation and extraordinary charges. The only cost that remains at this point is the payment of dividends. Net profit is the figure that is usually reported as profit. Other kinds of profit include paper profit, that is an expected profit not yet realized, and a windfall, that is an extraordinary profit not derived from sales.

Operating profit is important since this is the amount that is taxable. It is adjusted according to certain allowances such as depreciation, personal expenses, non-taxable income (such as government grants), and capital allowances (such as the purchase of certain fixed assets).

Profit forecasts are an increasingly common device for managing the company's relationship with financial markets. Firms try to calculate a figure that is both realistic in terms of what they expect, but one that also puts a positive spin upon their prospects to encourage share value. Profit warnings are the result of too optimistic a forecast. In volatile situations they can easily wipe out any benefit the forecast produced.

Managerial accounting makes use of additional profit definitions. A profit centre, for example, is an artificially created unit within the organization for which a profit can be derived. The idea is to encourage ownership of the benefit the unit provides for the company or to drive through efficiency measures. However, profit centres can also backfire when unit managers find that certain factors that impact the profit centre fall outside of their control.

See also: **Accounting, Finance**

Further reading: Bishop *et al.*, 1999; Muckian, 2000; Paxson and Wood, 1997; Shim *et al.*, 1997

PROJECT MANAGEMENT

Project managers work with a number of basic definitions that are goal oriented, that is designed to bring about the closure of the project. The number one rule is that projects should be clearly delineated to produce particular results with a limited scope. The scope of the project might be large or small but it must be defined. Project plans are devised to lay the project out within a certain timeframe and to coordinate the resources, schedules and budgets that are required for it. Gantt charts are particularly popular, showing how different elements within the project relate according to time. The project objective is specific, say the decoration of the office or the opening of new high street outlets, but it must fit into the overall strategy of the company, as in these two cases, to be regarded as a lively company or to be the first port of call for consumers respectively. The project slate coordinates the different projects that may be taking place within the organization at the same time.

So far so good. But project management is an area of management that is subject to particular scrutiny. This is particularly true in the age of information technology, since the implementation of computer systems is consistently seen to fail in up to half of all cases, and budget and time overruns are common. Project management is complicated because the scope is ill defined from the outset or may simply not really be known. Projects are treated as isolated activities within the organization, whereas in actual fact they affect normal operations and may even demand them to change. And as with all change, projects necessitate risk. Projects can suffer from bad planning, that overlooks events or miscalculates costs, and also from a certain power vacuum, when the managers concerned do not have the authority to drive through necessary decisions. Perhaps the most intractable problem that project managers face is the people factor, since the project must work with employees and ultimately be accepted by them. Team building is therefore central to project success.

This last factor is of rising significance because of notable trends in project management. For example, as businesses develop themselves as horizontal organizations, oriented towards processes or customers, projects have to include an increasingly diverse set of interest groups from across the enterprise. Alternatively, many projects now have an IT element, even those not primarily to do with computer systems, and this tends to complicate matters since technology brings its own set of issues, such as integration with legacy systems or erroneous expectations. Having said that, technology has also put a new set of tools at the disposal of the project manager, such as software designed to support projects by sharing information in a timely manner or making communication more easy.

We have noted that project management is defined by beginnings, middles and ends. This organization of projects is questioned by some management theorists, who regard it as outdated for the commercial environments faced by many businesses today that are characterized by continuous change. The argument is that project times are generally far longer than market cycles. This means that the advantage a company might have received as the result of a project is compromised before the project is completed, since it has become ineffective in the changed market. The goal, therefore, is to collapse project beginnings, middles and ends so that projects come to be viewed as ongoing, reflexive norms of operations. In other words the organization embodies the characteristic of continuous change that exists in its market.

See also: **Change management, Information and communications technology, Management, Systems analysis**

Further reading: Andersen *et al.*, 1999; Cleland, 1999; Field and Keller, 1998; Lintz and Rea, 1999; Lock, 2000; Tinnirello, 2000

PROTECTIONISM

An attitude that implements policies designed to secure markets against new or foreign entrants, often found in relation to trade laws made by governments.

Barriers to entry are the obvious manifestation of protectionist practices in business. At a macroeconomic level, governments are similarly engaged, often in the guise of opening up markets. For example, a regional trade agreement might produce a common market across the nations concerned, but is usually constructed with as much of an eye to the barriers it erects around the market it is creating to protect those operating within it. Commercial interests therefore have an uneasy relationship with ostensibly anti-protectionist, free trade laws. On the one hand they can open up new markets, but only by increasing competition.

See also: **Antitrust law, Barrier to market, Government, Monopoly**

PROTESTANT WORK ETHIC

The theory of Max Weber that capitalist success depends upon the religious idea that rewards and work are not causally connected.

The sociologist Max Weber asked why capitalism is so successful in the West. He noted that to take hold, capitalism needs people to save, in order to acquire capital. This in turn demands an attitude in which the pleasure that might be derived from spending money is rejected in favour of the greater returns that are anticipated in the future. Further, since many people cannot expect to experience the full pleasures that capital affords, the workforce must embody an attitude that is prepared to relinquish these pleasures, or at least trade them in for other benefits such as security.

Protestantism provides an effective framework within which this work ethos can flourish. Theologically, Protestant belief is that works do not bring divine rewards, faith does. Further, that 'reward' will be most fully enjoyed only after death. Faith has the advantage over works in that its rewards are secure since they are guaranteed by God, not by an individual's efforts.

The ethic is manifest in a range of attitudes: work is regarded as an obligation, it should be regulated by authorities, it is suspicious of leisure time that is not directed towards being recreative for more work. It is in this more general sense that the Protestant work ethic is usually meant today.

Further reading: Lehman and Roth, 1993; Weber, 1992

PUBLIC RELATIONS

The management of a company's profile in the public domain.

Public relations is an increasingly important business function. If managed well, PR contributes to many of the strategic goals of an organization, including intangible issues such as brand building and, PR managers would argue, tangible issues too, notably the bottom line. Tactically PR comes into its own when a company is launching a new product or announcing results. PR is also vital when it comes to crisis management.

PR is often linked to the marketing department of an organization, although typically its brief is to reach a wider audience than customers, markets and shareholders. PR is concerned with other groups that have a direct interest in the firm, such as employees and regulators, as well as groups that might have only a passing interest, that is the public at large. For example, if a company has to announce job losses PR will be used to manage the breaking news, especially to ensure that employees hear of redundancies from the correct sources. Bosses do not want such news to be first read in the newspaper on the way to work.

Alternatively, the management of the company's relationship with the wider public can be important too. For example, if there is environmentally sensitive information to announce, PR will try to ensure that the company's point of view is clearly presented to news outlets and that potentially damaging coverage is rebutted. At a more mundane level, PR is concerned with the long-term building of a company's reputation, which is achieved by regular communications with relevant parties, notably the press, analysts and public bodies.

PR can be the responsibility of an internal department, it can be outsourced to a PR agency, or a combination of both might be used. PR agencies typically have a number of non-competitive clients from a few industry sectors in which they specialize. The agency might be employed to work on isolated projects, such as a major announcement or campaign, or it will be used ongoing in the longer-term PR aims of the company.

At the heart of the management of PR is the gap that must be bridged between the company's own perspective and that of the media. This divide is another difference between PR and marketing. Whilst marketing can be extremely sophisticated, it basically speaks to its audience on its own terms. PR, on the other hand, operates on the terms of the media.

Successful PR is therefore facilitated by a deep understanding of the media. At one level this requires knowing how the media works, that journalists operate to deadlines, that they only focus on what is newsworthy, that different publications speak to very different audiences: so, a trade title might address the channel, the customer, or the industry itself, whereas a newspaper is addressed to the wider business audience or consumers at large. But good PR will also be able to advise on how to make the media itself work to the firm's best advantage. Doing a TV interview, for example, where two minutes is a very long time, is very different from talking to a newspaper journalist for half an hour or more. Or again, when it comes to issuing press releases, PR firms are able to raise their strategic significance, perhaps by linking an announcement with some current media interest, or by carefully managing the press release so that, for example, it might be given exclusively to one publication over another. Indeed, people in PR are often very skilled at playing the media at their own game, as in cases of the infamous spin doctors. This is a riskier strategy, though one that when done well can reap enormous benefits for the firm.

Crisis management is another issue again, discussed elsewhere.

Increasingly PR is finding a role that directly informs strategic decision making, rather than merely implementing it. This is partly because media are proliferating, especially in their online guises. However, large companies, in particular, are also finding that a poor public profile can be a major hindrance to ongoing success. So, as companies become more customer focused, PR is able to bring its own set of contributions. Another issue is that PR people have direct access to and are used to dealing with company bosses. How many others in the organization would have, and be happy to use, the CEO's personal mobile?

See also: **Crisis management, Marketing, Stakeholder**

Further reading: Ali, 1998; Jefkins and Yadin, 1998; Wilcox *et al.*, 2000

PUBLIC SECTOR

That part of the economy which is owned and administered by government.

The public sector is committed to the provision of goods and services that are valued by the society in which it exists. It can be thought of as providing the necessary infrastructure for business itself to function, as in the case of roads or postal services, or as providing services that if left to commercial means would not satisfy societal pressures for them, as in the case of hospitals or a criminal justice system.

The public sector differs from the private in that it is more or less exempt from market forces. Governments set public policy that they implement by legal statute and administer themselves. The public sector is therefore characterized by higher levels of bureaucracy and a trade-off between social and ethical concerns, and performance and innovation.

Public sector management is a particular skill. As already indicated, public sector organizations differ in their goals and cultures from those driven by the profit motive. They are coloured by their close involvement with government, so that management, for example, must be able to satisfy the demands of the regulator as much as the needs of the customer. The business of transforming policy into practice, and negotiating the gap that exists between the two, is another issue. Efficiency and effectiveness can take on very different meanings in the two contexts. The issue of accountability is important too. The private sector manager is ultimately accountable to shareholders for profit. The public sector manager will be accountable to many different individuals on many different accounts.

The role of the public sector in macroeconomics is a controversial one. Particularly under the influence of Keynesian economics, governments spend in the public sector to tackle unemployment and bolster the economy in general. However, experience has shown that using the public sector as a tool of macroeconomic policy is liable to backfire, since it causes instability elsewhere, notably in rising inflation.

Governments in the West have in recent years tended to blur the line between the private and public sector, and where outright privatization has not been possible or desirable have introduced private–public partnerships into the provision of public goods, such as the Private Finance Initiative in the UK, or market disciplines into the public sector itself. At the time of writing, there is a move to redress the balance between public and private, with a recognition that some public organizations are simply not amenable to the profit motive. The PFI, for example, which is primarily aimed at bringing the resources and rigour of commercial investment into the public sector, is plagued by problems that stem from the clash of cultures. Attitudes to risk, project management styles, and measures of return are common points of tension. Alternatively, the direct imposition of private sector management practices, such as performance management or an emphasis on the customer, can fall foul of the rational ethos that exists in public bureaucracies.

See also: **Bureaucracy, Government, Liberalization, Non-profit organizations**

Further reading: Brooks and Weatherston, 2000; Lee *et al.*, 1999

QUALITATIVE METHODS

The use of non-numerical methods in support of decision making.

Any area in which quantitative methods are used may also see qualitative methods being applied too. It may just be anecdotal testimony to back up the evidence of the bar chart. It may be that quantitative analysis can only provide approximate results when the matter in hand is extremely complex and the opinions of experts are likely to be of equal or more value. The Delphi method is a good example of this kind of qualitative approach.

A more general example of a qualitative method is the focus group. Unlike customer surveys that aim to produce statistical results from questionnaires, the value of focus groups is taken to stem directly from the comments, perceptions and opinions of participants: surveys always depend to some degree on the questions asked, focus groups try to uncover the spontaneous, unanticipated beliefs of real consumers. This is not to say that the structure of the focus group is not rigorous. Much effort is put into providing the kind of environment into which consumers can 'be themselves'. And again, sophisticated analysis of the qualitative results is also used to filter out the true and valuable result.

See also: **Delphi method**

Further reading: Gummesson, 2000a

QUALITY

The effort to ensure that products or services reach the standards that companies have set or customers expect.

Quality management is one of the key means by which organizational performance, effectiveness and ultimately success can be gained. The benefits that come with quality are perhaps obvious on one level, but can carry the company into a virtuous circle of growth when right or into a vicious spiral of decline if not. For example, whilst most customers will not tell the company when they are dissatisfied with product or service, they are likely to tell many friends and family, and vice-versa. The issue has become particularly critical with online channels to market, where research shows that for most customers just one bad experience on the phone, for example, will lead them to seek out a competitor.

Quality management uses a number of qualitative and quantitative methods, tools and techniques for improving the key elements that contribute to quality, such as uniformity of product or service characteristics, conformity to agreed standards, and satisfying customers. Process analysis maps processes to find the location of problems that impact quality; statistical methods for measuring quality adherence in mass production; benchmarking for comparing one company's quality standards with another; gap analysis that identifies why quality is not being delivered, because, say, customer and management expectations differ or because employees are inadequately resourced to deliver quality; projects that drive quality through the value chain, notably with suppliers and also customers (by encouraging customer feedback); organizational and job design tools that aim to provide the kind of environment within which quality can flourish. Quality management systems are concerned with the effectiveness of quality management, and provide standardized methods for documenting a company's quality record. The ISO 9000 series is the most widely used.

Perhaps the greatest effort in quality management at the time of writing is going into expanding the reach of quality projects across the enterprise and deepening the understanding of its role in organizational behaviour. Since the 1940s a number of 'quality gurus' have promoted the benefits of applying quality measures and improvement strategies to particular business functions.

See also: **Benchmarking, Gap analysis, Processes, Total quality management, Value**

Further reading: Antony and Kaye, 2000; Beckford, 1998; Dale and Plunkett, 1999; Hoyle, 1998; Kinney, 2000; Lamprecht, 2000; Mertins and Jochem, 1999; Munro-Faure *et al.*, 1998; Roth, 1999; Russell and Taylor, 1998; Straker, 1998;

QUANTITATIVE METHODS

Methods of analysis that use statistical or numerical data.

Quantitative methods in business used to be the specialist concern of the mathematician or statistician. However, their widespread study, use and reported success have led quantitative methods to be taught at virtually every level of business studies. Luckily for many, computers have put automated quantitative methods, as well as the tools for displaying their results, on the desktops of managers. Software has done for statistics what the calculator did for arithmetic.

Having said that, quantitative methods need not be that complicated. Basic and illuminating management information can be powerfully displayed on bar charts or as percentages. Statistics are generally used to present means and averages, or variances from averages. Project management, finances, logistics and quality management use their own set of quantitative tools. An understanding of the maths that underpins these functions can be enormously useful in applying them accurately to specific problems. This is why business studies teaches the basic principles, even though computers are likely to do the work in practice. Other kinds of analysis are more complex. Forecasting, for example, uses probability theory and regression analysis. Risk analysis uses calculus. For this reason, these disciplines still often lie in the hands of the specialist.

Wisniewski found that of the two-thirds of chief executives he researched in Europe who routinely use quantitative methods, most find them useful or essential. This is particularly the case in commercial environments that are complex because of international markets or rising competition. That said, he also points out that quantitative methods are used best as a support in decision making, in conjunction with qualitative methods and other intangible factors, such as the intuition of the manager.

See also: **Benchmarking, Chartism, Decision making, Finance, Forecasting, Modelling, Regression analysis, Risk, Sampling**

Further reading: Morris, 2000; Oakshott, 1998; Wisniewski, 1997

RATIONALIZATION

Changing an organization so that its structures are more clearly defined.

The aim of rationalization is to make the company more efficient. For example, an organization that has grown up organically over a number of years may well be duplicating processes or carrying out functions that are ineffective or not even required any longer. Rationalization therefore often results in job changes or losses, giving it a slightly sinister overtone in business. This is compounded by its origins in bureaucratic theories of the organization. The meaning was then slightly different, closer in fact to its common use of rendering logical. The belief was that organizations behave according to the principles of reason, always maximizing benefit. This has now largely been discredited. Further, theorists also recognize that many of the assets that an organization possesses, such as brand or people, are non-rational, if not irrational. Having said that, companies today may try to include an element of rationalization in their ongoing development as a component of feedback.

See also: **Bureaucracy, Management, Organic organization, Organization, Taylorism**

Further reading: Scott, 1992

REGRESSION ANALYSIS

The establishment of a mathematical relationship between the variables that have the greatest impact upon determining a business outcome.

Mathematically, regression analysis can be thought of in relation to the points that are plotted on a graph. These are determined empirically. So the question that the mathematician asks is, can an equation be devised that describes the relationship between these points? The problem arises because even accounting for the two variables that bear upon the distribution of the points, represented in the vertical and horizontal lines of the graph, makes the equations that regression analysis derives very complex. Mathematical tools called extrapolation, which formalize statistical and graphical means, are therefore deployed to describe the relationships. Regression analysis increases its sophistication by using computer models that simulate three and even more dimensions in graphical representations. However, the uncertainty associated with the results rises rapidly in these cases.

See also: **Modelling, Quantitative methods**

Further reading: Morris, 2000; Oakshott, 1998; Wisniewski, 1997

RELATIONSHIP MARKETING

Marketing techniques that focus on managing the long-term contact that a customer has with a company.

Relationship marketing can be contrasted with traditional marketing, since whereas the latter treats the relationship between customer and company as essentially transactional, the former regards it in a much more holistic frame.

For example, relationship marketing aims at retaining customers and building their loyalty as ends in themselves rather than as a means to increasing sales. Relationship marketing is customer oriented in that it targets what the customer wants and needs rather than simply what the product or service offers. It looks to the long term rather than seeing marketing as a series of autonomous projects: in a bank, for example, relationship marketing will not only target a customer segment according to, say, stage of life, but will target an individual over the course of their life so that the bank's services are tailored to their changing, long-term needs. Information of all contacts that the company has with the customer is retained and, ideally, brought to bear upon future interactions. And great attention is paid to the quality of these contacts so that bad situations between the customer and the company do not become entrenched, a common source of customer attrition.

Relationship marketing has developed for reasons of necessity and opportunity. Research has long shown that gaining new customers is far more expensive than cross-selling and up-selling to the existing customer base. Further, retaining customers by deepening the relationship they have with the company, say by selling one or more products to them, makes them very much more profitable in the long term. Proponents of relationship marketing also argue that it provides far more effective ways of marketing, that is it should not be thought of as an additional marketing activity but as a core approach to the discipline as a whole.

Relationship marketing also represents a relatively new, and therefore potentially more interesting, basis for the work of marketeers themselves, since rather than focusing on customers as sources of discrete, if repeated, transactions with the company, it looks to the wider picture of how the lives of the two entities intersect.

See also: **CRM, Marketing, Segmentation**

Further reading: Christopher *et al.*, 1991; Gummesson, 2000b; McKenna, 1991; Sheth and Parvatiyar, 2000; Stone *et al.*, 2000

R&D

The activity of scientists, theorists, strategists and designers who look for new products and services or new ways to improve existing products and services.

Although R&D – research and development – are linked in many companies, they are very often different activities altogether. Research tends to be the occupation of pure scientists and theorists; development that of strategists. The two may or may not meet in the person of the designer, according to the nature of the R&D and the ability of the organization to integrate the different cultures represented by these players.

It is the long length of typical R&D cycles that links the two functions. It is rare, for example, for a director to see a product through from earliest conception to release in the market, which explains much about why R&D departments have a special place in the life of the organization.

Research may be broken down into two broad areas of work. Blue sky research has little or no eye to output at all but rather seeks to develop technologies that could only possibly have some marketable application in the future. For example, many large pharmaceutical firms run laboratories that operate very much like their academic counterparts. Indeed, the two types increasingly overlap as business puts money into the university system. The brief is to build the intellectual capital of the firm.

Other types of research activity seek to advance products or services that the company already owns. For example, research departments in many professional services firms are currently engaged in developing new ways of accounting or auditing companies, in conjunction with IT companies and business academics – called strategic alliances, in response to perceived changes in the economy. The brief is to think relatively independently of existing practices in order to take the company forward into genuinely new territory. The only immediate benefit that companies may be able to derive from research is useful PR with, for example, stories about technological breakthroughs or achievements of human interest.

Development, on the other hand, is about taking the results of research and converting them into products that will ultimately return a profit. However, the development process may take many years to bring a product to market. That is, the return on the investment is not the primary driver in the development function, which is what links it economically to research.

R&D both carry high levels of risk. This lies at the heart of the management challenge. For example, consider the development of new IT products coping with deep uncertainty over market feasibility. (The shadow of Apple's failure to turn what was widely regarded as a superior product into a market-leading microcomputer still hangs over the computer industry.) Other complications include issues like product performance, which can be extremely variable once a product has left the controlled, un-scaled environment of the laboratory. The problem is that IT products often have a short market life, and so developers must try to reduce the uncertainty as early as possible in the development process. Apart from anticipating market trends, developers may therefore work closely with the marketing department, who will contribute to the strategic development of the product as well as try to influence the creation of a need for it in the market.

Companies are also increasingly looking to instil the insights of concepts of innovation into the organization, which in this area means closing the gap between development and sales. In this case, time to market is one of the central concepts in innovative organizations. The goal is to develop project management methodologies that re-engineer product development, manufacture and marketing into one continuous, reflexive process that works horizontally across the organization and is customer- or market-oriented.

See also: **Intellectual capital, Product, Time to market**

Further reading: Cooper and Schindler, 2001; Guerard and Bean, 1998; Johnson and Duberley, 2000; Miller and Morris, 1999

RESOURCES

The sources of the factors of production, land, labour and capital.

As the raw materials of business, resources are fundamental. How resources are allocated, appraised, exploited and renewed are basic managerial concerns. Many management methodologies and attitudes are therefore geared towards optimizing the use of resources.

Generally speaking, the greater the quantity of resources an organization has at its disposal, the greater its outcomes, within the constraints of the law of diminishing returns. This is offset by the competitive pressures it faces. An organization is also shaped and culturally determined by the different resources it has. A resource-based view of management therefore pays attention to the effective and efficient use of resources over and against these negative demands.

See also: **Asset, Capital, Labour, Supply and demand**

Further reading: Foss and Robertson, 2000

RESTRUCTURING

In general, changing the shape of the organization. The strict financial meaning is to change the capital debt to equity ratio.

Restructuring, in its broadest sense, covers a wide variety of corporate activity. Horne and Wachowicz list mergers, strategic alliances including joint ventures, divestitures including liquidation, sell-offs, spin-offs, equity carve-outs, ownership restructuring, and leveraged buyouts. However, the common driver is to increase shareholder value, which can be derived through restructuring in a number of ways. Economies of scale may be found. Points of entry into markets may become available, or at least new ways of cross-selling and up-selling. Management improvements may lead to increases in productivity or effectiveness. Companies may gain knowledge by sharing it in strategic alliances or acquisitions. Divestitures can simply rid the company of loss-making or inefficient activities. Moving the company offshore can bring enormous tax benefits. Restructuring the debt to equity ratio seeks to optimize the cost of capital to the organization according to the benefits that assets bring. M&As often represent the most high-profile of all restructuring activities.

The management of restructuring is therefore complex and multifaceted. However, it is worth pointing out that the value restructuring brings to the company is, at least in the early stages, often as much to do with stakeholder perceptions as it is with actual organizational change. So-called information effects are what drives shareholder value here. The idea is to positively influence the market's assessment of the company by showing that stock is undervalued. In their more tangible forms, information effects that give rise to an increase in share price occur because the restructuring exposes underlying profitability that was previously hidden. Less tangibly, restructuring may have the same effect because it is believed to improve the position of the company, positively impact assets such as brand, or simply because the restructuring fits current market fashions. In any restructuring it is certainly a priority of management to exclude or at least reduce any negative impact that announcements may have on share price.

Flotation, and the reverse process of privatization (here referring to non-government-owned organizations), is another form of restructuring that has become common on the back of market liberalization. However, both can be restructuring strategies in their own right. Flotation, or turning a private firm into a publicly owned company, is a way of increasing the investment resources available to the firm by gaining a massive in-flow of equity capital. It also has implications for management, such as increasing accountability, that are believed to be beneficial for the running of the company. In the UK, for example, a number of mutual companies, that is companies owned by customers, have been floated in recent years since first, it is perceived as the only way to compete in newly liberalized market sectors, and second, serious questions have been asked about the effectiveness of management that is not subject to market pressures. Returning a publicly owned company into private hands also occurs, though less frequently. The restructuring benefit here can be financial, since it reduces equity capital, though in the case of a leveraged buyout, when debt is taken on to finance the restructuring, the risks associated with defaulting can be high. But privatization may also be a strategic decision if it is believed that private companies are able to be more innovative because management has more direct control.

See also: **Capital, Finance, Liberalization, M&As**

Further reading: Gowing *et al.*, 1998; Harukiyo and Hook, 1998; Horne and Wachowicz, 1998; Ramu, 1999

RETAILING

The selling of products or services to consumers or end-users.

As Berman and Evans comment, retailing today is at a crossroads. In 1996, Wal-Mart became the first ever $100 billion retailer, and the productivity of retailing has increased significantly because of technological advances. But the challenges to retailing have, according to some, never been greater. Consumers are an increasingly savvy audience to sell to, service expectations continue to rise, and new channels to market provide new opportunities but also increased competition.

Retailing embraces a range of disciplines, including market research, merchandising and management. However, the key role that retailers play in the distribution chain is linking manufacturers to mass markets. Wholesalers, typically, do not have the organizational structures to efficiently buy or manufacture multiple goods and sell them to many customers. Retailers carry the economies of scale that wholesalers enjoy one step further down the value chain without compromising the potential for the goods to reach the widest possible audience. Retailers also add value. They engage in marketing activities, devise selling strategies, and add services to products, from receiving complaints to providing credit. Retail management focuses upon these unique business functions in particular.

However, retail management performs other roles too. An important one is managing the relationship with suppliers. This too is changing. For example, the balance of power in the distribution chain has shifted in favour of the retailers. As mentioned above and below, retailing is becoming a more sophisticated activity that makes wholesalers more dependent upon them. For example, a food manufacturer that designs its packaging on the basis that it will appear on the eye-level shelves of the supermarket may find its investment compromised when the store decides to move it to the bottom shelf. Alternatively, retailer decisions can backfire. A high street bookstore that recently demanded increased discounts from its small publishing house suppliers, arguing that it needed to turn a profit on a greater proportion of stock, was referred to the trading standards body in the UK, for exercising monopolistic power. These factors, and others, affect the distribution strategy in retailing, so that contractual relationships may variously be exclusive, extensive or selective.

The economics of retailing is different from other kinds of selling, too. For example, consumers tend to make a large number of small value purchases, which increases the impact of the logistical function upon profits. Purchase decisions are more complex than in other selling scenarios, since consumers may act on impulse or be strongly influenced by the retail environment. This increases uncertainty. Finally, in the retail case, customers come to a store, rather than salespeople going out to the customer, which means that the pull aspect of marketing is more significant in relation to the push.

Berman and Evans emphasize the significance of the retailing concept in retail strategic management: 'This concept requires a firm to have a customer orientation, use a coordinated effort, and be value-driven and goal-oriented.' They lament the fact that retailers are often not well trained in this respect and so fail to get the so-called retailing mix right. As a result customer service is poor, delivering neither expected service nor augmented service, that adds value in the eyes of the consumer. Further, relationship retailing, as the key strategic goal, that is contact with consumers that does not start from ground zero every time, never gets off the ground.

At the end of the twentieth century a rare thing happened in retailing. Two new channels to market emerged in only as many decades. The first was the telephone, which with the rapid deployment of call centres in the 1980s revolutionized retailing in certain respects, notably in terms of service. Customers now routinely expect to be able to speak to an agent seven days a week, twenty-four hours a day, in sectors as diverse as financial services and florists. Further, expectations on the telephone have spread back to the high street, so that opening hours have lengthened, stock delivery times have shortened, and customer convenience has increased.

The second was the internet, notably in its web form. Whilst there has been much debate as to the speed with which so-called B2C commerce will take off (that is business to consumer as opposed to business to business), few retailers are betting on it not doing so, and with dramatic effect on their business. The web has accentuated the changes that were already occurring because of the telephone. For example, service has now to be personalized, incidentally a quality that the web enhances not only at the customer end but in the call centre too, by providing the systems that can put customer information in front of the agent before the phone is even answered. But the web has also increased competition. As a channel to market it is very much cheaper than its high street cousin, by several orders of magnitude. But it has also, thus far, acted as a great leveller in retail since competition is now not a walk or drive away but instead no further than a click or two of the mouse. Having said that, there is much debate as to the extent that the web will continue to have a democratizing effect on retailing, since, for example, brand plays an important role and websites themselves are increasingly expensive to develop and run.

See also: **Direct operations, E-business, Inventory, Management, Merchandising, Sales management**

Further reading: Berman and Evans, 1998; Levy and Weitz, 1995; McGoldrick, 1990

RETURNS

The financial benefit that a company receives from its assets.

The return of an asset is calculated as the ratio of its performance, that is value earned, to the amount invested in it. The return can be in the form of income or capital gain. It is therefore a measure of its productivity.

Companies look for returns across a range of their activities. As indicated already, the most common is the return on an investment, which may be assets of many kinds including stocks, plant or information. However, returns can also be turned towards particular financial ends. The profitability of assets many be calculated by accountants as the return on assets or, in the particular case of capital assets, return on capital employed. Alternatively, financial markets may require information about the dividends that shareholders receive, called return on equity. The margin that is made upon a single sale, that is the amount that the price exceeds the marginal cost, is a basic measurement of profitability known as a return on sale.

The return on investment is an increasingly important gauge of the success of management projects. For example, whilst few companies would doubt the benefit of investing in IT, it has traditionally been treated as an unallocated cost because it does not have a direct impact upon revenue generation. This makes it hard to calculate investment returns and ensure efficient and effective implementations.

Various financial tools can be used to provide a specific figure for the return on investment. The payback period is one of the simplest. It calculates the length of time that it will take to recover the cost of the investment. The great advantage that this tool has is that it is a quantitative calculation, providing companies with a clear indicator of the risk they are taking. The drawback is that it tends to obscure certain elements associated with investing, notably the cash flow implications of a project: the same payback period might carry more risk because the return comes only at the end of the period rather than throughout.

Improving on this point is the net present value tool. It uses a formula that takes account of the higher risk associated with payback that increases as the payback period grows. The analysis derives a present value for future cash flows resulting from the investment that can be directly compared with present costs. However, uncertainty can creep in, since net present value requires a calculation of the risk over period of the investment. It is represented by so-called discount rates.

See also: **Finance, Yield**

Further reading: Oakshott, 1998; Paxson and Wood, 1997; Vandermerwe, 1999

RISK

The possibility of a loss or other adverse consequence in commercial activity. Financially, risk carries the specific meaning of the exposure that a security carries.

Risk is always present in business, since companies look for returns by operating in an environment characterized by risk, that is competitive markets. The general principle is that the greater the risk, the greater the potential reward *and* the greater the possibility of failure. Risk management is the effort to reduce the chance of failure in favour of the reward. However, risk is irreducible. So, organizations adopt very different attitudes to risk, as well as more or less successful strategies for dealing with it.

The mantra of risk management is 'Get real!'. The Austrian economist Fritz Machlup famously lamented his colleague whose system substituted a proxy for risk (and, he added, a dummy for sex, which is why the quote is remembered, though the point is that without taking on real risks there is no chance of real rewards).

The sophistication with which risk can be managed has increased dramatically in recent years. This has come with the advent of computers which employ applications such as value at risk systems that can provide detailed estimates of the risk the company is carrying. And there is in general much better communication of best practices. The difference can be likened to that of flying a jumbo and a fighter plane. The jumbo is old style and low risk: it is very safe even if you take your hands off the controls, though at the cost of poor performance. The fighter is high risk: it cannot be flown without computers to keep it in the air, but it comes with high performance and agility – the two key qualities for winning in competitive markets.

To be risk averse is therefore perceived as lacking entrepreneurial drive and probably indicative of poor productivity in today's commercial environment. Even the recent dramatic collapses of major financial institutions have served to highlight the necessity of risk. The trick is to take risk on, but strategically and cautiously, with as many controls in place as possible.

Kendall, writing as part of a government initiative in this spirit to promote better risk management, highlights five areas where controls should be applied. The first is market risk, that which stems from the external, competitive environment. Best practice is to establish risk management systems that are organizationally independent of those who reap the rewards, and to be as clear as possible about the position the company wants to take in the market.

Credit risk is the second area, that is the exposure which derives from trading with other companies. Best practice requires organizational change that introduces the credit department to risk management, a practice that is surprisingly rare, since the credit function has traditionally focused on contractual and remedial activities. Another increasingly important issue for international business is understanding the risk represented by trading with companies in foreign countries. Political instability or commercially immature legal systems are major sources of risk.

The third area is operational risk, that is the risk that the organization is to itself. It covers a multitude of sins, including human error, fraud and calamity, legal restrictions on activities, and risks to intangible assets such as reputation. Good business practices in general, such as corporate transparency, contingency planning and enlightened attitudes in management, are the best means of controlling these risks.

Legal risks, that is the risk that stems from legal obligations and/or litigation, vary from country to country, though in some parts of the world they represent a substantial threat, not because companies operate illegally deliberately but because the power that litigants have when something does go wrong is enormous. Lawyers, and common sense, are the only answer.

The fifth category of risks is assorted and includes concerns such as dependency upon computer systems. Again, good general business practice applies.

Financial markets are of course a specific application of risk management. Financial instruments are bought and sold to hedge against various kinds of risk. All that is required is one party who wants to avoid a risk and one who wants to take a risk on. The speculators may then devise means of reducing the risk they have bought into. Derivatives are the most common contracts, so called because their value derives from the asset they represent. Any number of contracts might be drawn up to deal with the risk represented by interest rate changes, foreign exchange rates, market falls and so on.

Some common derivatives are:

Futures – also called forwards, since the buyer of the contract wants to safeguard against a potential loss in the future by selling forward the source of the risk to the speculator, who in turn believes they will be able to sell the asset on at a profit.

Options – a contract that gives the purchaser of it the right but not the obligation to buy or sell an asset at some agreed price in the future, at the cost of a premium.

Swaps – a contract that allows two parties to exchange one kind of risk for another.

See also: **Exposure, Foreign exchange risk, Hedging, Insurance, Utility**

Further reading: Davis, 1992; Jorion, 1997; Kendall, 1998; Lonsdale and Cox, 1998; Wade and Wynne, 1999; Williams, C.A. *et al.*, 1998

SALES MANAGEMENT

The branch of marketing that focuses on the transfer of goods for payment. It includes the administration of the sales force and mechanisms for transacting, as well as the planning of a sales strategy.

Dalrymple and Cron define sales management as 'the planning, implementing, and control of personal contact programs designed to achieve the sales and profit objectives of the firm'.

The concerns of sales managers frequently coincide with those common to all managers, though specifically in relation to sales, productivity must be increased, costs reduced, and commercial changes negotiated. The differences tend to lie with the sales force itself. The management, recruitment, training and remuneration of these individuals and teams differ on certain accounts. Salesmen and women often work remotely and independently, for example, and compared to other employees they are often directly motivated on the basis of results, notably by commissions.

Sales forces are evaluated not only according to volume or value of sales, but also according to the profits they generate, the number of repeat orders, and the quality of after-sales service they provide. Salespersons are also expected to provide information about customer satisfaction and expectations in order that managers can respond to problems and emerging needs. This is a possible source of problems for the sales manager, because individuals in the sales force may well work alone and can become quite protective of their own client base. Devising the means of sharing information that is gleaned from the sales force brings enormous value to the organization as a whole.

Sales management involves direct contact with customers, either through personal selling or via account management. In this way it plays a leading role in the marketing mix. Advertising, public relations and sales promotions must all fit in with the strategies deployed by the sales force for personal selling. Indeed, salespersons may often be called upon to explain the meaning of other elements in the marketing mix that arise because of the communications gap that inevitably appears when contact is impersonal. The sales force is also on the frontline of cultural differences when working on the international stage.

In line with other business functions, sales management evolves according to the vagaries of the market. Customer needs are particularly important. Indeed, because they have a special relationship with customers and make it their business to understand the customer's point of view, salespersons can be treated as a valuable resource, not only in the matter of sales but for the organization as a whole if it is trying to become more customer oriented.

Today, the sales force is increasingly expected to spend more time with the customer, and possibly to reflect customer needs back more deeply into their own organization, providing input at the level of product development, for example. Another change that is currently sweeping through many sales forces is the roll out of remote computer technology. Laptops and wireless devices enhance the contact that salespersons have with their offices, as well as improve the quality of information that they have at their disposal when on site with customers. However, it brings its own problems too. Issues to do with control can be exacerbated by a sales force always on the road, and complementary systems such as intranets are often implemented to ensure salespersons stay in touch and feel well supported. Another issue is that of security. The installation of best practice when remote working is an important new area of training for the modern sales force.

See also: **Direct operations, E-business, Home working, Intranet, Management, Marketing, Retailing**

Further reading: Cummins, 1998; Dalrymple and Cron, 1998; Green, 1999; Jobber and Lancaster, 2000; Rackham and DeVincentis, 1999

SAMPLING

A statistical technique for determining the characteristics of a whole population by obtaining information from a representative subgroup.

Sampling is used to gain market research when the group under scrutiny is large, or when there are time constraints on the research. Sampling allows more detailed quantitative work to be done, since greater control can be exercised over the sources of information. Qualitative research is also possible by interviewing individuals.

In this way, sampling is different from a census in which the whole population is consulted. The advantage of the latter is that it does not depend upon the validity of the statistical methods that gear the sample up to represent the whole population.

The detection and elimination of errors is a critical process in sampling. Errors are defined as differences between the results provided by the sample and the reality in the population as a whole, and they originate in the sample itself, in which case it is a sampling error, or because the statistical techniques applied to the sample are at fault, in which case it is a non-sampling error. Sampling errors are the most easily remedied, notably by increasing the sample size. Non-sampling errors can go undetected altogether. The sampling process focuses on the trade-off between these factors and the production of results that would be useful to marketing.

See also: **Quantitative methods**

Further reading: Aaker *et al.*, 1998

SATURATION

The point at which supply just exceeds demand.

During the course of a typical product's lifecycle, sales increase, reach a maximum, and then decrease. The point at which they level out represents the phase in which the product achieves market saturation. The market ceases to grow and competition between producers often reaches its peak too. Competitive strategies are based upon the price proposition, so promotions and discounts are common. Alternatively, a product that has an effective monopoly must succeed in attracting its customer base to replacement sales which, for products that do not age, can be done by adding value to the product. Companies also seek to initiate new periods of market growth by diversification, that is developing the product for new markets. A company that relies upon saturated markets alone tends to see its profits fall.

See also: **Boston Consulting Group Model, Brand extension, Diversification, Market penetration, Price, Zero-sum game**

SEGMENTATION

A marketing strategy that targets the promotion of particular products at demographic groups or geographical areas.

The idea behind segmentation is that when treated as singular entities, markets only approximate to the real needs of customers. So, much can be gained in terms of attracting and satisfying customers if they are regarded in smaller groups. Segmentation therefore works best when customer groups with particular or unique preferences can be identified.

Segmentation lends itself to product diversification in that essentially the same good may be sold with different packaging or value-added services to a more diverse customer base. Segmentation can also provide the basis of a competitive strategy by, for example, enabling the company to appear closer to its customers. Smaller companies may in this way be able to compete against larger ones because they are able to develop a sales proposition that does not depend upon price alone and undermines the larger company's economies of scale.

See also: **Brand extension, Marketing**

Further reading: Davies, 1998; McDonald and Dunbar, 1998; Porter, 1998b

SEMIOTICS

The study of signs, especially in marketing and communications.

The use of semiotics in advertising was sparked by the publication of Roland Barthes' *Elements of Semiology*. He provided tools for the analysis of advertising messages by applying the ideas of denotation and connotation. Denotation is the primary meaning of a sign, that might be literal, dominant or intrinsic. Connotation points to the secondary meanings that accrue to the sign as it evolves in the environment around it. For example, an advertisement that features a photograph of the product carries a denotational meaning in the form of the image itself. This represents basic information about the product such as its look and utility. However, because of the cultural milieu into which the image is released and the associations that form around the image, partly triggered by the advertisement itself and partly stemming from those who see it, connotational meaning becomes attached to the sign. This transmits or creates meaning about brand, style, positioning and desirability.

The strict distinction between denotation and connotation was later questioned by Barthes himself, the point being that there could be no primary, pure meaning carried by a sign since signs exist already in a sociocultural setting. Even the utility of a product is designated in this way. Denotation, if it exists at all, is merely the lasting impression of connotational meaning.

Other thinkers have contributed alternative semiotic theories that can be applied to advertising and communications in general. Mick provides a survey of them. However, Barthes' legacy is the idea that advertisements can be read in a variety of ways, and that having some understanding of these possible readings is important if advertisers are to maintain any control on the reception of signs. As Nöth puts it,

> No advertisement can be successful if it fails to convey the message of the product (referential core) and when it does not have some appeal to purchase it (conative core). ... Even when the core messages of an advertisement are masked in the textual surface structure, the consumer will use his or her general text-pragmatic knowledge as a substitute.

See also: **Advertising, Communication**

Further reading: Barthes, 1967; Mick, 1988; Nöth, 1998

SMALL AND MEDIUM-SIZED ENTERPRISES

Quantitative definitions of an SME are notoriously contested. The European Union defines the SME sector as consisting of micro enterprises, from 0 to 9 employees; small enterprises, from 10 to 49 employees; and medium enterprises, from 100 to 250 employees. This classification does reflect some of the change phases that companies go through as they grow. However, the problem is that whilst small numbers in a manufacturer might indicate that the business is small too, they could represent a very large business in certain parts of the service sector. So, qualitative definitions of SMEs are common too. They indicate that SMEs have peculiar characteristics, such as possessing small market share and being organizationally flexible, entrepreneurial and autonomous.

For all the problems of definition, SMEs represent a vital part of the capitalist system. Since most companies start small, SMEs are engines of innovation and economic growth. For example, during the last major world recession, SMEs climbed to the top of the political agenda as a key to the recovery of an 'enterprise culture'. Alternatively, the fact that many developing countries do not seem able to enjoy the growth of the West is increasingly blamed on the factors that limit the growth of SMEs, notably restrictive property laws that inhibit the ability of SMEs to borrow. SMEs are becoming increasingly important in the contemporary economy for reasons including the growth of flexible working practices, in which individuals are self-employed, and the greater proportion of SMEs in the IT sector, often associated with entrepreneurialism.

SMEs are separated out in the economy not only because of the role they play but because of the issues they face. Stokes, noting that SMEs suffer from high mortality rates, identifies a number of influences on the small firm's formation and survival. Internal influences include a greater susceptibility to the motives of management who might also be owners; a greater sensitivity to the attributes of staff, especially when certain skills are lacking; higher proportionate risks in certain respects, notably in relation to technology, where recurrent and frequent problems can virtually hold the company to ransom; and greater problems in developing management competencies, especially in the fields of marketing, finance and human resources. External influences stem from the macroeconomic environment: political factors such as levels of taxation or the demands by employment law can have debilitating effects; SMEs are less able to withstand the downturns of economic cycles; and they can have greater problems adapting to commercial changes, notably in technology. And from the microeconomic environment: local socioeconomic factors play an important part since SMEs can do little to influence them; market developments can force SMEs out of their niche or render them powerless in the face of larger competitors; customer needs are often hard to meet when they change or diversify, since SMEs lose their economies of scale.

These factors mean that SMEs are particularly sensitive to time and place, growth strategies, market sector, barriers to entry, customer focus and commercial change. Whilst a large enterprise might be able to withstand unfavourable circumstances or a number of mistakes in these areas, SMEs are likely to go belly-up much more quickly. In short, small and medium-sized enterprise management is a specialist subject of its own.

Further reading: Ali, 1998; Good, 1998; Julien, 1998; Lasher, 1999; Maitland, 1998; Scarborough and Zimmerer, 2000; Stokes, 1998

SMALL OFFICE-HOME OFFICE

A place of work based in the home. Also called SOHO.

People who work from home face a particular set of productivity issues. On the one hand, home workers testify to increases in productivity due to a reduction in the distractions associated with a communal office. However, productivity can be detrimentally impacted by the lack of the intangible interaction that takes place in the communal office.

SOHOs represent a substantial investment for the individual. Given that they have space in their homes, technology is the critical issue here, not so much the cost of hardware and software as the ongoing costs of services from such as ISPs (internet service providers). Installing fast internet access is, at the time of writing, still very expensive in the SOHO. The problem is that telecommunications companies have yet to work out the right balance between economies of scale and service levels that will make it profitable for them to meet the needs of SOHOs, and for that matter SMEs as well.

See also: **Small and medium-sized enterprises**

SOCIAL AUDIT

A process that takes stock of a company's impact upon society and members of the public directly affected by the company's activities in particular.

Social auditing is in its infancy. Different approaches may use a variety of quantitative and qualitative tools to build up a picture of the company's relationship with the society around it.

The impulse to engage in a social audit stems from a number of imperatives. Public pressure is probably the most common when, like environmental auditing, companies wish to be seen to be considering the impact they have upon those around them seriously.

Companies may also realize that their own future success depends in part upon the social networks with which they are engaged through a variety of stakeholders. This might be a reflection of an entrepreneurial attitude which acknowledges that organizations are porous entities that can gain enormously from encouraging a flow of skills across their boundaries. It is also possibly a modern phenomenon in the sense that the limited neoclassical responsibilities of the firm, notably to its shareholders, are being extended to include other stakeholders. Inasmuch as this is happening it is because companies realize they play an important social, as well as commercial, role.

See also: **Audit, Environmental audit, Socioeconomics, Stakeholder**

Further reading: Brinckerhoff, 2000; Karake-Shalhoub, 1999; Marinetto, 1998

SOCIOECONOMICS

The study of the interaction between sociological and economic factors, in the academic context seeking to merge the sociological and economic sciences.

Socioeconomics has grown out of the paradoxical realization that classical economic factors are not adequate to explain human economic behaviour. The point is that people rarely act solely in order to satisfy material desires alone. Neither do they do so wholly rationally. Social factors play a role to a greater or lesser extent, and it is this element for which socioeconomics tries to account.

Social factors might include peer pressure. For example, this is a dynamic exploited by the advertising industry. Advertising does not in general try to engage audiences that are distant from its product, but individuals who might be customers because they are similar to those who are already. One means of persuading this group is to make them conscious of the peer pressure to obtain the product being advertised.

Social factors might also appear in more moral guise. For example, the success of the Body Shop can be attributed in large part to the stance the company has taken against the exploitation of the environment by the cosmetics industry. Clearly, economic factors are involved too: products have to be of the quality and ingenuity that people expect for the company to succeed in the long term. However, the Body Shop was also able to communicate not only the actuality of its 'environmentally friendly' products, but also its intention to change the industry as a whole for the good. This became a powerful socioeconomic driver of growth.

Socioeconomics takes on a more formal shape in certain branches of business studies, too. For example, the theory of communitarianism invented by Amitai Etzioni builds into its economic results the insight that social goods are important to the individual alongside economic goods. This challenges classical economic theory, which places the stress upon the individual as an economic player, to introduce a corrective balance that highlights the mutual interdependence between the individual and society. With this redress, ideas of community or society should be incorporated into economic theory, by, for example, analysing the role of shared moral values alongside individual material desires in the functioning of markets.

See also: **Advertising, Classical economics, Social audit**

Further reading: Etzioni, 1988; McAuliffe, 1997; Wheeler and Sillanpää, 1997

SOFT SELL

Unobtrusive techniques for encouraging individuals to buy products or services.

Soft selling takes a more subtle, seductive form than its hard-hitting relative. Seen as something of an art by the marketing department, the soft sell can be made in many ways. For example, many service companies will give information to customers for free in the hope that they will realize the value of what they have received and their need for more. Alternatively, the most powerful persuader in consumer markets is the personal recommendation: a soft sell here will try to imitate this with advertisements that have products endorsed by actors playing the 'man on the street'.

Contrasted with the hard sell, the irony is that the soft sell is often far more persuasive when it comes to encouraging people to buy.

See also: **Marketing**

SPECIALIZATION

Devoting a high percentage of a business's resources into excelling at certain functions or skills.

Specialization is a key strategy for increasing productivity. It aims to exploit the gains to be made by the division of labour. The theory is that an individual performing a large number of a few discrete tasks is able to increase their output. Specialization occurs at the organizational level too, meaning not so much that different departments perform different functions, but that businesses devise a strategy in which they carve out a niche for themselves in a competitive market by becoming specialists or experts.

Specialization does not necessarily imply that a company focuses on only one or a small number of skills. It may be that whilst different parts of the workforce become specialists, the overall effect in the organization is to increase the complexity of its output because of the way these specialisms are together. This might be an important factor for innovation, for example.

The degree to which companies specialize varies from nation to nation. Amongst white collar workers, for example, the UK and US are generally taken to prefer specialization when possible, whereas Germany and Japan favour employees taking on combinations of responsibilities.

Specialization can also carry a negative meaning in business. This occurs when tasks are given over to specialists whose subject area becomes so rarefied that their function serves itself rather than the organization as a whole. Further, whilst specialization is taken to increase productivity, it can also compromise the lateral thinking that is essential to innovation.

See also: **Core competency, Management, Productivity, Vertical integration**

STAKEHOLDER

The sum total of individuals and groups that can claim to have some kind of relationship with a business.

Stakeholders, that is those who have an interest or concern in a company, are diverse. They can be taken to include owners, shareholders, employees, customers, suppliers, regulatory bodies, governments, the press, and the public in general. Stakeholders will inevitably have conflicts of interests. In classical economics the interests of shareholders take priority. However, in many modern business theories the interests of customers take precedent, if only in the belief that the interests of shareholders will be best served in the long term as a result. Being able to relate to different stakeholders is certainly one of the skills required by senior management, although when stakeholder politics asserts the right of more tenuously linked individuals to influence company decision making, directors might feel the concept is being stretched a little far.

See also: **Activism, Environmental audit, Organization, Public relations, Social audit**

Further reading: Clarke and Clegg, 1998; Rutterford, 1998; Wheeler and Sillanpää, 1997

STRATEGY

A plan of action that embodies long-term goals.

The British politician Tony Benn once commented in relation to the development of commercial strategies, 'We have the benefit of much experience. Almost everything has been tried at least once.' Which is another way of saying that strategy is as old as commerce itself, although possibly a subject that has the dubious status of being the most fashionable of business fashions. In short, all decision making in business is taken to be strategic. Whether it is or not is another question entirely.

Strategy is a process that organizations undertake to decide the best way of bringing about corporate vision, mission and goals. In modern business studies its origins lie in military models from which many of the earliest ideas about strategy were drawn. Here is emphasized, for example, the need for clear objectives, respected lines of authority, and a sense of mutuality upon which everyone's future depends. More recently though, the approach has been seen to have a number of drawbacks. For example, it is top-heavy since the military is formed of hierarchical organizations. Alternatively, it is not so able to capture the importance of long-term goals, since military strategy tends to have more definite beginnings, middles and ends than businesses can provide. Or again, business strategy stems from its economic roots, that is the matching of needs and resources. Business strategy has tended as a result to become more focused on what opportunities lie ahead and how the organization might be geared up to exploit them. Another recent evolution is the spread of strategic thinking across the enterprise. Functions as mechanical as operations are now said to be strategic. The so-called strategic business unit is designed to bring strategic thinking as close as possible to actual operations. The great advantage of these kind of developments is the devolution of strategic thinking to local managers. Strategic management is therefore no longer the high level, cerebral activity it was once considered to be, but is a way of life and embodied in the day-to-day processes of individuals throughout the organization.

Thompson and Strickland outline the aims and objectives of strategic management in the following way:

(1) providing better guidance to the entire organization on the crucial point of 'what it is we are trying to do and to achieve'; (2) making managers more alert to the winds of change, new opportunities, and threatening developments; (3) providing managers with a rationale for evaluating competing budget requests for investment capital and new staff – a rationale that argues strongly for steering resources into strategy-supportive, results-producing areas; (4) helping to unify the numerous strategy-related decisions by managers across the organization; and (5) creating a more proactive management posture and counteracting the tendencies for decisions to be reactive and defensive.

See also: **Management, Marketing, Operations management and strategy, Performance**

Further reading: Bititci and Carrie, 1998; Buckley, 1998; Channon, 1997; Hussey, 1998; Morden, 1999; Thompson and Strickland, 1998

SUBLIMINAL ADVERTISING

Marketing techniques that try to make an impression on an audience without that audience being aware of it.

Subliminal advertising is hotly contested. Few would deny that it is possible for advertisements to influence people without them being fully conscious of it. However, this is usually taken to be only at the level of broad impressions that do not directly influence the buying decision. Subliminal advertising is therefore taken to carry a darker meaning, suggesting wanton manipulation of an audience or publishing images that would otherwise be illegal. This does not necessarily refer to elements such as sexual innuendo, but rather the communication of specific messages. For example, a TV advertisement might be cut with single frames that carry this message, the idea being that the viewer registers it without quite realizing what has happened. In some countries subliminal advertising has been outlawed.

See also: **Advertising**

SUPPLY AND DEMAND

The two forces in economics that determine, as oppose to merely influence, the behaviour of markets.

The term 'supply' is used in a variety of contexts. An elementary use refers to a product that is being supplied at a particular rate and price. A supply curve is one that charts the relationship between these two key supply variables. The supply function is one that seeks to incorporate all the factors that have a bearing upon supply, beginning with rate and price, but also including other market realities such as the level of competition, the availability of resources, and the prospects of the market. It may also include externalities, such as the supply of related products, that affect the demand for the product being studied.

The supply behaviour of producers is governed by the goal of profit maximization: producers aim to balance the factors that affect production to yield the greatest profits. For example, as production volumes increase, prices decrease and markets come closer to saturation. The firm will therefore try to determine the level of supply that optimizes the profits it can make. This balance is reached when the marginal revenue equals the marginal cost.

The supply of an industry sector is determined by the sum of these decisions made by all the players in the market, including the interaction between companies that indirectly affect supply. For example, externalities generated by one company may impact the profitability of another so that the latter's supply will be changed as a result. The empirical law of supply states that the quantity of a good that is supplied is directly and positively related to its price. The actual relationship between supply and price in a real market situation, which may obey economic laws more or less precisely, is mediated by the concept of elasticity, which can be described as the amount by which a market deviates from the laws of supply.

Demand can be used in similar contexts to that of supply. For example, that there is demand is taken to mean no more or less than that a product will sell at an indeterminate price. In economics, demand means the relationship between rate, price and other factors such as consumer behaviour or incomes. The demand function is therefore analogous to the supply function.

However, because the demand function depends directly on complex issues such as utility maximization in households – that is people spend their money in a way that brings them the greatest satisfaction – it is often less clearly determined. Statistical aggregates overcome many of the uncertainties associated with the demand function, and lead to additional concepts. For example, an inferior good is one whose price falls, not rises, as incomes rise. The law of demand is that as quantity rises prices fall, reflecting the law of supply. But it is often taken to be more robust than the law of supply, since it is enforced by the joint observations that when prices fall consumers tend to want more of the product and/or when incomes rise consumers extra purchasing power is usually spent on more of the product. The elasticity of demand mediates theoretical and actual demand behaviour.

Supply and demand together determine price, as described in neoclassical economics. The equilibrium price is the price that is arrived at when the quantity of a product demanded by customers matches the quantity of the product supplied by producers.

See also: **Economics, Neoclassical economics, Price, Resources**

Further reading: Magill, 1997; McAuliffe, 1997; Pindyck and Rubinfeld, 1995

SYNCHRONICITY

The simultaneous occurrence of events that have no apparent connection but significantly determine future outcomes.

Some would say that synchronicity is just another name for luck. But some business theorists believe that 'luck makes itself' or in other words, the entrepreneurial character is prepared to adopt certain attitudes to life that give rise to synchronicity and then success. For example, these individuals may be perceived by others to be on the edge, prepared to take risks, act quickly, and have powerful creative energies at their disposal that can make connections. The effort to structure this constellation of lucky causes, to bring about profitable business effects, is likely to only suit certain kinds of organization – those of the synchronous kind.

See also: **Entrepreneurship**

Further reading: Satori, 1999

SYNERGY

The theory that the result of combining businesses or functions is to enhance what the parts could achieve separately.

The signified of the signifier 'synergy' is hotly contested. Some say it is dishonest business consultants arguing that two plus two can make five. Others believe that synergy is at the heart of modern economic growth, with its increased links between businesses, markets and nations.

Others still argue that synergy is a valuable concept but no panacea, rather a strategic goal that must be approached cautiously. Campbell and Goold make a case for synergy that tries to steer a middle path. They point out that synergy is a difficult concept, both because it is hard to decide which synergies to structure the organization towards and because when synergies are manifest they are often intangible and not subject to ready cost-benefit analysis.

They recommend a number of management tactics for assessing possible synergies more carefully. First, bring clarity to the traditionally muddled discussion of synergies. For example, benefits should be disaggregated not compounded, initiatives should be structured not rolled together, and the full range of costs accounted for including opportunity costs. Second, synergy should be a goal that is sought selectively, not as a recipe for indiscriminate success. Third, and related to this second point, is that synergy depends upon human factors, so that the organization must either have established mechanisms for integrating the hoped-for synergistic elements or it must have a 'synergy champion' who can drive the benefits through. Fourth, they identify issues that can damage the opportunity, such as culture or organizational resistance, competition between managers, and a poor attitude towards innovation in general. Fifth, the decision needs to be based upon more than intuition: the point is that whilst two plus two may not be made to equal five, it is not hard to make them equal less than four. And finally, synergy should be part of the company's overall strategy for change and development.

See also: **Joint venture, M&As, Vertical integration**

Further reading: Campbell and Goold, 1998

SYSTEMS ANALYSIS

The study of interrelated parts but with particular reference to computer networks.

The systems analyst can be thought of as the person who coordinates the interests of the various parties involved in an IT project in order that the system being installed is designed, engineered and implemented to best advantage for all concerned. In this sense their role is that of the project manager, but specifically for IT projects. It is different largely because enterprise-wide computer systems are new to businesses. Computers have traditionally been installed on a departmental basis to fulfil specific, isolated functions. However, as computers are increasingly used in the context of networks, the design of these systems must to a high degree reflect the shape of the organizational structures and practices they aim to support. For example, an organization that views itself as an orderly body working towards clearly defined goals will look for systems defined by workflow processes. Alternatively, an organization that values innovative practices and knowledge sharing will want to ensure that the applications in place are able to support the more intuitive ways of working associated with this approach.

See also: **Information and communications technology, Open and closed systems, Project management**

Further reading: Currie and Galliers, 1999; Davis, 1997; Duffuaa *et al.*, 1999; Shelly *et al.*, 1998

TAYLORISM

The classical theory of management derived from the work of Frederick Taylor's book *Principles of Scientific Management*.

At the turn of the twentieth century, Taylor and others sought to devise principles from what they observed, that could be communicated to a rising class of managers. They borrowed from the rationalism of their day, such as the work of the sociologist Max Weber, to explain management as a logical process of optimization for the goals of the business. Management is presented as a series of problems for which solutions can be found. For example, the division of labour should be systematically structured so that it operates most effectively and efficiently, notably, in Taylorism, by the establishment of a working class equipped for operations and a managerial class equipped for administration and decision making. Taylorism is also characterized by respect for authority in companies and the use of financial remuneration alone. Today, Taylorism is not fashionable. Indeed, some would say it is unethical, with its scientific treatment of workers as production units and managers as rational robots.

See also: **Management, Rationalization**

Further reading: Taylor, 1911; Wren, 1979

TECHNOLOGY

In general, the use of applied sciences for the purposes of business. In particular, tools and devices that automate operations.

In common use, computers dominate references to technology, but in business studies technology has a much wider application. At a basic economic level, technology is that which is deployed by labour to convert land into commercial outputs. Technology therefore includes controls and tactics as well as computers and tools.

From what has been said it can be seen that the study of technology is fundamental to understanding economic growth. Technological progress is defined according to the productivity curve that relates inputs to outputs: as productivity increases technology can be said to progress. It is increasingly common, particularly in organizational studies, to regard technology as both external to the organization, that is autonomous with predictable consequences if applied to the organization, and integral to the organization itself, that is itself changing upon being applied to an organizational setting as well as changing the organization too. The latter case reflects the empirical evidence that the impact of technological innovation is complex and not always easily controlled, and is commensurate with the study of organizations as open systems, that is entities which adapt according to their environment. The study of the implementation of technology tries to integrate these various sociological factors. For example, it is widely acknowledged that technology can be perceived as a threat by a workforce, because it automates and therefore tends to reduce headcounts. However, another way of seeing the problem is to realize that technological change carries sociological change with it, and that both elements need to be managed in any particular project.

Technology is also subject to institutional controls such as the interests that govern research or the competitive forces that bring a technology to market. This means that technological superiority is only one factor in determining which technology will actually prevail.

Technology transfer is an increasingly important issue for international business. It describes the process by which technologies typically developed in the West are migrated for application in developing parts of the world. Technology transfer may be hindered by social and legal issues as well as purely technological ones, such as immature local technology infrastructures.

Technology is usually thought of as the application of science, science being the total body of physical knowledge that exists to be discovered. Science discovers the laws of nature and technologists apply them to particular problems. However, this is inadequate according to some theorists who try to understand how human beings make technological advances. They see technological advances as occurring in discrete steps rather than continuously: advances are made and the market develops standard versions of the new technology so that the old can be replaced with greatest application and least risk. The opposite theoretical idea therefore, after Heidegger, is to regard science as the abstraction of technology, which is itself primary as the bending of nature for the ends of human beings. This approach is also more powerful in an age that is wary of the abuses of technology, evidenced by human alienation or environmental damage.

For convenience, technology is often broken down into a number of different types. Common ones include information technology, that is electronic systems which handle data; process technology, that is the knowledge embedded in organizational systems; and object technology, which represents the knowledge embodied in objects such as tools, devices and machines. Technology is therefore a fundamental component of the value chain. However, although when first adopted by an organization technology's contribution to the value chain can be in the competitive advantage it provides, because technology tends to standardize across the market, the value it brings in the long term is more to do with the networks and partnerships it allows to be formed, that is the extension and deepening of the value chain. It is for this reason that companies feel a more or less constant imperative to invest in technological advances for fear of being excluded from the marketplace.

See also: **Automation, Productivity**

Further reading: Bijker *et al.*, 1987; Noble, 1984; Rosenbloom and Burgelman, 1989

TELECOMMUNICATIONS

The science and practice of exchanging information over a distance using the international network of land lines, terrestrial and satellite aerials, and devices including telephones, fax machines and PCs.

A number of physical characteristics define the kind of communication that is offered over telecommunications networks. For example, a switched network is one in which a user effectively opens up a dedicated connection between themselves and another for the duration of the communication. Such is the telephone. An unswitched network is online to multiple communicants continuously. Such is the internet. Broadcasting is the transmission of information to many simultaneous receivers that may or may not choose to pick up the signal. Radio and television fall into this category. Narrow-casting has a well defined body of receivers in view. Some websites can be thought of in this way. Interactivity, that is the ability to transmit as well as receive information, also varies according to technology. Because of the legacy of protocols that evolved for the sending and receiving of different kinds of telecommunication, be that voice, data or video, there is a major developmental effort under way to establish networks that can simultaneously cope with all three. With this so-called convergence, new economies of scale as well as new communications devices will become more widely available.

Apart from the technology itself, the defining issue of the telecommunications industry is regulation. The problem stems in migrating from the national monopolies that dominated the industry until recently to a marketplace of open competition for products and services. In Europe, for example, the liberalization of the telecommunications industry was still under way in the 1990s. The 1996 EU Telecommunications Liberalization Directive, for example, opened up international licences to new operators. In the UK, the monopoly that BT has on the final section of telephone line into domestic residences is still being unravelled at the time of writing.

This has stunted the growth of a number of new telecommunications services, notably unmetred access to the internet, since BT charges ISPs (internet service providers) for use per unit of time. However, the situation has changed dramatically in the last ten years, from one in which, typically, the market was controlled by what Hall *et al.* call a 'ménage à trois' of monopolistic operator, regulator and national government, to a dynamic environment in which the ménage is being broken up by independent market players such as mobile operators and anticompetitive enforcement bodies, allowing increasing space for new market entrants to compete. Indeed, the situation has become something of a political imperative. Consumers are demanding greater bandwidth online, and industry is complaining that restrictive telecommunications stifles productivity. Hall *et al.* see the regulatory issue as far from complete as aggressively competitive industry players work to seize market share. It is inevitable in an industry that effectively 'kills distance', that the issue will move from one that is played out on the national stage to one played out on the international stage. Not only will operators become international, but regulators will too, creating all sorts of problems from conflicts with bodies protecting national interests to conflicts between players who resort to litigious methods to advance their own interests.

See also: **Information and communications technology**

Further reading: Davis, 1997; Hall *et al.*, 2000

THIN MARKET

A market characterized by inactivity on the part of buyers and sellers.

Apart from hindering the transmission of value, thin markets do not operate efficiently in terms of setting prices. They therefore stifle the ability of businesses to generate profits, as well as simply reducing revenues. Thin markets may arise for a number of reasons. Seasonal variations may mean that markets thin out for limited periods only. Other markets are particularly susceptible to consumer attitudes, and so may grind to a halt if macroeconomic factors bring about a state of general nervousness. The housing market is a good example.

TIME TO MARKET

The period that elapses from the conception of a product to the point at which it generates profits.

Time to market is an important measure of the return that can be expected from the investment in new or upgraded products and services. It has become a particularly critical issue in the face of fast-paced and competitive environments. For example, in the IT sector, a company that cannot get its product to market quickly enough may find its investment rendered obsolete, since the technology upon which the product depends has been surpassed. A number of techniques are deployed to reduce time to market, including rapid prototyping, which collapses the development phase into the marketing phase so that a product is fine tuned for consumer reception more quickly.

See also: **R&D**

TOKENISM

The practice of employing a small number of individuals from minority groups to give the appearance of being anti-discriminatory.

Tokenism is merely a cynical exercise on the part of managers when it is done knowingly and only for show. However, it is a more widespread problem when organizations genuinely seeking to break up the dominance of certain demographic groups find they are not actually addressing the underlying issues. For example, positive discrimination, the practice of insisting that minorities are represented on shortlists, can become tokenistic. The failure here is the confusion of statistical results, that show the employee population merely reflecting the population of society at large, with actual changes to the organizational structures that give rise to the discrimination.

See also: **Discrimination, Glass ceiling**

Further reading: Good, 1998; Karake-Shalhoub, 1999; Maddock, 1999; Peters *et al.*, 1998; Wolkinson and Block, 1996

TOTAL CAPACITY MANAGEMENT

The effort to optimize the volume of goods that a company produces by understanding the role of unused, excess and idle capacity.

Determining operational capacity is a surprisingly tricky business. Many companies simply run at levels that are based upon past experience. But cost accounting methodologies in recent years have brought techniques to bear upon the scientific analysis of capacity. Total capacity management also brings many of the insights of value creation to the issue, and in this sense is similar to total quality management in attending to the minutiae of processes. The result is a number of models according to which capacity can be managed.

See also: **Inventory, Logistics, Operations management and strategy, Processes**

Further reading: McNair and Vangermeersch, 1998

TOTAL QUALITY MANAGEMENT

A quality management system that aims to enhance quality across all parts of the organization.

Dale and Bunney define it in the following way. TQM

> requires that the principles of quality management should be applied at every branch and at every level of the organization. ... The spread of the TQM philosophy would also be expected to be accompanied by greater sophistication in the application of tools and techniques and increased emphasis on people. The process will also extend beyond the organization to include partnerships with suppliers and customers. Activities will be reorientated to focus on the customer, internal and external.

They point out that TQM needs a number of key elements to work. Since it covers the whole enterprise, the commitment and leadership of senior management are required. TQM needs to be incorporated into the strategic planning of the organization, having a bearing upon other projects as well as implementing and improving measures specifically associated with quality. Employee involvement is essential, since it is employees who will use quality techniques and tools most intimately. Feedback is also key, since TQM is not a one-off project but a continuous process within the organization.

Robert Flood has devised eleven steps to TQM. They are:

1 developing an understanding of organization design and organizational behaviour
2 setting up a steering committee
3 setting organizational mission
4 setting up layers of Quality Councils
5 designing or choosing educational modules
6 setting up local missions
7 undertaking customer analysis
8 choosing projects for implementation
9 choosing tools for implementation
10 implementing educational and communications elements
11 implementing projects

See also: **Processes, Quality**

Further reading: Bank, 2000; Dale and Bunney, 1999; Flood, 1993; Madu, 1998; Stahl, 1999

TRAINING

The process of educating employees in new skills.

Orridge draws a distinction between education and training, which does serve to highlight the demands made by the latter: 'Education is concerned with the transfer of information or knowledge whilst training should not only impart knowledge but also develop skills and change attitudes.' He stresses the need for both management and specialist training staff to be involved in a structured approach. This is aimed at putting the aims of the employee and the goals of the organization on the same trajectory when it comes to acquiring skills, knowledge, experience and attitudes for the betterment of organizational performance and personal satisfaction. Training should be part of 'business as usual' within the organization, sponsored and driven by management, and devised to have measurable returns. Orridge also believes that training tends to be regarded as a secondary activity in many companies because of short-term attitudes or because not enough value is placed in staff. Management should therefore develop a proactive stance towards training that works to identify how people learn and what training they need, regardless of their position in the organization.

The benefits of training will then become evident. The organization, both collectively and at an individual level, will be better equipped to compete in a commercial environment of continuous change. Even if change is not a major concern, training, it is argued, enhances effectiveness since it works to bring personal skills and corporate goals into closer alignment. And at the very least, no successful business can afford to be complacent: companies do not hold on to other assets that do not grow. Why would they believe that staff should not develop too?

See also: **Human resources management, Learning organization**

Further reading: Boud and Garrick, 1999; Bruce and Wyman, 1998; Dunn and Dunn, 1998; Haskell, 1998; Orridge, 1998

TRANSFER PRICING

A notional amount that is charged for a product or service when it is bought or sold within the organization.

Transfer pricing is an accounting device that is used in a variety of situations. For example, if a large organization has developed shared cost centres, that is units which seek to realize economies of scale by offering services that are commonly used by many others, transfer pricing may be deployed. An alternative instance is profit centres, artificially created units within an organization that can then be held responsible for their own profitability. Transfer pricing can also be used as a tax avoidance measure when the profits of one subsidiary are accounted to another operating in a more favourable tax regime.

See also: **Accounting, Holding company**

TROUBLESHOOTING

The identification and correction of faults in the value chain.

Troubleshooting is usually taken to be a specialist job undertaken by one or more troubleshooters. The value these individuals bring to the analysis of a problem is the external perspective, since many process problems are confused with the vested interests of those concerned. Troubleshooting is therefore a limited activity, that aims quickly to identify and suggest remedies for the problem. When the troubleshooter is also briefed to correct a problem they need to be given the appropriate authority to do so. Their skills are similar to those required in crisis management, the difference being that the troubleshooter is also an outsider.

See also: **Crisis management**

UNITED NATIONS TRADE BODIES

A series of supranational organizations, sponsored by signatories of the United Nations, that aim to promote international trade.

The United Nations Centre on Transnational Corporations works to promote international standards and processes in accounting and reporting. It was established in 1974.

The United Nations Commission on International Trade Law (UNCITRAL) seeks to tackle the problems associated with differences in national legal regimes faced by companies operating between them. It is involved in disputes in international shipping, the protection afforded by and the enforcement of import and export licences. The overall aim is to reduce the confusion that is caused when individual nations rule on these matters without referring to the international community. It was established in 1966.

The United Nations Convention on Contracts for the International Sale of Goods (UNCISG) was first signed by some countries in 1980, and aims to standardize issues in import and export contracts.

The success of these and other UN initiatives is hotly debated. Some, for example, would argue that more success can be gained by regional bodies, such as the EU, or with agreements aimed at specific ends rather than as part of the work of larger bodies. Examples here are the North American Free Trade Agreement (NAFTA) which extends over America, Canada and Mexico, or the General Agreement on Tariffs and Trade (GATT) that led to the establishment of the World Trade Organization (WTO) in 1994 by a process of evolution and with more clout as a result. What is certain is that international trade disputes are set to continue and grow as more and more companies operate internationally.

See also: **Economic and Monetary Union**

Further reading: Helms, 1999; Litka, 1991; O'Connell, 1997; Wartick and Wood, 1998

UTILITY

The condition of being useful or profitable.

The utility of an item is therefore an informal measure of the extent to which it performs the function for which it was designed. Utility theory is a tool used in risk analysis to see how utility is assessed in a risk environment, the idea being that the actual utility of various positions can often be lost when set against factors such as the general attitude towards risk that the individual or organization has. Utilitarianism is the doctrine that actions are morally right if they benefit a majority or simply are useful, often associated with the writings of Jeremy Bentham.

See also: **Ethics, Risk**

VALUE

The perceived worth, desirability or utility of a good.

Value is one of those business concepts that tends to be over-employed, and to apparently cynical ends, in line with the Wildean substitution of price for value. The problem is that the concept of value is often confused because of the intrinsic difference between value and price (as in the consumer's question about getting value for money). On the one hand is the sense of value as the subjective measure of a item's worth that depends upon time, place, fashion and need. But value is also built on objective attributes such as quality, reputation and service. Companies can plan to increase the value of their products by improving on these objective attributes. Inflating the price because an item's subjective value will carry it is merely opportunistic.

Value is deliberately enhanced so as to be able to increase price by addressing issues of quality and service during production and sales. At any point in the process something may be altered, added to or omitted in order to increase the marginal value of the product or reduce its marginal cost. The sum total of processes is therefore called the value chain, a concept invented by Michael Porter in *Competitive Advantage: Creating and Sustaining Superior Performance.*

Value-based management is the result of the attempts to place this slippery subject at the heart of the organization. It is often presented as the next phase in the evolution of strategic management. Strategic management is about satisfying customers and performing well in markets whilst also staying one step ahead of competitors. Value-based management argues that the way to do this is to train the organization in the ways of value creation, in other words driving processes to add value at every stage. The additional element is that value-based management is defined as not only that which increases shareholder value, essentially increasing the returns upon investor capital, but that which builds value for customers and even for employees too. The idea is that the value-based company climbs a virtuous spiral on which investing and rewarding employees leads to better products and services, which leads to happier and more numerous customers, which leads to increased returns for investors.

Contrary to what was said above, value-based management is, according to Hedley (writing in Donovan *et al.*), actually a way of eliminating cynical attitudes in the organization, what he calls 'depoliticizing' the management process by identifying with the common aim of value maximization. The point is that value originates outside the organization, from the customer. It therefore provides an objective goal that motivates at an individual level without reference to the abilities or vision of management, which are so often experienced as limiting and frustrating. The trick is to know how to generate value in practice. According to Hedley this is more than just a trick pulled off by the advertising department, but is manifest in a management methodology, with tangible plans and means of assessment.

Whether the contemporary discovery of value is anything more than the reinvention of the traditional wheels on which business runs, that is price, performance, products and profit, time will tell. And it may have done little harm if that is all it is.

See also: **Brand, Economics, Marketing, Price, Quality, Processes**

Further reading: Bititci and Carrie, 1998; Brimson, 1999; Donovan *et al.*, 1998; Gomez, 1999; Lanning, 1998; Macredie *et al.*, 1998; Porter, 1998a

VENTURE CAPITAL

The money that is invested to start a new business or boost a young one.

Also called risk capital, venture capital is associated with high levels of risk since new businesses are unproven. Venture capital may come from a wealthy individual, also called an 'angel', or from a venture capital fund. Managed by venture capitalists, these businesses offset their risk by investing in a portfolio of new ventures on the expectation that whilst many may fail, a few will succeed with dramatic returns on the capital invested. Returns are expected in terms of capital gains, so companies with very high growth potentials are ideal for venture funding. Alternatively, a venture capital fund will also invest less speculatively, notably in established companies, to reduce the risk that it carries overall.

Venture capitalists bring more to the party than just money. They are often successful entrepreneurs in their own right and so bring that experience to bear upon the new venture, as well as moral support and industry contacts. However, as organizations that are particularly susceptible to the personalities of the key players, clashes between the different interests of those merely investing money and those for whom the venture represents their life and soul can raise the stakes.

At a macroeconomic level, venture capital plays different roles in economies from place to place. But it is closely associated with the entrepreneurial spirit that characterizes the American economy in particular. General George Doriot is sometimes called the father of modern American venture capital, following his investment in a company that became one of the early corporate computer giants, Digital Equipment Corporation. His $70,000 investment in 1957 was worth $355 million by the time it was sold in 1971. This kind of story is repeated many times over, so that the availability of venture capital is closely identified with the growth in the American economy since World War II. Having said that, it was not until the 1980s that the industry properly established itself, with the total amount of venture capital under management rising to tens of billions, enough to contribute significantly to a national Western economy.

The quintessential venture environment is Silicon Valley, where a concentration of high-tech companies celebrates the combined attitudes of business failure as an inevitable event on the path to success, and entrepreneurial risk which would in many other parts of the world be regarded as a gung-ho investment of venture capital. It is for this reason that a certain amount of schadenfreude was evident in the collapse of the so-called dotcoms.

Timmons advises entrepreneurs today to watch out for a number of factors in potential investors. Screening investors is important, since investors will have different attitudes towards the stage of development that the business is at, the kind of technology that will drive the growth, and the capital amounts required. Older funds are less likely to be actively investing, although they may take the time to investigate a proposal and put it on their books. Venture capitalists can also be very important when it comes to arranging future financing and generally building the market's confidence in the new company.

See also: **Entrepreneurship**

Further reading: Timmons, 1999

VERTICAL INTEGRATION

The assimilation of additional parts of the value chain into the organization.

Vertical integration usually refers to the acquisition of companies that perform other stages in the production or sales process. For example, a chain of high street shops may purchase a manufacturer in order to produce own-brand goods. The benefits vertical integration may bring are varied. The organization may be able to exert more control over processes and so develop competitive advantage. The exercise may simply be one of cutting costs.

Vertical integration has fallen somewhat out of fashion recently, with the emphasis on developing core skills and opting for outsourcing. The term can also be used in a less rigorous sense to describe management efforts to tighten up processes within a single organization.

See also: **Core competency, M&As, Outsourcing**

VIRTUAL CORPORATION

A company that employs only two factors of production, labour and capital.

Strictly speaking virtual organizations have no physical manifestation. In particular, they have no centralized offices. Instead the place of work and any other land resources that the virtual organization needs are devolved to individuals who work for the organization or to other companies that supply services. To put it another way, the virtual organization is the extreme case of an outsourcing policy in which every function is outsourced and the organization only exists as an entity that links these units together. Virtual organizations have become possible with advances in information technology. The company can exist because communication between its parts does not require any physical proximity, but can be carried out by electronic interaction. In reality, there are few cases of genuinely virtual organizations, but the term is used more loosely to describe the increasingly common phenomenon in which a brand heads up an organization that consists of many partner firms, linked electronically, to provide a service. Application Service Providers (ASPs) are a good example.

See also: **Information and communications technology, Outsourcing**

Further reading: Haywood, 1998; Lock, 1998

VOCATION

Employment to which an individual is particularly led because of personal calling or commitment.

Whilst vocation is increasingly used to refer to many kinds of profession or occupations in general, it traditionally referred to work that was dedicated to a particular mission, such as medicine or the church, or to work that was dedicated to a particular craft, such as painting or furniture making. The reason for the more general use stems from trends in human resources that are much more focused on the needs of the individual as well as those of the organization. So, vocational training is geared towards particular skills or future goals. The term is also used to refer to the increasing number of people who work self-employed or under various kinds of flexible contract.

See also: **Human resources management, Training**

WHISTLEBLOWING

The act of informing on an individual or activity to senior management.

Whistleblowing often carries pejorative connotations. However, increasingly it is encouraged as an invaluable means of halting a variety of activities that could be damaging to the organization. But it poses a number of legal, ethical and strategic dilemmas. Although whistleblowers are often model employees, they frequently suffer as a result. Legal protection is rarely available, although it is more common in the US. Best practices are hard to establish, but will include the need for reasonable evidence, and that the activity being revealed is dangerous, corrupt or involves mismanagement. Proper procedures for dealing with the complaint, including protection of the whistleblower, are also important. Written policies can also help to identify whether a whistleblower merely harbours a vendetta or is raising a genuine problem about company operations.

Further reading: Miethe, 1999; Vinten, 1994

YIELD

The output returned by land, labour or capital.

Although yield is most commonly used to refer to the return on a capital investment, typically calculated as a percentage of the profit over the initial investment, it can also refer to the output that is achieved from a physical resource, such as land farmed, or the output achieved by a workforce, that is employee performance.

In the case of capital investment a number of derivative uses pertain. The yield rate is the return over time. The yield to maturity is the amount gained when the investment matures. Yield variance is the difference between the expected return and the actual return.

See also: **Finance, Return**

Further reading: Oakshott, 1998; Paxson and Wood, 1997; Vandermerwe, 1999

ZERO-BASED BUDGETING

The calculation of financial needs afresh rather than basing upon previous estimates or usage.

Most items in a budget will be calculated by simply adding an increment to the amount in the last budget. However, zero-based budgeting does not make the assumption that the incremental value represents a realistic sum for the forthcoming period, and so works it out from basic principles. Apart from the likelihood that this will produce a more accurate budget, zero-based budgeting brings other benefits too. For example, it requires that all items be carefully justified. It also avoids the situation in which, because the amount set for the forthcoming period depends upon the amount spent previously, money is spent simply to sustain budgetary funding. Drawbacks to zero-based budgeting include the time taken to arrive at the estimates, as well as the fact that some budgetary values are in fact best derived by incremental methods.

See also: **Accounting**

ZERO-SUM GAME

A scenario in which for every winner there is an equal and opposite loser.

A zero-sum game is a particular situation within game theory. Consider the example of a saturated market. Activity within this environment is a zero-sum game because for every extra unit of market share gained by one player, a unit of market share must be lost by someone else. Another real-life situation that approximates to a zero-sum game is a static market, that is one in which there is no growth.

See also: **Game theory, Saturation**

BIBLIOGRAPHY

Aaker, D.A., Kumar, V. and Day, G.S. (1998) *Marketing Research*, 6th edn, Chichester: John Wiley.

Abe, J.M., Dempsey, P.E. and Bassett, D.A. (1998) *Business Ecology: Giving Your Organization the Natural Edge*, Oxford: Butterworth-Heinemann.

Ackoff, R.L. (1999a) *Ackoff's Best: His Classic Writings on Management*, Chichester: John Wiley.

——(1999b) *Re-creating the Corporation: A Design of Organisations for the 21st Century*, Oxford: Oxford University Press.

Adler, R.B. and Elmhorst, J.M. (1999) *Communicating at Work: Principles and Practices for Business and the Professions*, London: McGraw-Hill College.

Afuah, A. (1998) *Innovation Management: Strategies, Implementation and Profits*, Oxford: Oxford University Press.

Ali, M. (1998) *Practical Marketing and PR for the Small Business*, London: Kogan Page.

Allen, C., Kania, D. and Yaeckel, B. (1998) *Internet World Guide to One-to-one Web Marketing*, Chichester: Wiley Computer Publishing.

Altman, E. (1993) *Corporate Financial Distress and Bankruptcy*, New York: John Wiley.

Alvarez, J.L. (ed.) (1998) *The Diffusion and Consumption of Business Knowledge*, Basingstoke: Macmillan.

Anacona, A., Kochan, T., Scully, J., Van Maanen, J., Westney, A. (1999) *Organisational Behaviour and Processes*, Cincinnati: South-Western College Publishing.

Analoui, F. (ed.) (1998) *Human Resource Management Issues in Developing Countries*, Aldershot: Ashgate.

Anastasi, A. (1988) *Psychological Testing*, New York: Macmillan.

Andersen, E.S., Grude, K.V. and Haug, T. (1999) *Goal Oriented Project Management: Effective Techniques and Strategies*, 2nd edn, London: Kogan Page.

Antony, J. and Kaye, M. (2000) *Experimental Quality: A Strategic Approach to Achieve and Improve Quality*, London: Kluwer.

Armstrong, M. and Baron, A. (1998) *Performance Management: The New Realities*, London: Institute of Personnel and Development.

Armstrong, M. and Murlis, H. (1998) *Reward Management: A Handbook of Remuneration, Strategy and Practice*, 4th edn, London: Kogan Page.

Arnold, J.R.T. (1998) *Introduction to Materials Management*, 3rd edn, Upper Saddle River: Prentice Hall.

Aronson, J.E. and Zionts, S. (eds) (1998) *Operations Research: Methods, Models, and Applications*, London: Quorum Books.

Ashkanasy, N.M., Wilderom, C.P.M. and Peterson, M.F. (eds) (2000) *Handbook of Organizational Culture and Climate,* London: Sage.

Ashton, A.H. and Ashton, R.H. (eds) (1994) *Judgement and Decision Research in Accounting and Auditing*, Cambridge: Cambridge University Press.

Baets, W.R.J. (1998) *Organisational Learning and Knowledge Technologies in a Dynamic Environment*, London: Kluwer.

Bail, D.G. and Pepper, L.C. (1993) *Business Fluctuation: Forecasting Technique and Application*, 2nd edn, Englewood Cliffs: Prentice Hall.

Bain, J.S. (1956) *Barriers to New Competition*, Cambridge, MA: Harvard University Press.

Bakker, H.J.C. and Helmink, J.W.A. (2000) *Succesfully Integrating Two Businesses*, Aldershot: Gower.

Balachandran, S. (1999) *Customer-Driven Services Management*, London: Sage.

Ball, D. and McCulloch, W. (1999) *International Business: The Challenge of Global Competition*, London: Irwin McGraw-Hill.

Bank, J. (2000) *The Essence of Total Quality Management*, 2nd edn, Harlow: Pearson Education.

Baron, J.N. and Kreps, D.M. (1999) *Strategic Human Resources: Frameworks for General Managers*, Chichester: John Wiley.

Barthes, R. (1967) *Elements of Semiology*, trans. A. Lavers and C. Smith, New York: Hill & Wang.

Bartlett, C.A. and Ghoshal, S. (2000) *Transnational Management: Text, Cases, and Readings in Cross-border Management*, 3rd edn, London: Irwin McGraw-Hill.

Bass, B.M. (1990) *Handbook of Leadership: A Survey of Theory and Research*, New York: Free Press.

Bateson, J.E.G. and Hoffman, K.D. (1999) *Managing Services Marketing: Texts and Readings*, London: Dryden Press.

Beauchamp, T.L. (ed.) (1999) *Case Studies in Business, Society, and Ethics*, Upper Saddle River: Prentice Hall.

Beckford, J. (1998) *Quality: A Critical Introduction*, London: Routledge.

Beechler, S. and Stucker, K. (eds) (1998) *Japanese Business: Critical Perspectives on Business and Management*, 4 vols, London: Routledge.

Belch, G.E. and Belch, M.A. (1998) *Advertising and Promotion: An Integrated Marketing Communication Perspective*, 4th edn, Boston: McGraw-Hill.

Bell, T.B. and Wright, A. (eds) (1995) *Auditing Practice, Research and Education: A Productive Collaboration*, Washington DC: American Accounting Association, Auditing Section.

Bendell, T., Boulter, L. and Goodstadt, P. (1998) *Benchmarking for Competitive Advantage*, 2nd edn, London: Pitman.

Bentley, T. and Clayton, S. (1998) *Profiting from Diversity*, Aldershot: Gower.

Berman, B. and Evans, J.R. (1998) *Retail Management: A Strategic Approach*, 7th edn, Upper Saddle River: Prentice Hall.

Bernardin, H.J. and Russell, J.E.A. (1998) *Human Resource Management: An Experiential Approach*, London: Irwin McGraw-Hill.

Berry, M. (1998) *The New Integrated Direct Marketing*, Aldershot: Gower.

Bertalanffy, L. von (1975) *Perspectives on General System Theory*, New York: George Braziller.

Betteriss, M. (ed.) (1998) *Re-Inventing HR: Changing Roles to Create the High-performance Organisation*, Chichester: John Wiley.

Bhidé, A.V. (2000) *The Origin and Evolution of New Businesses*, Oxford: Oxford University Press.

Bidgoli, H. (1999) *Handbook of Management Information Systems: A Managerial Perspective*, London: Academic Press.

Bijker, W.E., Hughes, T.P. and Pinch, T.J. (1987) *The Social Construction of Technological Systems: New Directions in the Sociology and History of Technology*, Cambridge MA: MIT Press.

Billis, D. and Harris, M. (eds) (1996) *Voluntary Agencies: Challenges of Organisation and Management*, Basingstoke: Macmillan.

Birkinshaw, J. (2000) *Entrepreneurship in the Global Firm*, London: Sage.

Birkinshaw, J. and Hagström, P. (2000) *The Flexible Firm: Capability Management in Network Organisations*, Oxford: Oxford University Press.

Birn, R.J. (1999) *The Effective Use of Market Research: A Guide for Management to Grow the Business*, 3rd edn, London: Kogan Page.

Bishop, M., Evans, J., Hughes, M. and Woods, M.M. (1999) *Financial Reporting, Analysis and Planning*, 2nd edn, Canterbury: CIB Publishing.

Bititci, U.S. and Carrie, A.S. (eds) (1998) *Strategic Management of the Manufacturing Value Chain*, London: Kluwer.

Bland, M. (1998) *Communicating out of a Crisis*, London: Macmillan Business.

Boaz, D. (ed.) (1998) *The Libertarian Reader: Classic and Contemporary Writings from Lao-Tzu to Milton Friedman*, New York: Free Press.

Boddy, D. and Paton, R. (1998) *Management: An Introduction*, London: Prentice Hall.

Bogan, C.E. and English, M.J. (1994) *Benchmarking for Best Practices, Winning through Innovative Adaptation*, New York: McGraw-Hill.

Boston Consulting Group (1971) *Growth and Financial Strategies*, Boston MA: Boston Consulting Group.

Boud, D. and Garrick, J. (eds) (1999) *Understanding Learning at Work*, London: Routledge.

Bowie, N. and Freeman, R.E. (eds) (1992) *Ethics and Agency Theory*, New York: Oxford University Press.

Boyett, J.H. and Boyett, J.T. (1998) *The Guru Guide: The Best Ideas of the Top Management Thinkers*, Chichester: John Wiley.

Branch, M.C. (1998) *Comprehensive Planning for the 21st Century: General Theory and Principles*, London: Praeger.

Brickley, J.A., Smith, C.W. Jr and Zimmerman, J.L. (2001) *Managerial Economics and Organizational Architecture*, 2nd edn, London: Irwin McGraw-Hill.

Brierly, S. (1995) *The Advertising Handbook*, London: Routledge.

Brimson, J.A. (1999) *Driving Value Using Activity-based Budgeting*, Chichester: John Wiley.

Brinckerhoff, P.C. (2000) *Social Entrepreneurship: The Art of Mission-based Venture Development*, Chichester: John Wiley.

Bristow, N., Buckner, K., Folkman, J. and McKinnon, P. (1999) *The Leadership Skills Audit: A Guide to Measuring and Improving the Effectiveness of Leaders at Every Level in Your Organisation*, Cambridge: Cambridge Strategy Publications.

Brooks, I. and Weatherston, J. (2000) *The Business Environment: Challenges and Changes*, 2nd edn, Harlow: Pearson Education.

Brown, A.D. (1999) *The Six Dimensions of Leadership*, London: Random House.

Bruce, R. and Wyman, S. (1998) *Changing Organizations: Practicing Action Training and Research*, London: Sage.

Buckley, P.J. (1998) *International Strategic Management and Government Policy*, Basingstoke: Macmillan.

Burnett, R. (1998) *Outsourcing IT: The Legal Aspects*, Aldershot: Gower.

Butler, R.J. and Wilson, D.C. (1989) *Managing Voluntary and Non-profit Organisations: Strategy and Structure*, London: Routledge.

Cabena, P., Hadjinian, P., Stadler, R., Verhees, J. and Zanasi, A. (1998) *Discovering Data Mining: From Concept to Implementation*, Upper Saddle River: Prentice Hall.

Callaway, R.L. (1999) *The Realities of Management: A View from the Trenches*, London: Quorum Books.

Cameron, K. and Whetten, D.A. (1983) *Organisational Effectiveness: A Comparison of Multiple Models*, New York: Academic Press.

Campbell, A. and Goold, M. (1998) *Synergy: Why Links between Business Units Often Fail and How to Make Them Work*, Oxford: Capstone.

Campkin, P., Duncan, W. and Morgan, D. (1999) *The Operating Environment*, London: Pitman.

Cappells, T.M. (1999) *Financially Focused Quality*, London: St Lucie Press.

Carnall, C.A. (1999) *Managing Change in Organizations*, 3rd edn, Hemel Hempstead: Prentice Hall Europe.

Carroll, T. (1998) *The Role of the Finance Director*, 2nd edn, London: Financial Times Management.

Carter, R.L. (1983) *Reinsurance*, 2nd edn, Brentford: Kluwer.

Carter, S. (1999) *Renaissance Management: The Rebirth of Energy and Innovation in People and Organisations*, London: Kogan Page.

Carysforth, C. (1998) *Communication for Work*, Oxford: Heinemann.

Castells, M. (1998) *The Networked Age*, 3 vols, Oxford: Blackwell.

Chandler, A.D. (1962) *Strategy and Structure: Chapters in the History of the Industrial Enterprise*, Cambridge MA: MIT Press.

Chandler, A.D. Jr, Hagström, P. and Sölvell, Ö. (1998) *The Dynamic Firm: The Role of Technology, Strategy, Organization and Regions*, Oxford: Oxford University Press.

Channon, D.F. (ed.) (1997) *The Blackwell Encyclopedic Dictionary of Strategic Management*, Oxford: Blackwell.

Chase, R.B., Aquilano, N.J. and Jacobs, F.R. (1998) *Production and Operations Management: Manufacturing and Services*, London: Irwin McGraw-Hill.

Chen, H.T. (1991) *Theory-Driven Evaluations*, Newbury Park CA: Sage.

Chernatony, L. de (ed.) (1998) *Brand Management*, Aldershot: Ashgate.

Chesworth, N. and Pine-Coffin, S. (1998) *The EMU Fact Book*, London: Kogan Page.

Chorafas, D.N. (2000) *Reliable Financial Reporting and Internal Control: A Global Implementation Guide*, Chichester: John Wiley.

Christopher, M. (1998) *Logistics and Supply Chain Management: Strategies for Reducing Cost and Improving Service*, 2nd edn, London: Pitman.

Christopher, M.G., Payne, A. and Ballantyne, D. (1991) *Relationship Marketing*, Oxford: Butterworth-Heinemann.

Clarke, T. and Clegg, S. (1998) *Changing Paradigms: The Transformation of Management Knowledge for the 21st Century*, London: HarperCollins Business.

Clegg, B. and Birch, P, (1998) *DisOrganization: The Handbook of Creative Organizational Change*, London: Pitman.

Cleland, D.I. (1999) *Project Management: Strategic Design and Implementation*, 3rd edn, London: McGraw-Hill.

Clemente, M.N. and Greenspan, D.S. (1998) *Winning at Mergers and Acquisitions: The Guide to Market-focused Planning and Integration*, Chichester: John Wiley.

Clements-Croome, D. (ed.) (2000) *Creating the Productive Workplace*, London: E. & F.N. Spon.

Codling, S. (1998) *Benchmarking*, Aldershot: Gower.

Coen, D. (1997) 'The European business lobby', *Business Strategy Review*, 8(4): 17–25.

Cohen, S.S. and Boyd, G. (2000) *Corporate Governance and Globalisation: Long Range Planning Issues*, Cheltenham: Edward Elgar.

Cole, R.E. and Scott, W.R. (eds) (2000) *The Quality Movement and Organization Theory*, London: Sage.

Collins, D. (1998) *Organizational Change: Sociological Perspectives*, London: Routledge.

Compaine, B.M. and Read, W.H. (eds) (1999) *The Information Resources Policy Handbook: Research for the Information Age*, Cambridge MA: MIT Press.

Conger, J.A. and Kanungo, R.N. (1998) *Charismatic Leadership in Organizations*, London: Sage.

Conway, C. (1998) *Strategies for Mentoring: A Blueprint for Successful Organizational Development*, Chichester: John Wiley.

Cook, M.F. (1999) *Outsourcing Human Resources Functions: Strategies for Providing Enhanced HR Services at Lower Cost*, New York: AMACOM.

Cooper, C.L. and Argyris, C. (eds) (1998) *The Concise Blackwell Encyclopedia of Management*, Oxford: Blackwell.

Cooper, C.L. and Robertson, I.T. (eds) (1990), *International Review of Industrial Psychology*, Chichester: John Wiley.

Cooper, D. (1998) *Improving Safety Culture: A Practical Guide*, Chichester: John Wiley.

Cooper, D.R. and Schindler, P.S. (2001) *Business Research Methods*, 7th edn, New York: McGraw-Hill.

Corbett, E.N. and Wilson, J.R. (1995) *Evaluation of Human Work: A Practical Ergonomics Methodology*, London: Taylor & Francis.

Cortada, J.W. (2001) *21st Century Business: Managing and Working in the New Digital Economy*, London: Prentice Hall.

Cosh, A. and Hughes, A. (eds) (1998) *Takeovers*, 3 vols, Aldershot: Ashgate.

Costin, H. (1998) *Readings in Strategy and Strategic Planning*, Fort Worth: Dryden Press.

Cox, A. (1997) *Business Success: A Way of Thinking about Strategy, Critical Supply Chain Assets and Operational Best Practice*, Bath: Earlsgate Press.

Cox, A., Harris, L. and Parker, D. (1999) *Privatisation and Supply Chain Management: On the Effective Alignment of Purchasing and Supply after Privatisation*, London: Routledge.

Craig-Lees, M., Joy, S. and Browne, B. (1995) *Consumer Behaviour*, Chichester: John Wiley.

Crainer, S. (1998) *Key Management Ideas: Thinkers That Changed the Management World*, London: Financial Times Management.

Creelman, J. (1998) *Building and Developing a Balanced Scorecard: International Best Practice in Strategy Implementation*, London: Business International.

Cronin, A.M. (2000) *Advertising and Consumer Citizenship: Gender, Image and Rights*, London: Routledge.

Cronje, G.J. de, Toit, G.S. du and Motlatla, M.D.C. (2000) *Introduction to Business Management*, 5th edn, Cape Town: Oxford University Press.

Cross, R. (1998) *Revenue Management: Hard-core Tactics for Profit-making and Market Domination*, London: Orion Books.

Cummins, J. (1998) *Sales Promotion: How to Create and Implement Campaigns That Really Work*, 2nd edn, London: Kogan Page.

Currie, W. and Galliers, B. (eds) (1999) *Rethinking Management Information Systems: An Interdisciplinary Perspective*, Oxford: Oxford University Press.

Cyert, R. and March, J. (1963) *A Behavioural Theory of the Firm*, Englewood Cliffs: Prentice Hall.

d'Herbemont, O. and César, B. (1998) *Managing Sensitive Projects: A Lateral Approach*, London: Macmillan Business.

Dale, B. and Bunney, H. (1999) *Total Quality Management Blueprint*, Oxford: Blackwell Business.

Dale, B. and Plunkett, J. (1999) *Quality Costing*, 3rd edn, Aldershot: Gower.

Dalrymple, D.J. and Cron, W.L. (1998) *Sales Management: Concepts and Cases*, Chichester: John Wiley.

Danford, A. (1999) *Japanese Management Techniques and British Workers*, London: Mansell.

Davenport, T.H. (1993) *Process Innovation: Reengineering Work through Information Technology*, Boston MA: Harvard Business School.

Davia, H.R., Coggins, P.C., Wideman, J.C. and Kastantin, J.T. (2000) *Accountant's Guide to Fraud Detection and Control*, Chichester: John Wiley.

Davidson, M.J. and Cooper, C.L. (1992) *Shattering the Glass Ceiling*, London: Paul Chapman.

Davies, A. (1999) *A Strategic Approach to Corporate Governance*, Aldershot: Gower.

Davies, M.A.P. (1998) *Understanding Marketing*, London: Prentice Hall.

Davis, D. (2000) *Business Research for Decision Making*, 5th edn, London: Duxbury.

Davis, E.P. (1992) *Debt, Financial Fragility, and Systemic Risk*, Oxford: Clarendon Press.

Davis, G.B. (ed.) (1997) *The Blackwell Encyclopedic Dictionary of Management Information Systems*, Oxford: Blackwell.

Davis, W. (1998) *Great Myths of Business*, revised paperback edn, London: Kogan Page.

Dawson, T. (1998) *Principles and Practice of Modern Management*, 2nd edn, London: Tudor.

Dearlove, D. (1998) *Key Management Decisions: Tools and Techniques of the Executive Decision-maker*, London: Pitman.

Dearlove, D. and Crainer, S. (1999) *The Ultimate Book of Business Brands: Insights from the World's 50 Greatest Brands*, Oxford: Capstone.

DeCenzo, D.A. and Robbins, S.P. (1999) *Human Resource Management*, 6th edn, Chichester: John Wiley.

Deering, A. and Murphy, A. (1998) *The Difference Engine: Achieving Powerful and Sustainable Partnering*, Aldershot: Gower.

Deise, M.V., Nowikow, C., King, P. and Wright, A. (2000) *Executive's Guide to E-Business: From Tactics to Strategy*, Chichester: John Wiley.

Denning, S.L. (1998) *The Practice of Workplace Participation: Management–Employee Relations at Three Participatory Firms*, London: Quorum Books.

Denton, J. (1998) *Organisational Learning and Effectiveness*, London: Routledge.

Dessler, G. (2000) *Human Resource Management*, 8th edn, Upper Saddle River: Prentice Hall.

——(2001) *Management: Leading People and Organizations in the 21st Century*, Upper Saddle River: Prentice Hall.

Dew, J.R. (1997) *Empowerment and Democracy in the Workplace: Applying Adult Education Theory and Practice for Cultivating Empowerment*, London: Quorum Books.

Diacon, S. (ed.) (1990) *A Guide to Insurance Management*, Basingstoke: Macmillan.

Dilworth, J.B. (2000) *Operations Management: Providing Value in Goods and Services*, 3rd edn, London: Dryden Press.

Dobson, J. (1999) *The Art of Management and the Aesthetic Manager: The Coming Way of Business*, London: Quorum Books.

Domberger, S. (1998) *The Contracting Organisation: A Strategic Guide to Outsourcing*, Oxford: Oxford University Press.

Donaldson, L. (1999) *Performance-driven Organizational Change*, London: Sage.

Donovan, J., Tully, R. and Wortman, B. (1998) *The Value Enterprise: Strategies for Building a Value-based Organisation*, London: McGraw-Hill Ryerson.

Dowell, D. (1998) *Understanding Business: The Connections Between Common Sense and Good Commercial Decisions*, London: Century Business.

Dowling, P.J., Welch, D.E. and Schuler, R.S. (1999) *International Human*

Resource Management: Managing People in a Multinational Context, 3rd edn, Cincinnati: South-Western College Publishing.

Doyle, P. (1998) *Marketing Management and Strategy,* 2nd edn, London: Prentice Hall Europe.

Doyle, P. and Bridgewater, S. (eds) (1998) *Innovation in Marketing,* Oxford: Butterworth-Heinemann.

Drucker, P. (1989) *The New Realities,* London: Mandarin.

Dubois, A. (1998) *Organising Industrial Activities Across Firm Boundaries,* London: Routledge.

Dubois, B. (2000) *Understanding the Consumer: A European Perspective,* London: Prentice Hall.

Duffuaa, S.O., Raouf, A. and Campbell, J.D. (1999) *Planning and Control of Maintenance Systems: Modeling and Analysis,* Chichester: John Wiley.

Dunn, R. and Dunn, K. (eds) (1998) *Practical Approaches to Individualizing Staff Development for Adults,* London: Praeger.

Dunnette, M.D. (1990) *Handbook of Industrial and Organizational Psychology,* 2nd edn, Palo Alto: Consulting Psychologists Press.

Dussauge, P. and Garrette, B. (1999) *Cooperative Strategy: Competing Successfully through Strategic Alliances,* Chichester: John Wiley.

Dutta, S. and Manzoni, J.F. (1999) *Process Reengineering, Organizational Change and Performance Management,* London: McGraw-Hill.

Dyson, R.G. and O'Brien, F.A. (eds) (1998) *Strategic Development: Methods and Models,* Chichester: John Wiley.

Ekelund, R.B. and Herbert, R.H. (1996) *A History of Economic Theory and Method,* 4th edn, New York: McGraw-Hill.

Elkouri, F. and Elkouri, E. (1985) *How Arbitration Works,* 4th edn, Washington DC: Bureau of National Affairs.

Ellis, S. and Dick, P. (2000) *Introduction to Organisational Behaviour,* London: McGraw-Hill.

Eltis, W. (2000) *Britain, Europe and EMU,* London: Palgrave.

Elton, E.J. and Gruber, M.J. (1995) *Modern Portfolio Theory and Investment Analysis,* New York: John Wiley.

Emery, D.R., Finnerty, J.D. and Stowe, J.D. (1998) *Principles of Financial Management,* Upper Saddle River: Prentice Hall.

Engel, J.F., Blackwell, R.D. and Miniard, P.W. (1990) *Consumer Behaviour,* 6th edn, Harlow: Addison-Wesley.

Etzioni, A. (1988) *The Moral Dimension: Toward a New Economics,* New York: Free Press.

Evans, J.R. and Olson, D.L. (2000) *Statistics, Data Analysis, and Decision Modeling,* Upper Saddle River: Prentice Hall.

Evans, M. and Moutinho, L. (1999) *Contemporary Issues in Marketing,* London: Macmillan Business.

Evans, P.A.L. (2000) 'The dualistic leader: thriving on paradox', in S. Chowdhury, *Management 21C,* London: Financial Times/Prentice Hall.

Fairholm, G.W. (1998) *Perspectives on Leadership: From the Science of Management to Its Spiritual Heart,* London: Quorum Books.

Fellenstein, C. and Wood, R. (2000) *Exploring E-commerce, Global E-business, and E-societies,* Upper Saddle River: Prentice Hall.

Field, M. and Keller, L. (1998) *Project Management,* London: The Open University/Thomson Business Press.

Flamholtz, E.G. (1999) *Human Resource Accounting: Advances in Concepts, Methods and Applications*, London: Kluwer.

Fleidner, G. and Vokurka, R.J. (1997) 'Agility: competitive weapon of the 1990s and beyond', *Production and Inventory Management Journal*, 3rd quarter, 19–24.

Fletcher, G.P. (1993) *Loyalty: An Essay on the Morality of Relationships*, Oxford: Oxford University Press.

Fletcher, W. (1999) *Advertising Advertising*, London: Profile Books.

Flood, R.L. (1993) *Beyond TQM*, Chichester: John Wiley.

——(1999) *Rethinking the Fifth Discipline: Learning Within the Unknowable*, London: Routledge.

Foot, M. and Hook, C. (1999) *Introducing Human Resource Management*, 2nd edn, Harlow: Addison Wesley Longman.

Forrest, E. (1996) *Activity-based Management: A Comprehensive Implementation Guide*, New York: McGraw-Hill.

Forsyth, P. (1999) *Understanding Office Politics*, Abingdon: Hodder & Stoughton.

Foss, N.J. and Robertson, P.L. (eds) (2000) *Resources, Technology and Strategy: Explorations in the Resource-based Perspective*, London: Routledge.

Foster, P. (1999) *Business Administration Level 2*, Harlow: Longman.

Foxall, G., Goldsmith, R. and Brown, S. (1998) *Consumer Psychology for Marketing*, 2nd edn, London: International Thomson Business Press.

Francesco, A.M. and Gold, B.A. (1998) *International Organisational Behaviour: Text, Readings, Cases, and Skills*, Upper Saddle River: Prentice Hall.

Fraser, A. (1998) *Reinventing Aristocracy: The Constitutional Reformation of Corporate Governance*, Aldershot: Ashgate.

Friedman, L.G. and Furey, T.R. (2000) *The Channel Advantage: Going to Market with Multiple Sales Channels to Reach More Customers, Sell More Products, Make More Profit*, Oxford: Butterworth-Heinemann.

Fry, F.L., Stoner, C. R. and Hattwick, R.E. (1998) *Business: An Integrative Framework*, London: Irwin McGraw-Hill.

Fudenberg, D. and Tirole, J. (1991) *Game Theory*, Cambridge MA: MIT Press.

Fuller, D.A. (1999) *Sustainable Marketing: Managerial-Ecological Issues*, London: Sage.

Furham, A. (1998) *The Psychology of Managerial Incompetence: A Sceptic's Dictionary of Modern Organizational Issues*, London: Whurr Publishers.

Gabbott, M. and Hogg, G. (1998) *Consumers and Services*, Chichester: John Wiley.

Galegher, J., Kraut, R.E. and Egido, C. (eds) (1990) *Intellectual Teamwork: The Social and Technological Bases of Cooperative Work*, Hillsdale: Lawrence Erlbaum.

Gallagher, M., Austin, S. and Caffyn, S. (1997) *Continuous Improvement in Action: The Journeys of Eight Companies*, London: Kogan Page.

Galliers, R.D. and Baets, W.R.J. (eds) (1998) *Information Technology and Organisational Transformation: Innovation for the 21st Century Organisation*, Chichester: John Wiley.

Gay, C.L. and Essinger, J. (2000) *Inside Outsourcing: The Insider's Guide to Managing Strategic Outsourcing*, London: Nicholas Brealey.

Gemünden, H.G., Ritter, T. and Walter, A. (1997) *Relationships and Networks in International Markets*, Oxford: Pergamon.

Geringer, M.J. (1998) *Joint Venture Partner Selection*, Westport: Quorum Books.

Glass, N. (1998) *Management Masterclass: A Practical Guide to the New Realities of Business*, London: Nicholas Brealey.

Goffee, R. and Jones, G. (1998) *The Character of a Corporation: How Your Company's Culture Can Make or Break Your Business*, London: HarperCollins Business.

Gomez, P. (1999) *Integrated Value Management*, London: International Thomson Business Press.

Good, D.C. (1998) *Gender and Successful Human Resource Decisions in Small Businesses*, London: Garland.

Gormley, W.T. Jr and Weimer, D.L. (1999) *Organizational Report Cards*, Cambridge MA: Harvard University Press.

Gosney, J.W. and Boehm, T.P. (2000) *Customer Relationship Management Essentials*, Roseville CA: Prima Tech.

Gottlieb, B.H., Kelloway, E.K. and Barham, E. (1998) *Flexible Work Arrangements: Managing the Work/Family Boundary*, Chichester: John Wiley.

Gowing, M.K., Kraft, J.D. and Quick, J.C. (eds) (1998) *The New Organizational Reality: Downsizing, Restructuring, and Revitalization*, Washington DC: American Psychological Association.

Goyder, M. (1998) *Living Tomorrow's Company*, Aldershot: Gower.

Graeser, V. and Willcocks, L. with Pisanias, N. (1998) *Developing the IT Scorecard*, London: Business International.

Grandori, A. (ed.) (1999) *Interfirm Networks: Organization and Industrial Competitiveness*, London: Routledge.

Green, P. (1999) *Sales Management and Organisation*, London: Hawksmere.

Greenberg, J. (1999) *Managing Behaviour in Organisations*, 2nd edn, Upper Saddle River: Prentice Hall.

Greenberg, J. and Baron, R.A. (2000) *Behaviour in Organisations: Understanding and Managing the Human Side of Work*, 7th edn, Upper Saddle River: Prentice Hall.

Greiner, L.E. (1972) 'Evolution and revolution as organisations grow', *Harvard Business Review*, July.

Griggs, L.B. and Louw, L-L. (1995) *Valuing Diversity: New Tools for a New Reality*, London: McGraw-Hill.

Gronstedt, A. (2000) *The Customer Century: Lessons from World-class Companies in Integrated Marketing and Communications*, London: Routledge.

Gross, M.J. Jr, Larkin, R.F. and McCarthy, J.H. (2000) *Financial and Accounting Guide for Not-for-profit Organisations*, Chichester: John Wiley.

Gruenfeld, D.H. (1998) *Research on Managing Groups and Teams*, vol. 1, London: JAI Press.

Guerard, J.B. Jr and Bean, A.S. (1998) *R&D Management and Corporate Financial Policy*, Chichester: John Wiley.

Gummesson, E. (2000a) *Qualitative Methods in Management Research*, Thousand Oaks: Sage.

——(2000b) *Total Relationship Marketing: From the 4Ps – Product, Price, Promotion, Place – of Traditional Marketing Management to the 30Rs – the Thirty Relationships – of the New Marketing Paradigm*, Oxford: Butterworth-Heinemann.

Gupta, K. (1999) *A Practical Guide to Needs Assessment*, San Francisco: Jossey-Bass Pfeiffer.

Haines, S.G. (2000) *The Systems Thinking Approach to Strategic Planning and Management*, London: St Lucie Press.

Haksever, C., Render, B., Russell, R.S. and Murdick, R.G. (2000) *Service Management and Operations*, 2nd edn, Upper Saddle River: Prentice Hall.

Hale, R. and Whitlam, P. (2000) *Powering Up Performance Management: An Integrated Approach to Getting the Best from Your People*, Aldershot: Gower.

Hall, C., Scott, C. and Hood, C. (2000) *Telecommunications Regulation: Culture, Chaos and Interdependence Inside the Regulatory Process*, London: Routledge.

Hall, L. and Torrington, D. (1998) *The Human Resource Function: The Dynamics of Change and Development*, London: Financial Times Pitman.

Hamel, G., Prahalad, C.K., Thomas, H. and O'Neal, D. (1998) *Strategic Flexibility: Managing in a Turbulent Environment*, Chichester: John Wiley.

Hammer, M. (1996) *Beyond Reengineering*, New York: HarperCollins Business.

Hammer, M. and Champy, J. (1993) *Re-engineering the Corporation: A Manifesto for Business Revolution*, New York: HarperCollins.

Handy, C.B. (1988) *Understanding Voluntary Organisations*, Harmondsworth: Penguin.

——(1999) *Inside Organisations*, Harmondsworth: Penguin.

Hannagan, T. (1998) *Management: Concepts and Practices*, 2nd edn, London: Pitman.

Hannan, M.T. and Freeman, J. (1989) *Organisational Ecology*, Cambridge MA: Harvard University Press.

Hanson, D.S. (1997) *Cultivating Common Ground: Releasing the Power of Relationships at Work*, Oxford: Butterworth-Heinemann.

Harding, S. and Long, T. (1998) *Proven Management Models*, Aldershot: Gower.

Harrington, H.J. (1991) *Business Process Improvement*, New York: McGraw-Hill.

Harrington, H.J. and Lomax, K.C. (2000) *Performance Improvement Methods: Fighting the War on Waste*, London: McGraw-Hill.

Harrington, H.J., Conner, D.R. and Horney, N.L. (2000) *Project Change Management: Applying Change Management to Improvement Projects*, London: McGraw-Hill.

Hartley, R.F. (1998) *Marketing Mistakes and Successes*, London: John Wiley.

Harukiyo, H. and Hook, G.D. (eds) (1998) *Japanese Business Management: Restructuring for Low Growth and Globalisation*, London: Routledge.

Haskell, R.E. (1998) *Reengineering Corporate Training: Intellectual Capital and Transfer Learning*, London: Quorum Books.

Haywood, M. (1998) *Managing Virtual Teams: Practical Techniques for High-Technology Project Managers*, London: Artech House.

Heath, J. (1998) *Teaching and Writing Case Studies: A Practical Guide*, Wharley End: European Case Clearing House.

Heath, R. (1998) *Crisis Management for Managers and Executives*, London: Pitman.

Helliegel, D., Jackson, S.E. and Slocum, J.W. Jr (1999) *Management*, 8th edn, Cincinnati: South-Western College Publishing.

Helms, M.M. (1999) *Encyclopedia of Management*, 4th edn, London: Gale Group.

Helmstetter, G. and Metivier, P. (2000) *Affiliate Selling: Building Revenue on the Web*, Chichester: John Wiley.

Hennell, A. and Warner, A. (1998) *Financial Performance Measurement and Shareholder Value Explained*, London: Financial Times Management.

High, J. (1990) *Maximising, Action and Market Adjustment*, Munich: Philosophia Verlag.

Hill, E. and O'Sullivan, T. (1999) *Marketing*, 2nd edn, Harlow: Longman.

Hill, N. and Alexander, J. (2000) *Handbook of Customer Satisfaction and Loyalty Measurement*, 2nd edn, Aldershot: Gower.

Hindle, T. (2000) *Pocket MBA*, London: Economist Books.

Hooley, G.J. (1998) *Marketing Strategy and Competitive Positioning*, 2nd edn, London: Prentice Hall Europe.

Hooper, A. and Potter, J. (2000) *Intelligent Leadership: Creating a Passion for Change*, London: Random House Business Books.

Hopt, K.J., Kanda, H., Roe, M.J., Wymeersch, E. and Prigge, S. (eds) (1998) *Comparative Corporate Governance: The State of the Art and Emerging Research*, Oxford: Oxford University Press.

Horgen, T.H., Joroff, M.L., Porter, W.L. and Schön, D.A. (1999) *Excellence by Design: Transforming Workplace and Work Practice*, Chichester: John Wiley.

Horne, J.C. van and Wachowicz, J.M. Jr (1998) *Fundamentals of Financial Management*, 10th edn, Upper Saddle River: Prentice Hall.

Hosking, D. and Anderson, N. (eds) (1992) *Organisational Change and Innovation: Psychological Perspectives and Practices in Europe*, London: Routledge.

Hosmer, L.T. (1991) *The Ethics of Management*, 2nd edn, Homewood: Irwin.

Howard, R. (1983) *Antitrust and Trade Regulation*, Englewood Cliffs: Prentice Hall.

Howard, S. (1998) *Corporate Image Management: A Marketing Discipline for the 21st Century*, Singapore: Butterworth-Heinemann Asia.

Hoyle, D. (1998) *ISO 9000 Quality Systems Handbook*, 3rd edn, Oxford: Butterworth-Heinemann.

Hussey, D. (1998) *Strategic Management: From Theory to Implementation*, 4th edn, Oxford: Butterworth-Heinemann.

Hussey, D. and Jenster, P. (1999) *Competitor Intelligence: Turning Analysis into Success*, Chichester: John Wiley.

Ilgen, D.R. and Hulin, C.L. (eds) (2000) *Computational Modeling of Behaviour in Organisations: The Third Scientific Discipline*, Washington DC: American Psychological Association.

Innes, J. and Mitchell, F. (1998) *A Practical Guide to Activity-based Costing*, London: Kogan Page.

Ivancevich, J.M. and Matteson, M.T. (1999) *Organizational Behaviour and Management*, London: McGraw-Hill.

Jablin, F.M., Putman, L.L., Roberts, K.H. and Porter, L.W. (2001) *The Handbook of Organisational Communication*, Newbury Park CA: Sage.

Jackson, P. (ed.) (1999) *Virtual Working: Social and Organisational Dynamics*, London: Routledge.

Jagolinzer, P. (2000) *Cost Accounting: An Introduction to Cost Management Systems*, Cincinnati: South-Western College Publishing.

James, K. and Arroba, T. (1999) *Energizing the Workplace: A Strategic Response to Stress*, London: Gower.

Jefkins, F. and Yadin, D. (1998) *Public Relations*, 5th edn, London: Pitman.

Jenkins, M. (1997) *The Customer-centred Strategy: Thinking Strategically about Your Customers*, London: Pitman.

Jobber, D. and Lancaster, G. (2000) *Selling and Sales Management*, 5th edn, London: Financial Times/Prentice Hall.

Johnson, B. (1999) *Introducing Management: A Development Guide for New Managers*, Oxford: Butterworth-Heinemann.

Johnson, P. and Duberley, J. (2000) *Understanding Management Research*, Thousand Oaks: Sage.

Johnson, R. and Redmond, D. (1998) *The Art of Empowerment: The Profit and Pain of Employee Involvement*, London: Financial Times Management.

Jonash, R.S. and Sommerlatter, T. (1999) *The Innovation Premium*, London: Century/Arrow.

Jones, J.P. (ed.) (1998) *How Advertising Works: The Role of Research*, London: Sage.

Jorion, P. (1997) *Value at Risk: The New Benchmark for Controlling Market Risk*, London: Irwin.

Julien, P. (1998) *The State of the Art in Small Business and Entrepreneurship*, Aldershot: Ashgate.

Juliff, P., Kado, T. and Barta, B. (eds) (1999) *Educating Professionals for Network-centric Organisations*, London: Kluwer.

Kalakota, R. and Robinson, M. (1999) *E-Business: Roadmap for Success*, Harlow: Addison-Wesley.

Kanfer, R. (1992) 'Work motivation: new directions in theory and research', in C.L Cooper and I.T. Robertson (eds) *International Review of Industrial and Organisational Psychology*, 7: 1–53, London: John Wiley.

Kaplan, R.S. and Atkinson, A.A. (1998) *Advanced Management Accounting*, 3rd edn, Upper Saddle River: Prentice Hall.

Kaplan, R.S. and Norton, D.P. (1996) *The Balanced Scorecard*, Boston MA: Harvard Business School Press.

Karake-Shalhoub, Z.A. (1999) *Organizational Downsizing, Discrimination, and Corporate Social Responsibility*, London: Quorum Books.

Kasper, H., Helsdingen, P. van and Vries, W. de Jr (1999) *Services Marketing Management: An International Perspective*, Chichester: John Wiley.

Kasper, L.J. (1997) *Business Valuations: Advanced Topics*, London: Quorum Books.

Katz, D., Kahn, R.L. and Adams, S. (1980) *The Study of Organisations*, San Francisco: Jossey-Bass.

Keller, K.L. (1998) *Strategic Brand Management: Building, Measuring, and Managing Brand Equity*, Upper Saddle River: Prentice Hall.

Kendall, R.A.H. (1998) *Risk Management for Executives: A Practical Approach to Controlling Business Risks*, London: Pitman.

Kennedy, G. (1998) *The New Negotiating Edge: The Behavioural Approach for Results and Relationships*, London: Nicholas Brealey.

Keuning, D. (1998) *Management: A Contemporary Approach*, London: Pitman.

Keyes, J. (ed.) (2000) *Best Practice Series: Internet Management*, London: Auerbach.

Keynes, J. (1971–89) *The Collected Writings of John Maynard Keynes: In 30 Volumes*, London: Palgrave.

Kinney, W.R. Jr (2000) *Information Quality Assurance and Internal Control for Management Decision Making*, London: Irwin McGraw-Hill.

Kipping, M. and Bjarnar, O. (1998) *The Americanisation of European Business: The Marshall Plan and the Transfer of US Management Models*, London: Routledge.

Klatt, B., Murphy, S. and Irvine, D. (1999) *Accountability: Practical Tools for Focusing on Clarity, Commitment, Results*, London: Kogan Page.

Klein, D.A. (ed.) (1998) *The Strategic Management of Intellectual Capital*, Oxford: Butterworth-Heinemann.

Klostermann, J.E.M. and Tukker, A. (1998) *Product Innovation and Eco-efficiency*, London: Kluwer.

Kmetz, J.L. (1998) *The Information Processing Theory of Organization: Managing Technology Accession in Complex Systems*, Aldershot: Ashgate.

Kock, N. (1999) *Process Improvement and Organizational Learning: The Role of Collaboration Technologies*, London: Idea Group Publishing.

Kock, R. (1998) *The 80/20 Principle: The Secret of Achieving More with Less*, London: Nicholas Brealey.

Korper, S. and Ellis, J. (2000) *The E-Commerce Book: Building the E-Empire*, London: Academic Press.

Kotler, P. (1994) *Marketing Management: Analysis, Planning, Implementation and Control*, 8th edn, London: Prentice Hall International.

Kotler, P. and Armstrong, G. (1999) *Principles of Marketing*, 8th edn, Upper Saddle River: Prentice Hall.

Kotter, J.P. and Schlesinger, L.A. (1979) 'Choosing strategies for change', *Harvard Business Review*, March.

Kovaleff, T. (1990) 'A symposium on the 100th anniversary of the Sherman Act', *Antitrust Bulletin*, 35.

Kraft, R.J. (1998) *Utilizing Self-managing Teams: Effective Behaviour of Team Leaders*, London: Garland.

Kransdorff, A. (1998) *Corporate Amnesia: Keeping Know-how in the Company*, Oxford: Butterworth-Heinemann.

Kroeber, A.L. and Kluckholn, C. (1952) *Culture: A Critical Review of Concepts and Definitions*, London: Vintage.

Krogh, G. von, Ichijo, K. and Nonaka, I. (2000) *Enabling Knowledge Creation: How to Unlock the Mystery of Tacit Knowledge and Release the Power of Innovation*, Oxford: Oxford University Press.

Kuhn, I. (ed.) (1988) *Handbook for Creative and Innovative Management*, New York: McGraw-Hill.

Lacey, H. (2000) *How to Resolve Conflict in the Workplace*, Aldershot: Gower.

Lake, C. (1999) *Activities Management: Team Leader Development Series*, Oxford: Butterworth-Heinemann.

Lambkin, M., Foxall, G., Raaij, F. van and Heilbrunn, B. (1998) *European Perspectives on Consumer Behaviour*, London: Prentice Hall.

Lamming, R. and Cox, A. (eds) (1999) *Strategic Procurement Management: Concepts and Cases*, London: Earlsgate Press.

Lamprecht, J. (2000) *Quality and Power in the Supply Chain: What Industry Does for the Sake of Quality*, Oxford: Butterworth-Heinemann.

Lancaster, G. and Massingham, L. (1999) *Essentials of Marketing: Text and Cases*, 3rd edn, London: McGraw-Hill.

Lane, H.W., DiStefano, J.J. and Maznevski, M.L. (2000) *International Management Behaviour: Texts, Readings and Cases*, 4th edn, Oxford: Blackwell Business.

Lanning, M.J. (1998) *Delivering Profitable Value: A Revolutionary Framework to Accelerate Growth, Generate Wealth and Rediscover the Heart of Business*, Oxford: Capstone.

Larsson, M. and Lundberg, D. (1998) *The Transparent Market: Management Challenges in the Electronic Age*, London: Macmillan.

Lasher, W.R. (1999) *Strategic Thinking for Smaller Business and Divisions*, Oxford: Blackwell.

Le Sueur, A. and Sunkin, M. (1997) *Public Law*, London: Addison Wesley Longman.

Leach, P. (1991) *The Family Business*, London: Kogan Page.

Leather, P., Brady, C., Lawrence, C., Beale, D. and Cox, T. (1999) *Work-related Violence: Assessment and Intervention*, London: Routledge.

Lee, P.L., Newell, R.B. and Cameron, I.T. (1998) *Process Control and Management*, London: Blackie Academic & Professional.

Lee, T.H., Shiba, S. and Wood, R.C. (1999) *Integrated Management Systems: A Practical Approach to Transforming Organisations*, Chichester: John Wiley.

Leebaert, D. (ed.) (1998) *The Future of the Electronic Marketplace*, Cambridge MA: MIT Press.

Lehman, H. and Roth, G. (eds) (1993) *Weber's Protestant Ethic: Origins, Evidence, Contexts*, Cambridge: Cambridge University Press.

Leibenstein, H. (1975) 'Aspects of the x-efficiency theorem of the firm', *Bell Journal of Economics*, 6(2): 580–606.

Lessem, R. and Palsule, S. (1999) *From Management Education to Civic Reconstruction: The Emerging Ecology of Organizations*, London: Routledge.

Letts, C.W., Ryan, W.P. and Grossman, A. (1999) *High Performance Nonprofit Organisations: Managing Upstream for Greater Impact*, Chichester: John Wiley.

Levy, M. and Weitz, B.A. (1995) *Retailing Management*, Chicago: Irwin McGraw-Hill.

Linstone, H.A. and Turoff, M. (1975) *The Delphi Method: Techniques and Applications*, London: Addison Wesley.

Lintz, B.P. and Rea, K.P. (1999) *Breakthrough Technology Project Management*, London: Academic Press.

—— (2000) *On Time Technology Implementation: How to Achieve Implementation Success with Limited Time and Resources*, London: Academic Press.

Litka, M. (1991) *International Dimensions of the Legal Environment of Business*, 2nd edn, Boston MA: PWS-Kent Publishing Company.

Lloyd, P. and Boyle, P. (1998) *Web-Weaving: Intranets, Extranets and Strategic Alliances*, Oxford: Butterworth-Heinemann.

Lock, D. (2000) *Project Management*, 7th edn, Aldershot: Gower.

——(ed.) (1998) *The Gower Handbook of Management*, Aldershot: Gower.

Lonsdale, C. and Cox, A. (1998) *Outsourcing: A Business Guide to Risk Management Tools and Techniques*, London: Earlsgate Press.

Loose, P., Griffiths, M. and Impey, D. (2000) *The Company Director: Powers, Duties and Liabilities*, 8th edn, Bristol: Jordans.

Lord, R. (2000) *The Net Effect*, London: Random House.

Lower, M. (1998) *Internal Audit*, London: Pitman.

Mabey, C., Salaman, G. and Storey, J. (eds) (1998) *Strategic Human Resource Management: A Reader*, London: Sage.

Macchiette, B. and Roy, A. (2001) *Taking Sides: Clashing Views on Controversial Issues in Marketing*, Guilford CT: McGraw-Hill/Dushkin.

Macdonald, S. (1998) *Information for Innovation: Managing Change from an Information Perspective*, Oxford: Oxford University Press.

Mack, C.S. (1989) *Lobbying and Government Relations*, New York: Quorum Books.

Mackenzie, C.R. (1993) *The Shareholder Action Handbook*, Newcastle-upon-Tyne: New Consumer.

Macredie, R.D., Paul, R.J., Lehaney, B., Anketell, D.R. and Warwick, J. (eds) (1998) *Modelling for Added Value*, Berlin: Springer.

Maddock, S. (1999) *Challenging Women: Gender, Culture and Organization*, London: Sage.

Madu, C.N. (1998) *Handbook of Total Quality Management*, London: Kluwer.

Magill, F.N. (ed.) (1997) *International Encyclopaedia of Economics*, London: Fitzroy Dearborn.

Mahimi, A. and Turcq, D. (1993) 'The three faces of European deregulation', *McKinsey Quarterly*, no. 3, 35–50.

Mailick, S. and Stumpf, S.A. (1998) *Learning Theory in the Practice of Management Development: Evolution and Applications*, London: Quorum Books.

Maister, D. H. (1997) *True Professionalism: The Courage to Care about Your People, Your Clients, and Your Career*, London: The Free Press.

Maitland, I. (1998) *The Small Business Marketing Handbook*, London: Cassell.

Malthus, T.R. (1999) *Essay on Population*, Oxford: Oxford University Press.

Marcousé, I. (ed.) (1999) *Business Studies*, London: Hodder & Stoughton.

Marinetto, M. (1998) *Corporate Social Involvement: Social, Political and Environmental Issues in Britain and Italy*, Aldershot: Ashgate.

Market Tracking International (1999) *Recruitment Strategies*, London: Haymarket.

Markowitz, H. (1959) *Portfolio Selection: Efficient Diversification of Investments*, New York: John Wiley.

Marksick, V.J. and Watkins, K.E. (1999) *Facilitating Learning Organizations: Making Learning Count*, Aldershot: Gower.

Marshall, A. (1999) *Principles of Economics*, 8th edn, London: Macmillan.

Martin, E.W., Brown, C.V., DeHayes, D.W., Hoffer, J.A. and Perkins, W.C. (1999) *Managing Information Technology: What Managers Need to Know*, 3rd edn, Upper Saddle River: Prentice Hall.

Marx, K. (1999) *Capital*, Oxford: Oxford University Press.

——(2000) *Karl Marx: Selected Writings*, ed. David McLellan, Oxford: Oxford University Press.

Marx, K. and Engels, F. (1985) *The Communist Manifesto*, London: Penguin.

Maslow, A. (1970) *Motivation and Personality*, 2nd edn, New York: Harper & Row.

Masterton, A. (1997) *Getting Results with Time Management*, London: Library Association Publishing.

Mauss, M. (1954) *The Gift*, New York: Norton.

Maynard, M. (1998) *The Global Manufacturing Vanguard: New Rules from the Industry Elite*, Chichester: John Wiley.

McAlpine, A. (1998) *The New Machiavelli: The Art of Politics in Business*, Chichester: John Wiley.

McAuliffe, R. (ed.) (1997) *The Blackwell Encyclopedic Dictionary of Managerial Economics*, Oxford: Blackwell.

McDonald, M. and Dunbar, I. (1998) *Market Segmentation*, 2nd edn, London: Macmillan.

McDonald, W.J. (1998) *Cases in Strategic Marketing Management: An Integrated Approach*, Upper Saddle River: Prentice Hall.

McGoldrick, P.J. (1990) *Retail Marketing*, Maidenhead: McGraw-Hill.

McIntosh, M., Leipziger, D., Jones, K. and Coleman, G. (1998) *Corporate Citizenship: Successful Strategies for Responsible Companies*, London: Pitman.

McKean, J. (1999) *Information Masters: Secrets of the Customer Race*, Chichester: John Wiley.

McKenna, R. (1991) *Relationship Marketing*, London: Century Business.

McMahan, G.C. and Woodman, R.W. (1992) 'The current practice of organisational development within the firm', *Group and Organisation Management*, no. 17, 117–34.

McNair, C.J. and Vangermeersch, R. (1998) *Total Capacity Management: Optimising at the Operational, Tactical, and Strategic Levels*, London: St Lucie Press.

Menascé, D.A. and Almeida, V.A.F. (2000) *Scaling for E-Business: Technologies, Models, Performance, and Capacity Planning*, Upper Saddle River: Prentice Hall PTR.

Mendenhall, M., Punnett, B. and Ricks, D. (1995) *Global Management*, Cambridge MA: Blackwell.

Meredith, J.R. and Shafer, S.M. (1999) *Operations Management for MBAs*, Chichester: John Wiley.

Mertins, K. and Jochem, R. (1999) *Quality-oriented Design of Business Processes*, London: Kluwer.

Meyer, G.D. and Heppard, K.A. (eds) (2000) *Entrepreneurship as Strategy: Competing on the Entrepreneurial Edge*, London: Sage.

Mick, D.G. (1988) 'Contributions to the semiotics of marketing and consumer behaviour', in T.A. Sebeok and A. Umiker-Sebeok, *The Semiotic Web 1987*, Berlin: Mouton de Gruyter, 535–84.

Miethe, T.D. (1999) *Whistleblowing at Work: Tough Choices in Exposing Fraud, Waste, and Abuse on the Job*, London: Westview Press.

Mill, J.S. (1998) *Principles of Political Economy and Chapters on Socialism*, Oxford: Oxford Paperbacks.

Miller, D. (1998) *A Theory of Shopping*, Cambridge: Polity Press.

Miller, K. (1999) *Organizational Communication: Approaches and Processes*, 2nd edn, London: Wadsworth Publishing.

Miller, W.L. and Morris, L. (1999) *4th Generation R&D: Managing Knowledge, Technology, and Innovation*, Chichester: John Wiley.

Mintzberg, H. and Quinn, J.B. (eds) (1998) *Readings in the Strategy Process*, 3rd edn, Upper Saddle River: Prentice Hall.

Mockler, R.J. and Dologite, D.G. (1997) *Multinational Cross-cultural Management: An Integrative Context-specific Process*, London: Quorum Books.

Modis, T. (1998) *Conquering Uncertainty: Understanding Corporate Cycles and Positioning Your Company to Survive the Changing Environment*, London: McGraw-Hill.

Morden, T. (1999) *Introduction to Business Strategy: A Strategic Management Approach, Text and Cases*, 2nd edn, London: McGraw-Hill.

Morgan, B.W. (1998) *Strategy and Enterprise Value in the Relationship Economy*, London: Van Nostrand Reinhold.

Morosini, P. (1998) *Managing Cultural Differences: Effective Strategies and Execution across Cultures in Global Corporate Alliances*, Oxford: Pergamon.

Morris, C. (2000) *Quantitative Approaches in Business Studies*, 5th edn, Harlow: Pearson Education.

Morris, J.M. (1998) *Joint Ventures: Business Strategies for Accountants*, 2nd edn, Chichester: John Wiley.

Morse, S. (1998) *Successful Product Management: A Guide to Strategy, Planning and Development*, London: Kogan Page.

Muckian, M. (2000) *Prentice Hall's One-day MBA in Finance and Accounting*, Upper Saddle River: Prentice Hall.

Mudambi, R. and Ricketts, M. (eds) (1997) *The Organisation of the Firm*, London: Routledge.

—— (1998) *The Organisation of the Firm: International Business Perspectives*, London: Routledge.

Munn G.M., Garcia, F.L. and Woelfel, C.J. (eds) (1991) *Encyclopedia of Banking and Finance*, 9th edn, London: McGraw-Hill.

Munro-Faure, L., Teare, R. and Sheuing, E.E. (eds) (1998) *Quality Improvement: Teamwork Solutions from the UK and North America*, London: Cassell.

Nagle, T.T. and Holden, R.K. (1995) *The Strategy and Tactics of Pricing*, Englewood Cliffs: Prentice Hall.

Newell, A. (1990) *Unified Theories of Cognition*, Cambridge MA: Harvard University Press.

Nicholas, J. (1998) *Competitive Manufacturing Management: Continuous Improvement Lean Production Customer-focused Quality*, London: Irwin McGraw-Hill.

Noble, D. (1984) *Forces of Production: A Social History of Industrial Automation*, New York: Knopf.

Nohria, N. and Eccles, R. (eds) (1992) *Networks and Organisations: Structure, Form and Action*, Boston MA: Harvard Business School Press.

Norris, G., Hurley, J.R., Hartley, K.M., Dunleavy, J.R. and Balls, J.D. (2000) *E-Business and ERP: Transforming the Enterprise*, Chichester: John Wiley.

Nöth, W. (1998) 'Advertising', in P. Bouissac (ed.) *Encyclopedia of Semiotics*, Oxford: Oxford University Press, 13–16.

O'Connell, J. (ed.) (1997) *The Blackwell Encyclopedic Dictionary of International Management*, Oxford: Blackwell.

O'Malley, L., Patterson, M. and Evans, M. (1999) *Exploring Direct Marketing*, London: International Thomson Business Press.

O'Shea, J. and Madigan, C. (1998) *Dangerous Company: The Consulting Powerhouses and the Businesses They Save and Ruin*, London: Nicholas Brealey.

Oakshott, L. (1998) *Essential Quantitative Methods for Business, Management and Finance*, London: Macmillan Business.

Oddou, G. and Mendenhall, M. (eds) (1998) *Cases in International Organizational Behaviour*, Oxford: Blackwell.

Ohmae, K. (1995) 'Putting global logic first', *Harvard Business Review*, Jan.–Feb.

Oliver, D. and Roos, J. (2000) *Striking a Balance: Complexity and Knowledge Landscapes*, London: McGraw-Hill.

Olve, N., Roy, J. and Wetter, M. (1999) *Performance Drivers: A Practical Guide to Using the Balanced Scorecard*, Chichester: John Wiley.

Orna, E. (1999) *Practical Information Policies*, 2nd edn, Aldershot: Gower.

Orridge, M. (1998) *How To Deliver Training*, Aldershot: Gower.

Ostroff, F. (1999) *The Horizontal Organisation: What the Organisation of the Future Looks Like and How it Delivers Value to Customers*, Oxford: Oxford University Press.

Owens, K. (1997) *Law for Business Studies Students*, London: Cavendish Publishing.

Palmer, A. and Hartley, B. (1999) *The Business and Marketing Environment*, 3rd edn, London: McGraw-Hill.

Park, A. (1998) *Facilities Management: An Explanation*, 2nd edn, London: Macmillan.

Parker, D.B. (1998) *Fighting Computer Crime: A Framework for Protecting Information*, Chichester: John Wiley.

Parkinson, M. (1999) *Using Psychology in Business: A Practical Guide for Managers*, Aldershot: Gower.

Parsons, N. (1997) *Employee Participation in Europe: A Case Study in the British and French Gas Industries*, Aldershot: Avebury.

Pasternack, B.A. and Visco, A.J. (1998) *The Centerless Corporation: A New Model for Transforming Your Organization for Growth and Prosperity*, New York: Simon & Schuster.

Paxson, D. and Wood, D. (eds) (1997) *The Blackwell Encyclopedic Dictionary of Finance*, Oxford: Blackwell.

Peach, T. (ed.) (2001) *David Ricardo: 4 Volume Set*, London: Routledge.

Pearson, G. (1999) *Strategy in Action: Strategic Thinking, Understanding and Practice*, London: Pearson Education.

Pendlebury, M. and Groves, R. (1999) *Company Accounts: Analysis, Interpretation and Understanding*, 4th edn, London: International Thomson Business Press.

Perren, L. and Berry, A. (1998) *Selecting and Managing a Non-executive Director*, London: Financial Times Publishing.

Peters, L.H., Greer, C.R. and Youngblood, S.A. (eds) (1998) *The Blackwell Encyclopedic Dictionary of Human Resource Management*, Oxford: Blackwell.

Peters, T. (1998) *The Circle of Innovation*, London: Hodder & Stoughton.

Pfeffer, J. (1981) *Power in Organisations*, London: Pitman.

Phillips, C., Pruyn, A. and Kestemont, M. (2000) *Understanding Marketing: A European Casebook*, Chichester: John Wiley.

Phillips, K. and Shaw, P. (1998) *A Consultancy Approach for Trainers and Developers*, 2nd edn, Aldershot: Gower.

Pindyck, R.S. and Rubinfeld, D.L. (1995) *Microeconomics*, 3rd edn, Englewood Cliffs: Prentice Hall.

Pinto, M. (1998) *The Management Syndrome ... How to Deal with It!*, London: Minerva Press.

Player, S. and Keys, D.E. (eds) (1999) *Activity-based Management*, Chichester: John Wiley.

Png, I. (1998) *Managerial Economics*, Oxford: Blackwell.

Pollard, A. (1999) *Competitor Intelligence: Strategy, Tools and Techniques for Competitive Advantage*, London: Pitman.

Poole, M. (ed.) (1999) *Human Resource Management: Critical Perspectives on Business and Management*, 3 vols, London: Routledge.

Porter, G.A. and Norton, C.L. (1995) *Financial Accounting: The Impact on Decision Makers*, London: Dryden Press.

Porter, M.E. (1998a) *Competitive Advantage: Creating and Sustaining Superior Performance*, London: The Free Press.

——(1998b) *Competitive Strategy: Techniques for Analysing Industries and Competitors*, London: The Free Press.

Posner, M.I. (1989) *Foundations of Cognitive Science*, Cambridge MA: MIT Press.

Post, J.E., Lawrence, A.T. and Weber, J. (1999) *Business and Society: Corporate Strategy, Public Policy, Ethics*, London: Irwin McGraw-Hill.

Power, M. (1997) *The Audit Society: Rituals of Verification*, Oxford: Oxford University Press.

Pringle, H. and Thompson, M. (1999) *Brand Spirit: How Cause Related Marketing Builds Brands*, Chichester: John Wiley.

Proctor, T. (1999) *Creative Problem Solving for Managers*, London: Routledge.

Pruijt, H. D. (1997) *Job Design and Technology: Taylorism vs. Anti-Taylorism*, London: Routledge.

Quinn, J.J. and Davies, P.W.F. (eds) (1998) *Ethics and Empowerment*, London: Macmillan Business.

Rackham, N. and DeVincentis, J.R. (1999) *Rethinking the Sales Force: Redefining Selling to Create and Capture Customer Value*, London: McGraw-Hill.

Ramsden, P. (1998) *The Essentials of Management Ratios*, Aldershot: Gower.

Ramu, S.S. (1999) *Restructuring and Break-ups: Corporate Growth through Divestitures, Spin-offs, Split-ups and Swaps*, London: Response Books.

——(2000) *Corporate Crisis Management: Challenges for Survival*, London: Sage.

Randall, H. (ed.) (1996) *Business Guide to Lobbying in the EU*, London: Cartermill.

Rashad Abdel-Khalik, A. (ed.) (1998) *Encyclopedic Dictionary of Accounting*, Oxford: Blackwell Business.

Rasmusen, E. (1990) *Games and Information: An Introduction to Game Theory*, Cambridge MA: Blackwell.

Rathgeb Smith, S. and Lipsky, M. (1995) *Nonprofits for Hire: The Welfare State in the Age of Contracting*, Cambridge MA: Harvard University Press.

Rawls, J. (1971) *A Theory of Justice*, Cambridge MA: Harvard University Press.

Reid, J.L. (2000) *Crisis Management: Planning and Media Relations for the Design and Construction Industry*, Chichester: John Wiley.

Reimpp, G. (1998) *Wide Area Workflow Management: Creating Partnerships for the 21st Century*, London: Springer.

Remenyi, D., Williams, B., Money, A. and Swartz, E. (1998) *Doing Research in Business and Management: An Introduction to Process and Method*, Thousand Oaks: Sage.

Reuters (1998) *EMU Explained*, London: Kogan Page.

ReVelle, J.B., Moran, J.W. and Cox, C.A. (1998) *The QFD Handbook*, Chichester: John Wiley.

Rima, I.H. (1996) *Development of Economic Analysis*, 5th edn, London: Routledge.

Rollins, T. and Roberts, D. (1998) *Work Culture, Organisational Performance, and Business Success: Measurement and Management*, London: Quorum Books.

Rook, D.W. (ed.) (1999) *Brands, Consumers, Symbols and Research: Sidney J. Levy on Marketing*, London: Sage.

Rosenbloom, R.S. and Burgelman, R.A. (eds) (1989) *Research on Technological Innovation, Management and Policy*, Greenwich CT: JAI Press.

Rosenfeld, R.H. and Wilson, D.C. (1999) *Managing Organisations: Text, Readings and Cases*, Maidenhead: McGraw-Hill.

Rossiter, J.R. and Danaher, P.J. (1998) *Advanced Media Planning*, London: Kluwer.

Roth, W. (1999) *Quality Improvement: A Systems Perspective*, London: St Lucie Press.

——(2000) *The Roots and Future of Management Theory: A Systems Perspective*, London: St Lucie Press.

Runci, M.A. and Albert, R.S. (eds) (1990) *Theories of Creativity*, London: Sage.

Russell, R.S. and Taylor, B.W. III (1998) *Operations Management: Focusing on Quality and Competitiveness*, Upper Saddle River: Prentice Hall.

Rutterford, J. (ed.) (1998) *Financial Strategy: Adding Stakeholder Value*, Chichester: John Wiley.

Sadler, P. (1999) *Leadership in Tomorrow's Company*, London: The Centre for Tomorrow's Company.

Salmon, R. and Linares, Y. de (1999) *Competitive Intelligence: Scanning the Global Environment*, London: Economica.

Satori, J. (1999) *Synchronicity: The Entrepreneur's Edge*, Oxford: Butterworth-Heinemann.

Scarborough, J. (1998) *The Origins of Cultural Differences and Their Impact on Management*, London: Quorum Books.

Scarborough, N.M. and Zimmerer, T.W. (2000) *Effective Small Business Management*, Upper Saddle River: Prentice Hall.

Scherer, F.M. (1990) *Industrial Market Structure and Economic Performance*, Boston: Houghton Mifflin.

Schmidt, H.V. (1994) 'Occupational clinical psychology', in R.J. Corsini (ed.) *Encyclopedia of Psychology*, 2nd edn, Chichester: John Wiley, 507–12.

Schniederjans, M.J. (1998) *Operations Management in a Global Context*, London: Quorum Books.

Schniederjans, M.J. and Olson, J.R. (1999) *Advanced Topics in Just-in-time Management*, London: Quorum Books.

Schönsleben, P. (2000) *Integral Logistics Management: Planning and Control of Comprehensive Business Processes*, London: St Lucie Press.

Schorr, J.E. (1998) *Purchasing in the 21st Century: A Guide to State-of-the-art Techniques and Strategies*, Chichester: John Wiley.

Schuler, R.S. and Van de Ven, A.H. (eds) (1997) *The Blackwell Encyclopedic Dictionary of Organizational Behaviour*, Oxford: Blackwell.

Schwandt, D.R. and Marquardt, M.J. (2000) *Organizational Learning: From World-class Theories to Global Best Practices*, New York: St Lucie Press.

Schwartz, A.E. (1992) *Delegating Authority*, Happauge: Barron.

Scott, M.C. (1998) *The Intellect Industry: Profiting and Learning from Professional Services Firms*, Chichester: John Wiley.

Scott, W.R. (1992) *Organisations: Rational, Natural and Open Systems*, Englewood Cliffs: Prentice Hall.

Senge, P.M. (1990) *The Fifth Discipline: The Art and Practice of the Learning Organisation*, New York: Currency/Doubleday.

Seymour, M. and Moore, S. (2000) *Effective Crisis Management: Worldwide Principles and Practice*, London: Cassell.

Shapiro, M. (1999) *Understanding Neuro-Linguistic Programming*, Abingdon: Hodder & Stoughton.

Sheal, P. (1999) *The Staff Development Handbook*, London: Kogan Page.

Shelly, G.B., Cashman, T.J. and Rosenblatt, H.J. (1998) *Systems Analysis and Design*, 3rd edn, Cambridge MA: Course Technology.

Shepherd, W.G. (1996) *The Economics of Industrial Organisation*, Upper Saddle River: Prentice Hall.

Sherrington, M. (1999) 'Branding and brand management', in M.J. Baker (ed.) *The IEBM Encyclopedia of Marketing*, London: Thomson Business Press.

Sheth, J.N. and Parvatiyar, A. (2000) *Handbook of Relationship Marketing*, London: Sage.

Shim, J.K. (2000) *Information Systems and Technology for the Noninformation Systems Executive: An Integrated Resource Management Guide for the 21st Century*, London: St Lucie Press.

Shim, J.K. and Siegel, J.G. (2000) *Modern Cost Management and Analysis: Understanding Your Cash Flow for a More Profitable Business*, Happauge: Barron.

Shim, J.K., Siegel, J.G. and Simon, A.J. (1997) *The Vest-pocket MBA*, Upper Saddle River: Prentice Hall.

Silbiger, S. (1994) *The 10-day MBA: A Step-by-step Guide to Mastering the Skills Taught in Top Business Schools*, London: Piatkus Books.

Simon, H.A. (1976) *Administrative Behaviour*, 3rd edn, New York: Free Press.

Singer, P. (1980) *Marx*, Oxford: Oxford University Press.

Skidelsky, R. (1983–2000) *John Maynard Keynes: In Three Volumes*, London: Macmillan.

Skyrme, D.J. (1999) *Knowledge Networking: Creating the Collaborative Enterprise*, Oxford: Butterworth-Heinemann.

Slack, N. (ed.) (1997) *The Blackwell Encyclopedic Dictionary of Operations Management*, Oxford: Blackwell.

Small, P. (2000) *The Entrepreneurial Web: First, Think like an E-business*, London: Pearson Education.

Smith, A. (2000), *The Wealth of Nations*, London: Modern Library.

Smith, C. and McWilliams, F. (1999) *Successful Flexible Working*, Abingdon: Hodder & Stoughton.

Smith, C.L. Sr. (1998) *Computer-supported Decision Making: Meeting the Decision Demands of Modern Organisations*, London: Ablex Publishing.

Sparrow, J. (1998) *Knowledge in Organisations: Access to Thinking at Work*, London: Sage.

Spears, L.C. (ed.) (1998) *Insights on Leadership: Service, Stewardship, Spirit, and Servant-Leadership*, Chichester: John Wiley.

Stahl, M.J. (ed.) (1999) *Perspectives in Total Quality*, Oxford: Blackwell.

Stair, R.M. (1999) *Principles of Information Systems*, 4th edn, London: Course Technology.

Statt, D.A. (1999) *Concise Dictionary of Business Management*, 2nd edn, London: Routledge.

Stauble, V.R. (2000) *Marketing Strategy: A Global Perspective*, London: The Dryden Press.

Steers, R.M., Lyman, W.P. and Gregory, A.B. (1996) *Motivation and Leadership at Work*, 6th edn, New York: McGraw-Hill.

Steinbock, D. (2000) *The Birth of Internet Marketing Communications*, London: Quorum Books.

Stern, C.W. and Stalk, G. Jr (1998) *Perspectives on Strategy from the Boston Consulting Group*, Chichester: John Wiley.

Sternberg, R.J. (ed.) (1988) *The Nature of Creativity*, Cambridge: Cambridge University Press.

Sterne, J. and Priore, A. (2000) *Email Marketing: Using Email to Reach Your Target Audience and Build Customer Relationships*, Chichester: Wiley Computer Publishing.

241

Stevenson, W.J. (1999) *Production Operations Management*, Boston: Irwin McGraw-Hill.

Steward, C. (1999) *Developing Strategic Partnerships: How to Leverage More Business from Major Customers*, Aldershot: Gower.

Stewart, D.M. (ed.) (1998) *Gower Handbook of Management Skills*, Aldershot: Gower.

Stokes, D. (1998) *Small Business Management: A Case Study Approach*, 3rd edn, London: Letts.

Stone, M., Woodcock, N. and Machtynger, L. (2000) *Customer Relationship Marketing: Get to Know Your Customers and Win Their Loyalty*, London: Kogan Page.

Straker, D. (1998) *The Quality Conspiracy*, Aldershot: Gower.

Stredwick, J. and Ellis, S. (1998) *Flexible Working Practices: Techniques and Innovations*, London: Institute of Personnel and Development.

Sullivan, P.H. (1998) *Profiting from Intellectual Capital: Extracting Value from Innovation*, Chichester: John Wiley.

——(2000) *Value-driven Intellectual Capital: How to Convert Intangible Corporate Assets into Market Value*, Chichester: John Wiley.

Summers, M.R. (1998) *Analysing Operations in Business: Issues, Tools, and Techniques*, London: Quorum Books.

Sundbo, J. (1998) *The Theory of Innovation: Entrepreneurs, Technology and Strategy*, Cheltenham: Edward Elgar.

Sutton, C. (1998) *Strategic Concepts*, London: Macmillan Business.

Syrett, M. and Lamminman, J. (1998) *Managing Live Innovation*, Oxford: Butterworth-Heinemann.

Takashi, O. (1991) *The 5 Ss*, Tokyo: Asian Productivity Organisation.

Tapscott, D., Lowy, A. and Ticoll, D. (eds) (1998) *Blueprint to the Digital Economy: Creating Wealth in the Era of E-Business*, London: McGraw-Hill.

Taylor, F.W. (1911) *Principles of Scientific Management*, New York: Harper.

Thomas, A. (1999) *An Introduction to Financial Accounting*, 3rd edn, London: McGraw-Hill.

Thomas, P. (1999) *Fashions in Management Research: An Empirical Analysis*, Aldershot: Ashgate.

Thompson, A.A. and Strickland, A.J. (1998) *Strategic Management: Concepts and Cases*, 10th edn, New York: Irwin McGraw-Hill.

Thorp, J. (1998) *The Information Paradox: Realising the Business Benefits of Information Technology*, London: McGraw-Hill.

Thorpe, R. and Homan, G. (eds) (2000) *Strategic Reward Systems*, Harlow: Pearson Education.

Tichy, N.M. and Sherman, S. (1993) *Control Your Own Destiny or Someone Else Will*, London: HarperCollins.

Tidd, J. (ed.) (2000) *From Knowledge Management to Strategic Competence: Measuring Technological, Market and Organisational Innovation*, London: Imperial College Press.

Tiemann, H.A. (1996) 'Industrial and organisational psychology', in F.N. Magill (ed.) *International Encyclopedia of Psychology*, London: Fitzroy Dearborn, 878–82.

Timmons, J.A. (1999) *New Venture Creation: Entrepreneurship for the 21st Century*, 5th edn, London: McGraw-Hill International Editions.

Tinnirello, P.C. (ed.) (2000) *Project Management*, London: Auerbach.
Toomey, J.W. (2000) *Inventory Management: Principles, Concepts and Techniques*, London: Kluwer.
Toplis, J., Dulewicz, V. and Fletcher, C. (1991) *Psychological Testing: A Manager's Guide*, 2nd edn, London: Institute of Personnel Management.
Trott, P. (1998) *Innovation Management and New Product Development*, London: Pitman.
Trout, J. (1999) *The Power of Simplicity: A Management Guide to Cutting Through the Nonsense and Doing Things Right*, London: McGraw-Hill.
Turban, E., Lee, J., King, D. and Chung, H.M. (2000) *Electronic Commerce: A Managerial Perspective*, Upper Saddle River: Prentice Hall.
Turney, P.B.B. (1996) *The Activity Based Costing Performance Breakthrough*, London: Kogan Page.
Tyndall, G., Gopal, C., Partsch, W. and Kamauff, J. (1998) *Supercharging Supply Chains: New Ways to Increase Value through Global Operational Excellence*, Chichester: John Wiley.
Udom, U.E. (1998) *Adminisprudence: A Behavioural Approach to Managing Ourselves and Others*, Ibadan: Spectrum Books.
Ungson, G.R. and Trudel, J.D. (1998) *Engines of Prosperity: Templates for the Information Age*, London: Imperial College Press.
Vandermerwe, S. (1999) *Customer Capitalism: The New Business Model of Increasing Returns in New Market Spaces*, London: Nicholas Brealey.
Vink, P., Koningsveld, E.A.P. and Dhondt, S. (eds) (1998) *Human Factors in Organizational Design and Management – VI*, Amsterdam: Elsevier.
Vinten, G. (ed.) (1994) *Whistleblowing: Subversion or Corporate Citizenship?*, London: St Martin's Press.
Vollmann, T.E., Berry, W.L. and Whybark, D.C. (1992) *Manufacturing Planning and Control Systems*, Burr Bridge: Irwin.
Vries, M.S. de (1999) *Calculated Choices in Policy-making: The Theory and Practice of Impact Assessment*, Basingstoke: Macmillan.
Wade, K. and Wynne, A. (eds) (1999) *Control Self Assessment: For Risk Management and Other Practical Applications*, Chichester: John Wiley.
Wagner, J.A. and Hollenbeck, J.R. (1998) *Organizational Behaviour: Securing Competitive Advantage*, 3rd edn, Upper Saddle River: Prentice Hall.
Wallace, W. McD. (1998) *Postmodern Management: The Emerging Partnership between Employees and Stockholders*, London: Quorum Books.
Walley, L. and Smith, M. (1998) *Deception in Selection*, Chichester: John Wiley.
Walton, J. (1999) *Strategic Human Resource Development*, London: Financial Times.
Warner, M. (ed.) (2000) *Management in the Americas*, London: Business Press.
Wartick, S.L. and Wood, D.J. (1998) *International Business and Society*, Oxford: Blackwell Business.
Webb, R.C. (1999) *Psychology of the Consumer and Its Development: An Introduction*, London: Kluwer.
Weber, M. (1979) *Economy and Society*: 2 vol. set, Berkeley, University of California Press.

——(1992) *The Protestant Ethic and the Spirit of Capitalism*, London: Routledge.

Weinreich, N.K. (1999) *Hands-on Social Marketing: A Step-by-step Guide*, London: Sage.

Wellings, F. (1998) *Forecasting Company Profits*, Cambridge: Woodhead Publishing.

Werhane, P.H. and Freeman, R.E. (eds) (1997) *The Blackwell Encyclopedic Dictionary of Business Ethics*, Oxford: Blackwell.

West, T.L. and Jones, J.D. (eds) (1999) *Handbook of Business Valuation*, 2nd edn, Chichester: John Wiley.

Westland, J.C. and Clark, T.H.K. (1999) *Global Electronic Commerce: Theory and Case Studies*, Cambridge MA: MIT Press.

Wheeler, D. and Sillanpää, M. (1997) *The Stakeholder Corporation: A Blueprint for Maximizing Stakeholder Value*, London: Pitman.

Wilcox, D.L., Ault, P.H., Agee, W.K. and Cameron, G.T. (2000) *Public Relations: Strategies and Tactics*, 6th edn, Harlow: Longman.

Williams, C.A. Jr, Smith, M.L. and Young, P.C. (1998) *Risk Management and Insurance*, Boston MA: Irwin McGraw-Hill.

Williams, R., Faulkner, W. and Fleck, J. (1998) *Exploring Expertise: Issues and Perspectives*, Basingstoke: Macmillan.

Wilmshurst, J. and Mackay, A. (1999) *The Fundamentals of Advertising*, 2nd edn, Oxford: Butterworth-Heinemann.

Wilson, J.Q. (1989) *Bureaucracy*, New York: Basic Books.

Winter, M. and Steger, U. (1998) *Managing Outside Pressure: Strategies for Preventing Corporate Disasters*, Chichester: John Wiley.

Wisniewski, M. (1997) *Quantitative Methods for Decision Makers*, 2nd edn, London: Pitman.

Wolkinson, B.W. and Block, R.N. (1996) *Employment Law*, Oxford: Blackwell.

Wooding, J. and Levenstein, C. (1999) *The Point of Production: Work Environment in Advanced Industrial Societies*, London: The Guilford Press.

Worthington, I. and Britton, C. (2000) *The Business Environment*, 3rd edn, Harlow: Prentice Hall.

Wren, D.A. (1979) *The Evolution of Management Thought*, New York: John Wiley.

Wren, D.A. and Greenwood, R.G. (1998) *Management Innovators: The People and Ideas that have Shaped Modern Business*, New York: Oxford University Press.

Wright, R.J. (1997) *Beyond Time Management: Business with Purpose*, Oxford: Butterworth-Heinemann.

Xerox Corporation (1987) *Leadership Through Quality: Implementing Competitive Benchmarking*, London: Xerox Corporation.

Yeatts, D.E. and Hyten, C. (1998) *High-performing Self-managed Work Teams: A Comparison of Theory to Practice*, London: Sage.

Yukl, G. (1994) *Leadership in Organisations*, 3rd edn, Englewood Cliffs: Prentice Hall.

Zairi, M. (1998) *Effective Management of Benchmarking Projects: Practical Guidelines and Examples of Best Practice*, Oxford: Butterworth-Heinemann.

Zimmerman, F.M. (1991) *The Turnaround Experience: Real World Lessons in Corporate Revitalisation*, New York: McGraw-Hill.

Zwell, M. (2000) *Creating a Culture of Competence*, Chichester: John Wiley.

Zyman, S. (1999) *The End of Marketing as We Know It*, London: HarperCollins Business.

INDEX